LUTHER AS AN EDUCATOR

By

GUSTAV MARIUS BRUCE, M.A., S.T.D., Ph.D., D.D.
Professor of New Testament Literature and Exegesis, Symbolics and Ethics
LUTHER THEOLOGICAL SEMINARY
ST. PAUL, MINNESOTA

With An Introduction by
HANS GERHARD STUB, D.D., LL.D., Litt.D., L.H.D.
President Emeritus of the Norwegian Lutheran Church of America

Wipf and Stock Publishers
EUGENE, OREGON

Wipf and Stock Publishers
199 West 8th Avenue, Suite 3
Eugene, Oregon 97401

Luther as an Educator
By Bruce, Gustav Marius
Copyright©1928 Bruce, Gustav Marius
ISBN: 1-59244-080-0
Publication date: October, 2002
Previously published by Augsburg Publishing House, 1928.

To

MY BELOVED WIFE

For twenty-five years a bosom companion, a devoted and successful homemaker, and a constant source of inspiration and support

THIS VOLUME IS AFFECTIONATELY
DEDICATED

MARTIN LUTHER

That which he knew he uttered,
  Conviction made him strong;
And with undaunted courage
  He faced and fought the wrong.
No power on earth could silence him
  Whom love and faith made brave,
And though four hundred years have gone,
  Men strew with flowers his grave.

A frail child, born to poverty,
  A German miner's son;
A poor monk searching in his cell,
  What honors has he won!
The nations crown him Faithful,
  A man whom truth made free:
God give us for these easier times
  More men as real as he!

—MARIANNE FARNINGHAM.

FOREWORD

It was the day after Christmas in 1538. Guests were gathered around the table as Martin Luther spoke these words:

> You parents can provide no better gift for your children than an education in the liberal arts. House and home burn down, but an education is easy to carry along.

Luther was well-versed in the classics. He frequently commended a liberal arts education — but much of that had been forgotten by succeeding generations.

Today, however, classical Lutheran education is enjoying a renaissance. This book is being reprinted in hopes of renewing such an interest among those who educate in school or at home.

This reproduction has been made possible through some generous gifts from the Biblical Charities Foundation and from the Consortium for Classical Lutheran Education together with the expert help of Wipf and Stock Publishers.

Rev. Joel A. Brondos, Headmaster
Zion Lutheran Academy, Fort Wayne, IN
November, 2002

A Word of Introduction

TO comply with the request of the author to accompany his work, *Luther as an Educator*, with some words of introduction, has been a pleasure to me, because the presentation of the great Reformer of the Church as also a Reformer of education, has, to my knowledge, never been brought out in a more comprehensive and convincing manner than in this book.

The author has laid a broad foundation, but this foundation was necessary in order to prove the position taken. It is evident that a great deal of preliminary work had to be done by the author before directly placing before us his arguments for Luther's unique position in the field of education.

Any church historian who would do justice to a presentation of Luther as the great Reformer of the Church, would have to give a thorough survey of the social and political affairs, and more especially of the conditions in the Church before the Reformation, and then proceed to present the Reformer and his preparation for the work. In the same manner the author of this book has placed before us in the first chapter the very interesting and true condition of education in Europe, and especially in Germany, before and after the time of Luther. Without knowledge of the principles and practices in vogue in the realm of education before Luther, we would not be able to realize to any appreciable extent the important changes wrought by the Reformation in the field of education.

Then Martin Luther appears. The author does not intend to give a biography of Luther. He only desires to give the salient points in the life of Luther that have some bearing upon moulding him into the educator he became. Therefore the education and training which Martin Luther received, both in his home and at the schools he attended as a young boy, as well as a student at the university and as a monk, must be considered. Later we find him as a teacher, as a professor, and learn something about his own way of teaching and dealing with his students. A presentation of Luther in the family circle also has its place here, because in his family life he gives a practical illustration of his principles in the education and training of children.

In order to do justice to his subject the author could not omit a summary of Luther's theology, because the theological views of Luther were fundamental in their relation to his views on education.

Luther now stands before us as well prepared and equipped for his great task of being an educator. Therefore the author introduces his pedagogical writings and by studying the copious extracts from Luther's works that either directly or more indirectly treat of education in its different aspects, we receive a vivid impression of the deep interest Luther had in the education and training of the young people.

Based upon the study of his pedagogical works, the author gives Luther's "Principles of Education," which certainly deserve to be studied and compared with the principles of education in our own times.

One thing we must remember is that the State schools, of which Luther speaks, were at the same time Church schools, because the Church and State were united and constituted what we call a State Church. It would therefore be wrong to infer from Luther's position that in our country, where we have no State Church, religion should be taught in our public schools. The home and the church must take care of the religious instruction.

Luther also made significant contributions to Christian worship, and these are also entitled to consideration in a presentation of Luther as an educator. The statement made by Weigle and Tweedy that "training in worship is an essential element in the religious education of our children," is true. Because Luther fully realized the importance of this truth, worship became an essential element in the schools which he advocated. It should also be borne in mind that what Luther taught concerning Christian worship in general is of the utmost significance for worship in our homes, Week-day schools, Sunday schools, churches, academies, and colleges.

The last chapters have the headings: *Evaluation of the Man and his Work,* and: *Verdict of History.* Witnesses from medieval and modern times, not only from Lutherans, but also from Reformed and even Catholics, have been called upon to prove the greatness of Luther's personality and his work, more particularly as an educator.

Dr. Bruce has done historic truth a great service by so forcibly and convincingly bringing to the fore Luther as an educator. It certainly is significant that the most widely known Teachers' College in the United States, that of Columbia University, whose latest building is inscribed to the memory of outstanding modern educators, omits the name of Luther entirely, beginning its inscription with the names of Melanchthon and Sturm. It is not generally known what, according to Dr. Bruce, Dr. Schmidt says in his *History of Pedagogy*: "Luther himself was one of the greatest educators and school masters. He stood at the head of the workers in the field of education, because he called attention to a large number of grave abuses in the school, brought new life to the teachers and young people through the school visitations, which he directed and commended, urged a thorough language study as the basis of learning and culture and as the source of pure religious conceptions, wrote new books for religious instruction, proposed suitable methods of teaching the various branches of knowledge, and because, in association with Melanchthon, he trained a large number of excellent teachers for higher and lower schools and enjoined upon rulers and governments to provide for schools and the education of the young."

Finally, we have an imposingly large bibliography, showing that the author has made extensive use of the libraries at Hartford, Yale and many other places.

We hope that this work, which brought the author the degree of Ph. D. from Hartford Seminary Foundation, may be received everywhere as an important contribution to that kind of literature which impresses upon the citizens of the State and upon the members of the Church the responsibility for the education and training of the children and the young people, and indicates how this training may be effected in the very best way.

—H. G. STUB, *President Emeritus,*
The Norwegian Lutheran Church of America.

Preface

FOR over a quarter of a century the author has been engaged in some form of educational work, having taught in the public schools, two church academies, a church college, and two theological seminaries. During all of this time he has been an interested and devoted student of education, its history, theory, and practice. For a number of years he has taught catechetics, child psychology, and the principles and methods of religious education, and for the past eight years he has been a member of the Board of Elementary Christian Education of the Norwegian Lutheran Church of America. He has thus had ample opportunity to keep in close and constant contact with educational theory and practice, especially in the field of religious education.

The author's interest in Luther and his educational work is of long standing. Twenty years ago he prepared a thesis on the subject, *The Relation of Education to Crime and Delinquency,* to be presented to the University of South Dakota for the degree of Master of Arts, and discovered that Luther had said some very fine things on the nature and aim of education. About the same time he prepared a paper on *Christian Religious Education* to be read at a pastoral conference and again found occasion to refer to Luther and his educational ideas. Since then he has had occasion to dip into Luther's works considerably in connection with various theological researches, and his admiration and appreciation of Luther have grown with the passing years. While much of the study of Luther and his work has not been directly concerned with his contributions to education, the author's interest in education as such has naturally led him to pay some attention to this aspect of Luther's work even though the objects sought may have been outside the educational field.

In this more or less casual study of Luther and his educational contributions which the author thus for years has carried on, there has come to him a deepening conviction that writers on the history of education, a few German writers excepted, have in a large measure failed to accord the miner's son who set the world on fire at the beginning of the sixteenth century the place in the history of education to which the distinguished services he rendered to education justly entitle him. Dr. F. V. N. Painter pointed the way to a fuller and better appreciation of him in his two excellent volumes published over a generation ago, *History of Education* and *Luther on Education*, but the lead has not been followed up, and Luther, the religious reformer, still continues to eclipse almost totally Luther, the educational reformer, even in Lutheran consciousness. Dr. A. R. Wentz of Gettysburg Seminary, Gettysburg, Pa., deserves great credit for his splendid article on *Luther's Significance for Education* in the recently published *Lutheran World Almanac for 1928*, in which he very ably and convincingly sets forth some of Luther's great contributions to education.

Owing to a heavy teaching load and various duties of a practical and administrative nature that have made large demands upon time and energy, the author has not found the time and leisure so essential to engaging in intensive study and painstaking researches; hence a long cherished desire to undertake something on the order attempted in this work has not been realized sooner. During the school year of 1926-27, however, a golden opportunity to carry on extensive research along this line presented itself, it being the author's turn to avail himself of the liberal and commendable provision made by the Church he has the honor to serve, whereby her theological professors are accorded a sabbatical year in rotation for travel, study, and recreation. The author takes this opportunity to express to the officers and members of the Norwegian Lutheran Church of America his deep and sincere gratitude for the leave of absence from active duties thus afforded.

In casting about for a base of operations, the choice finally fell on the Hartford Seminary Foundation of Hartford, Conn., because of the excellent opportunities which this institution offers for post-graduate study, and, especially, because it was reported to have the best Lutherana of any educational institution in America. The author's personal examination of the largest libraries in the East for works on Luther, leads him to believe that the report is well within the bounds of truth. The Foundation library has a remarkably large and well selected collection of Lutherana, especially in the German language.

During his stay at Hartford, the author met the requirements of the School of Religious Education of the Foundation for the degree of Doctor of Philosophy, and submitted the thesis on *Luther as an Educator* as part of the requirement for that degree. The present volume is the outgrowth of that thesis. Much additional work has been spent in research, and considerable new matter has been added, so that the thesis submitted for the Doctor's degree now appears in an enlarged and revised form. The work is based primarily upon Luther's own works in the original language, but, as the bibliography and constant references show, a large number of Luther biographies and other works germane to the subject have been consulted throughout, in the English, German, and Scandinavian languages. Wherever English translations have been available, these have been used in making quotations from Luther's works or other books consulted; where no such translations have been available, the author has made his own translations. A few translations made by authors quoted have been modified, where in the author's judgment the original could be more closely rendered into the English.

Next year will be the quadricentennial of the publication of Luther's Catechisms and throughout the Lutheran Church over the entire globe there will be memorial celebrations commemorating this significant event. It is to be hoped that on these various festive occasions efforts will be made everywhere to stress Luther's significance as an educator and bring home to the people as never before the great contributions he made to a general and broad Christian education through his distinctively pedagogical works, his preaching, his extensive and varied writings in other fields, his theology, his liturgical writings, his hymns, and his personal influence and example. The author takes great pleasure in offering the present work as a testimony and tribute to Luther as an educator, and trusts that he by means of this volume may contribute a small share to the task of placing Luther in the proper light before the educators, pastors, and people generally preparatory to the memorial celebrations of 1929.

The author wishes to ackowledge his indebtedness and express his sincere gratitude to the Hartford Seminary Foundation Faculty, especially those who had direct charge of his work, for encouragement and helpful criticisms and suggestions. In this connection special mention should be made of Dean Edward Hooker Knight, Dr. A. J. William Meyers, and Dr. Charles Stoddard Lane, of the School of Religious Education, and Dean Melanchthon W. Jacobus and Dr. Elmer E. S. Johnson of the Theological Seminary. To his friend, Dr. Hans Gerhard Stub, scholar, educator, and churchman, the author expresses his sincere thanks for so kindly reading the book in manuscript and accompanying it with a word of introduction. Last but not least, the author feels deeply indebted to his wife for her keen interest, constant support, and helpful criticisms during the pursuit of this study, in token whereof the book is gratefully inscribed to her.

Luther Theological Seminary, St. Paul, Minn., March 27, 1928.

THE AUTHOR.

Contents

CHAPTER		PAGE
I.	EDUCATION IN EUROPE AT THE BEGINNING OF THE SIXTEENTH CENTURY	19
II.	LUTHER'S CHILDHOOD AND EARLY EDUCATION	54
III.	THE STUDENT AND MONK	66
IV.	IN THE PROFESSOR'S CHAIR	78
V.	IN THE FAMILY CIRCLE	86
VI.	LUTHER'S THEOLOGY	105
VII.	PEDAGOGICAL WORKS	131
VIII.	PEDAGOGICAL WORKS	152
IX.	PEDAGOGICAL WORKS	172
X.	PEDAGOGICAL WORKS	189
XI.	PEDAGOGICAL PRINCIPLES	211
XII.	LUTHER'S CONTRIBUTIONS TO CHRISTIAN WORSHIP	237
XIII.	EVALUATION OF THE MAN AND HIS WORK	269
XIV.	THE VERDICT OF HISTORY	285
	BIBLIOGRAPHY	300
	INDEX OF SUBJECTS	313
	INDEX OF NAMES	317

CHAPTER I

EDUCATION IN EUROPE AT THE BEGINNING OF THE SIXTEENTH CENTURY

I. Introductory

As a background for our study of Luther as an educator we shall present a brief sketch of the state of education in Europe at the beginning of the sixteenth century. No detailed and comprehensive survey can be attempted, however, as that would carry us beyond the scope and purpose of this study. For a fuller presentation of the state of education and the nature and progress of educational reform during the thirteenth, fourteenth, and fifteenth centuries, the reader is referred to the standard works on the history of education given in the bibliography of this volume.

To give a brief and yet sufficiently comprehensive view of education at the beginning of the Reformation, to serve as a fitting background for an intelligent and profitable study and evaluation of Luther and his contributions to educational theory and practice, is by no means an easy matter. While there is an abundance of available data on which to base general views and impressions, there is unfortunately a dearth of definite, specific, and detailed information covering sufficiently large areas to give clear and unquestioned results as to the general nature and status of education, the number and character of schools, the qualifications of teachers, the subjects taught, the methods of teaching and discipline, and the general school equipment. There is a number of outstanding schools of secondary and higher education throughout Europe during the closing decades of the Middle Ages, and at least a few examples of elementary schools, but it cannot be shown conclusively that they are very numerous and generally accessible to all classes of society as some, especially Catholic writers, contend. There were also a number of educational reformers who made their appearance and registered their influence from the days of Alcuin to the time of Luther, but to what extent their educational reforms were put into actual operation is still a mooted question. It is, therefore, very difficult to arrive at definite and absolute conclusions.[1] Hence it is not strange that authorities on the history of education differ widely in their characterization of many of the essential aspects of medieval education. There is especially a wide divergence of views expressed by Catholic and Protestant writers. Catholic writers are ever on the defensive when it comes to speaking and writing about the Reformation, its nature and effects, and therefore they are prone to present a more favorable view of the conditions that obtained before the Reformation than the facts in the case will warrant. On the other hand, it must be admitted that Protestant writers may go to the other extreme and picture the conditions in darker hues than a full knowledge of facts may sustain.

---

1) The following remark by Dr. Paul Monroe, noted American writer on the history of education, is very much to the point: "It is with the greatest difficulty that one obtains concrete information concerning educational activities in the past, especially any connected and tolerably complete account of school life. In lieu of such knowledge the student of the history of education accepts a very general view of educational development drawn partially from inference or more largely by generalization from the work or writings of prominent men." *Thomas Platter*, p. 1.

EDUCATION IN EUROPE

In proof of these assertions we submit, on the Catholic side, the following glowing picture of medieval education by the Catholic scholar Janssen: "The period of German reform, which began in the middle of the fifteenth century, produced the most splendid intellectual results. It was a time when culture penetrated to all classes of society, spreading its ramifications deep and wide, a time of extraordinary activity in art and learning by catechetical teaching, by sermons, by the translation of the Holy Scriptures, by instructional and devotional publications of all sorts. Religious knowledge was zealously diffused and the development of religious life abundantly fostered. In the lower elementary schools and the advanced middle schools a sound basis of popular education was established. The universities attained a height of excellence and distinction undreamt of before and became the burning centers of all intellectual activity. And more even than learning, art was seen to blossom and develop on the soil of national religious life, beautifying all departments of life, public and private, secular and ecclesiastical in the worthiest manner, while in its many grand and comprehensive works, inspired by the then prevailing sense of Christian brotherhood, it manifested the real core of German genius and character." [2]

In this view Janssen is very able supported by his American co-religionist, McCormick, who says: "In addition to the cathedral and monastic institutions, other types of elementary schools flourished in the countries of Europe in the later Middle Ages. Chief among them were the parish, chantry, town, and guild schools, and these were so numerous and widely extended that we must conclude elementary education

---

2) Janssen, *History of the German People*, vol. II, p. 287.

was then well provided for in cities and rural districts, and not only for boys but also for girls. The Church was solicitous for the education of all. This is clear from the decrees of councils and general legislative actions of her officials. As in the earlier Middle Ages, there is notable provision of free schools for the poor."[3] The same writer also states that in Germany, at the beginning of the Reformation, educational institutions were flourishing everywhere.[4]

It is not very common to find Protestant writers expressing themselves very favorably as to the conditions that obtained at the close of the Middle Ages, but we find some exceptions to the rule. The German philosopher Friedrich Paulsen says: "There seems to be little doubt that towards the end of the fifteenth century nearly every city had a school of its own and that even in small market towns and villages schools were by no means rare. Knepper's survey of Alsatian schools affords an instance, and many a school must have existed besides those whose names have not been handed down to posterity."[5] Even the American educator Paul Monroe, though brought up in a Protestant manse, lends support to the Catholic writers in his *Textbook in the History of Education*. It should be noted that Dr. Monroe cites Janssen as one of his authorities which may, to some extent, account for the following favorable characterization: "The later Middle Ages were well supplied with schools, not all of which were dominated by the Church. For a century before the Reformation it is probable that schools were as numerous and that as wide an opportunity for study existed as for a century afterward. Monastic schools never recovered their importance after the

---

3) *History of Education*, p. 154.
4) Ibid. p. 211.
5) *German Education, Past and Present*, p. 29

Renaissance of the thirteenth century. Cathedral schools that grew into new prominence in the early University period were insufficient for the demand. Not only secondary but elementary education was provided in the fourteenth and fifteenth centuries in a much more general way than ever before." [6]

Compayre, the French educator, however, has an entirely different view of the situation. After sketching the history of education during the Middle Ages, he concludes: "It is thus that the Middle Age in drawing to a close came nearer and nearer, in the way of continuous progress, to the decisive emancipation which the Renaissance and the Reformation were soon to perpetuate. But the Middle Age in itself, whatever effort may be put forth at this day to rehabilitate it and to discover in it the golden age of modern societies, remains an ill-starred epoch. A few virtues, negative for the most part, virtues of obedience and consecration, cannot atone for the real faults of those rude and barbarous centuries. A higher education, reserved to ecclesiastics and men of noble rank; an instruction which consisted in verbal legerdemain, which developed only mechanism of reasoning and made of the intelligence a prisoner of the formal syllogism; agreeably to the barbarism of primitive times; a fantastic pedantry which lost itself in superficial discussions and in verbal distinctions; popular education almost null and restricted to the teaching of the catechism in Latin; finally a Church absolute and sovereign, which determined for all, great and small, the limits of thought, of belief, and of action—such was, from all points of view, the condition of the Middle Age. It was time for the coming of the Renaissance to affranchise the human mind, to excite and to reveal

---

6) P. 337.

to itself the unconscious need of instruction, and by the fruitful alliance of the Christian spirit and profane letters to prepare for the coming of modern education." [7]

The same writer also says: "Save claustral and cathedral schools, to which must be added some parish schools, the earliest example of our village schools, the sole educational establishment of the Middle Age was what is called the University." [8]

While the picture presented by Compayre may seem almost too dark when contrasted with the glowing picture of Janssen and McCormick, his view is substantially supported by most Protestant writers. Says Painter: "No general effort was made to reach and elevate the common people by education. The ecclesiastical schools were designated chiefly for candidates for the priesthood; the parochial schools fitted the young for church membership, the burgher schools were intended for commercial and artisan classes of the cities; knightly education gave a training for chivalry. Thus the laboring classes were left to toil on in ignorance and want. They remained in a dependent and servile condition, their lives unillumined by intellectual pleasures. If here and there, as claimed by Roman Catholic writers, popular schools were established, they were too few in numbers and too weak in influence to deserve more than a passing mention." [9]

We might go on to quote other authorities on educational history, such as Carl von Raumer, Schmidt, Kemp, but this will suffice to show that the educational conditions during the Middle Ages and at the

---
7) *History of Pedagogy*, pp. 80-81.
8) Ibid., p. 77.
9) *Luther on Education*, p. 87.

beginning of the sixteenth century are variously interpreted.[10]

However difficult it may be to sketch briefly and accurately the educational situation at the close of the Middle Ages, due to lack of many essential facts and the wide divergence of views on the part of writers on the history of education, there are, nevertheless, certain well established facts, the consideration of which will give us fairly correct notions of the actual status of education at the beginning of the Reformation.

II. Educational Movements and Influences during the Middle Ages

THE SOCIAL CLASSES.—During the greater part of the Middle Ages there were three well marked social classes, the clergy, the nobility, and the peasants. The clergy lorded it over the other two classes, holding as they did the keys of both knowledge and salvation in their hands. Though the education of the clergy was, as a rule, very meager, they constituted the learned class in society, for the nobility were largely ignorant, except in matters pertaining to war and hunting, and depended upon the clergy for advice and counsel in secular as well as in spiritual matters. But the peasant class was the most ignorant. There was little desire or need on the part of the peasants for education and virtually no opportunities for them to receive any. The monasteries were the repositories of knowledge and the monks, together with some of the more intelligent parish priests, were dispensers of it, meager and limited though it was.

---

10) On the intellectual, religious, and moral state of Europe during the Middle Ages, see Hallam, *The Middle Ages*, Colonial Press, ed., vol. III, pp. 3-231, or Harper's ed. pp. 559-684; Draper, *The Intellectual Development of Europe*, vol. II.; Adams, *Civilization During the Middle Ages*.

LUTHER AS AN EDUCATOR

THE REFORMATION OF CHARLEMAGNE.—In the latter part of the eighth century Charlemagne began very earnestly to bring about both an educational and moral reform in his domains. In the proclamation issued in 787, directed to Abbot Baugulf, he says, among other things: "Be it known, therefore, to your devotion, pleasing to God, that we, together with our faithful, have considered it to be useful that the bishoprics and monasteries, entrusted by the favor of Christ to our control, in addition to the order of monastic life and the intercourse of holy religion in the culture of letters, also ought to be zealous in teaching those who, by the gift of God, are able to learn according to the capacity of each individual, so that just as the observance of the rule imparts order and grace to honesty of morals, so also zeal in teaching and learning may do the same for sentences, so that those who desire to please God by living rightly should not neglect to please Him also by speaking correctly. . . . Therefore, we exhort you not only not to neglect the study of letters but also with most humble mind, pleasing to God, to study earnestly in order that you may be able more easily and more correctly to penetrate the mysteries of the divine Scriptures." He then directs that copies of this decree be sent to all the bishops and monasteries under the direction of Baugulf. In another proclamation issued two years later, he says: "And let schools be established in which boys may learn to read. Correct carefully the psalms, the signs in writing, the songs, the calendar, the grammar in each monastery or bishopric and the Catholic books; because often some desire to pray to God properly, but they pray badly because of the incorrect books. And do not permit your boys to corrupt them in reading or writing." In 802 he issued an order commanding "that laymen shall learn throroughly the Creed and the Lord's Prayer." [11]

Through his effort a large number of parish schools were established which were to receive even children of the common people who were willing to send them and instruct them free of charge. He established a model school at his palace for the children of the nobility with Alcuin, the most learned man of his day, at its head. This school was attended by four of Charlemagne's own sons and by two daughters. Even Charlemagne himself attended this school at times, learning Latin, Greek, and writing. While he gave a new impetus to educational activities and his efforts had very beneficial effects upon conventual and parish schools, his work was in a large measure a failure due to the lack of interest shown by both the nobility and the clergy. Already in 817 the conventual schools were closed to the day pupils at Aix-la-Chapelle (Aachen) because the large number that flocked to these schools interfered with the maintenance of monastic discipline. Charlemagne's successors did not share his educational views nor his zeal for education and consequently education was again neglected. "Under Louis the Pious and Charles the Bald," says Compayre, "there were constructed more castles than schools." [12]

THE CRUSADES.—The Crusades began toward the close of the eleventh century and continued for about 200 years. They brought together as never before all peoples and classes in the Christian world in behalf of a common cause and against a common foe, Mohammedanism. Although there was a fearful waste of human life and accumulated wealth, the Crusades were not without their good results. They were a mass movement, dominated by religious zeal and the

---
11) Cubberly, *Readings in History of Education*, pp. 90-91.
12) *History of Education*, p. 73.

spirit of adventure; they established hitherto unknown contacts between people of different nationalities and stations in life; they kindled new ideas and new aspirations among many, even of the common people; they brought to the West many of the treasures of art and literature of the East; they stimulated intellectual and commercial intercourse among the nations of Europe and led to the development of trade and industry on a larger scale than ever before. The expansion of industry and trade led to the rise of the third estate, the merchant class, and with their increasing wealth and influence the merchant class established burgher schools to teach their children reading, writing, and arithmetic and thus fit them for the occupation of merchants.

The Crusades also developed the earlier German institution of chivalry to its height and led to the establishment of a system of education for the knight separate and distinct from that given by the parish schools of the Church. This education was mainly secular, training the boy for secular pursuits, but his religious education was not altogether neglected. The education of the boy was completed when at the age of 21 he was solemnly knighted. Some provision was also made in the chivalric system of education for the girls, but it consisted chiefly in providing tutoring at the castle in household duties, good manners, music, dancing, and pleasing conversation. Only exceptionally were girls of nobility taught the languages and literature. Chivalry and chivalric education declined rapidly throughout the fifteenth century and finally passed off the stage of history.

SCHOLASTICISM.—One of the most powerful and influential intellectual movements of the Middle Ages was scholasticism. It arose about the middle of the ninth century and reached the height of its development during the twelfth and thirteenth centuries, after which it began to decline. It left quite a pronounced impress, however, upon the educational thought and methods in the cathedral and conventual schools as well as the universities. It was characterized by speculative thinking, interminable analysis, hair-splitting niceties of distinction and long drawn-out discussions about the most insignificant and puerile matters. While it helped to sharpen the intellect and develop skill in dialectics and to some extent improved methods of teaching in higher institutions of learning, yet it cannot be said that scholasticism was an unmixed educational good.

RELIGIOUS ORDERS.—During the Middle Ages there arose three great religious orders which exerted considerable influence educationally, namely, the Franciscans, Dominicans, and Augustinians. The order of Benedict, which was founded in 529, wielded a very beneficial influence educationally until its decline in the twelfth century. It conducted both elementary and higher instruction in the convents, many of which received both boys and girls for elementary instruction.[13] As the Benedictine order declined, the Franciscan and Dominican orders came into being and soon manifested great activity, especially in the field of higher education, although neither order was founded for educational purposes. The Dominican order became especially a powerful educational factor, its men being more highly trained so that they soon established themselves as teachers in the now rapidly multiplying universities. They count among their number such men as Albertus Magnus, and his distinguished pupil Thomas Aquinas. While the Franciscans did not at first become directly connected with

---

13) Schmidt, *Geschichte der Pädagogik*, vol. II, p. 144.

the universities, they also came to share very largely in the development of university teaching. Among their number were found such schoolmen as Duns Scotus and William of Occam. Both orders followed the methods of scholasticism very closely. The Augustinian order was founded in the middle of the thirteenth century by Popes Innocent IV and Alexander IV to check the rising power of the Franciscans and the Dominicans. The Augustinians were directly under the authority of the Popes, and while they were not so active in educational matters as either of the other two, they nevertheless had a number of their men on university faculties and at one time maintained no less than 2,000 cloisters. The famous Erfurt professors, Johann von Platz and Johann Staupitz, as well as Luther were members of this order.

THE RISE OF THE UNIVERSITIES.—An educational movement of still greater significance than scholasticism was the university movement. It had its origin in some of the old cathedral and conventual schools in Italy during the twelfth century and spread rapidly to the other European countries. The first school, generally dignified with the name of university, was the one at Salerno, Italy. Concerning the origin of the universities, Laurie says: "To fix precisely the date of the rise of the first specialized schools or universities is impossible for the simple reason that they were not founded. Europe was at the beginning of a new intellectual movement and had to feel its own way to the forms which might provide a fitting channel. . . . The simplest account of the new university origins is the most correct. It would appear that certain active-minded men of marked eminence began to give instruction in medical subjects at Salerno and in law at Bologna in a spirit and manner not previously attempted, to youths who had left the monastery and cathedral school and who desired to equip themselves for professional life. Pupils flocked to them, and the more able of these students, finding that there was a public demand for this higher specialized instruction, remained at headquarters and themselves became teachers and doctors. The Church did not found universities any more than it founded the order of chivalry. They were founded by a concurrence (not wholly fortuitous) of able men who had something they wished to teach and of youths who desired to learn. None the less were the acquiescence and protection of the Church and State necessary in those days for the fostering of these infant seminaries. Free, voluntary, self-supporting centers of learning, independent of ecclesiastical control and of civil direction, they certainly were in their beginnings. Free teaching and free learning were in the very heart of them."[14]

During the same century the universities of Bologna, Paris, and Oxford were founded in Italy, France, and England, respectively. During the following century many new universities were founded in Italy; the universities of Orleans and Toulouse in France, Cambridge in England, and some universities in Spain. Not until the middle of the fourteenth century were universities founded in central Europe, the University of Prague being founded in 1347, Vienna 1365, Erfurt 1379-92, Heidelberg 1385, and Cologne 1382. So popular were these seats of specialized and professional learning that their number throughout Europe at the close of the Middle Ages had reached a total of 80.[15]

THE MOORS.—After the Mohammedans were defeated at Tours in 732, many of them settled in Spain,

---

14) *Rise and Constitution of Universities*, pp. 106-8; see also Haskins, *Renaissance of the Twelfth Century*, pp. 368-396.
15) Haskins, *The Rise of Universities*, p. 29.

which had been conquered by them in 711, and there established themselves in the provinces of Seville, Cordova, Toledo, and Granada, where they built a civilization of their own which persisted to the close of the fifteenth century, when the Moors were conquered by the Spaniards and driven into exile. During the seventh and eighth centuries the Mohammedans of the East made very rapid progress in science and art and developed a learning superior in many respects to that of the Christian lands. Damascus and Bagdad became centers of Moslem learning where Greek, Jewish, and Arab scholars labored zealously both as students and teachers. As already indicated above, the Christian world came in contact with some of this learning during the Crusades. More of the Moslem learning, however, was brought westward by the gradual migration of Moslem scholars to the Moorish kingdom of Granada, and especially by the flight to the West of the Brothers of Sincerity, due to the fanatical persecutions by their fellow Moslems at home. The Brothers of Sincerity were a society which carried on the rationalizing of Moslem theology and the advancement of learning generally. They incurred the suspicion and hatred of the orthodox Moslems and were forced to flee to Spain, where they continued their work and established both elementary and higher schools at which were taught besides the Koran, mathematics, physics, astronomy, biology, medicine, logic, and metaphysics. The works of Aristotle were held in high esteem by the Moslem scholars. Averroes, one of their greatest scholars, born at Cordova in 1126, says of him: "Aristotle was the wisest of the Greeks and constituted and completed logic, physics, and metaphysics. I say that he constituted the sciences, because all the works on these subjects previous to him do not deserve to be mentioned and were completely eclipsed by his writings. I say that he put the finishing touches on these sciences, because none of those who have succeeded him up to this time, to wit, during nearly fifteen hundred years, have been able to add anything to his writings or to find in them any error of any importance. Now that all this should be found in one man is a strange and miraculous thing, and this privileged being deserves to be called divine rather than human." [16]

The great contribution of the Moors to Christian education during the Middle Ages, especially after the rise of the universities, was the enrichment of the university curricula with the study of the works of Aristotle, particularly his works on philosophy, physics, mathematics, and medicine.[17]

THE RENAISSANCE. — The intellectual movement known as the Renaissance, renascens, as some English and American scholars insist on terming it, arose in Italy in the thirteenth century. It awakened new interest in classical literature and culture and brought to light ancient literature, treasures long since lost and forgotten. Rising simultaneously with the university movement and the spread of Moslem learning, it naturally received stimuli from both these movements and in turn reacted upon them. The early leaders of the Renaissance in Italy were Petrarch (1304-74) and Boccaccio (1313-75). The movement in time also spread to other European countries, especially to France, Holland, England, and Germany, where it became known as Humanism. The most noted English humanists were Thomas Linacre (1460-1524), William Grocyn (1446-1514), and John Colet (1467-1519). Linacre and Grocyn, as professors of medicine

---

16) Cubberly, *Readings in History of Education*, p. 137.
17) On contributions of the Moors to the Renaissance, see Haskins, *The Renaissance of the Twelfth Century*, p. 281 seq.

and Greek, respectively, were the first to introduce Humanism at Oxford. From there it spread to Cambridge. It was Colet, however, who rendered the cause of education the greatest service by the establishment of the English secondary or grammar school, for which his school at St. Paul's Cathedral, founded in 1509, became the model. The first German to embrace Humanism seems to have been Peder Luder (1415-96) who, upon his return from Italy in 1456 began to lecture on the new learning at the Universities of Heidelberg, Erfurt, and Leipsic, but evoked little or no response. More successful were the Dutch humanists, Johann Wessel (1420-89), and Rudolph Agricola, or Husmann (1443-85). Neither of these men was an actual teacher, and yet they wielded a very extensive and wholesome influence on both men and studies, and especially did they promote the study of the classics.[18] Erasmus (1467-1536) was the greatest of the Dutch humanists and did a great deal to advance the cause of Greek study. He was the first to produce a Greek edition of the New Testament, which was published in 1516. Erasmus also wrote quite extensively on various phases of studies and teaching. Johann Reuchlin (1455-1522) was the most influential German humanist of his day. He was the greatest Hebrew scholar, as Erasmus, his great contemporary, was the greatest Greek scholar of the day. Reuchlin learned Hebrew in Italy, and on his return to Germany became a professor of Hebrew at Heidelberg. In 1506 he published his first Hebrew grammar. He was in his youth greatly influenced by Wessel and exerted a powerful influence upon his nephew Melanchthon who, at his suggestion, became professor of Greek and philosophy at the newly established University of Wittenberg.

---

18) Raumer, *Geschichte der Pädagogik*, vol. I, pp. 61-71.

Erfurt was the first German university to embrace Humanism, a professorship in poetry and eloquence being established there in 1493. It is thus evident that Humanism had not materially affected either the content of the curriculum or the methods of teaching at the universities outside of Italy at the close of the fifteenth century.

Among the educational reformers of the Italian Renaissance should especially be mentioned Vittorino da Feltre (1378-1446), Guarino da Verona (1374-1460), and Pier Paolo Vergerio (1349-1420). They wrote very extensively on educational topics, and Feltre and Verona maintained famous schools for boys from 9 to 20 years of age at Mantua and Ferrara. Their educational ideas were very advanced, sound, and practical.[19] The influence of these writers, however, was mainly local. At any rate, their educational ideas had not reached northern and central Europe by the close of the fifteenth century.

THE HIERONYMIANS.—The Hieronymians were a semi-monastic and communistic religious order which was organized at Deventer, Holland, in 1376, by Geert Groote, also known as Gerhard Magnus (1340-84), and Florentius Radewin, or Radewyns (1350-1400). Groote, who had been a student at the University of Paris, devoted himself in his early life to magic, astrology and necromancy, but following a severe illness he ordered all his books on magic and astrology to be burned and became a canon of Aachen and Cologne. For a time he devoted himself to the study of theology and the work of his office, but he soon retired to the monastery of Monnikhuizen, where he remained for three years, being especially devoted to a study of the Bible. He then went about as a preacher of repentance

---
[19] Woodward, *Vittorino da Feltre and Other Humanistic Educators; Education During the Renaissance.*

among the common people, preaching in the vernacular language. He very severely castigated the priests and monks for their parasitic, luxurious, and licentious living, and thus aroused their animosity. The hostility of clergy and monks finally brought an order from the bishop of Utrecht prohibiting Groote from preaching. He now retired to his birthplace, Deventer, and gathered about him a circle of pious young clericals, especially students of the school of Deventer, for meditation, reading of good books, and copying manuscripts. He was strongly opposed to the mendicant orders and would not permit anyone to join his circle who supported himself by begging. Florentius became a member of this circle, and one day he proposed to his master that the members of their little band form a voluntary association, pool their income and live in common. Groote at first opposed the idea but finally yielded, and the order of the Brethren of Good Will (Fratres Bonae Voluntatis) was organized. The order chose St. Jerome and St. Gregory as their patron saints and were, therefore, also known as Hieronymians and Gregorians. They also became known as the Brethren of the Common Life (Fratres Vitae Communis) and School Brethren (Fratres Scholares). The order was often severely persecuted by both mendicant monks and the lower and higher clergy. It was, however, recognized by the Council of Constance in 1418 and finally also by Pope Eugene IV in 1437 and Sixtus IV in 1474.

The first fraternity house was established at Deventer in 1384, and two years later another one was established at Windesheim, near Zwolle. So rapidly did the order grow that by 1430 there were no less than 45 fraternity houses. The last house to be established was the one at Cambrai, France, which was founded in 1505. Houses were established throughout Holland, France, and northern Germany and attracted a number of inmates. Not only did the order establish houses for men but also for women. There were no vows to be taken and absolutely no begging to be done, but otherwise very strict monastic discipline was observed. Both the men and the women were engaged in copying manuscripts and in other useful and productive occupations. Especially were they active in educational work, teaching the children of the common people both in their fraternity houses and in schools, either such as they themselves established— as the ones at Deventer and Zwolle—or in schools that were already established. The men taught the boys and the women the girls. The girls were mainly taught in the sisterhood houses, learning to read and write and doing various kinds of handiwork and household duties.

At first the curriculum of the Brethren was very narrow, Groote excluding geometry, arithmetic, rhetoric, dialectics, grammar, poetry, and astrology. Philosophy, science, and art were given a very subordinate place. Reading, writing, and the study of the Bible, especially the Gospels, Acts, and Paul's Epistles and the devotional writings of Bernhard, Anselm, and the early church fathers, were taught. While the order later on also promoted higher education, it was from the beginning a movement in behalf of the education of the common people. They used the vernacular language in teaching and preaching, and labored zealously to promote the translation of the Bible into the language of the people. Yet they very strictly enforced the teaching and speaking of the ecclesiastical Latin of the day in their higher institutions.

Among the leaders of this order and the men trained in its schools may be mentioned Thomas a Kempis, the author of *Imitation of Christ;* Gerhard von Zütphen, a great champion for the translation of the Bible into the vernacular, and Wessel, Agricola, Reuchlin, and Erasmus, whom we have already mentioned in connection with the Humanistic movement. Through these men Humanism was introduced into the schools of the order, but the introduction of the new learning did not alter their fundamental character and educational work. The teaching of the Bible to the common people, the use of the vernacular, and the cultivation of a pious life still continued to be the chief aim and ambition of the order. While the Italian Renaissance led away from the Scriptures to pagan literature and philosophy, the Brethren of the Common Life, through whom Humanism reached Holland and Germany, made the new learning a tool for a more profound study of Scripture and a better understanding and appreciation of it.

Concerning the educational work of the Hieronymians, Graves well says: "Naturally they at first stressed the instruction of the Bible and the vernacular, and taught reading, writing, singing, and conversation in ecclesiastical Latin. But as the Italian influence began to be felt in the upper countries, although the Hieronymians still held to the moral and religious motives, they broadened the course by the addition of humanistic elements. They retained their Christian training, but added the classic literature and Hebrew. While the education they offered was generally elementary and secondary, and consisted mostly of Latin and Greek, it included rhetoric and theology in the higher classes, and the Brethren often expanded the course so that in several instances it covered the work of the faculty of arts in a university. The constant visits of the members of the order to Italy and the frequent change of their teachers brought about an interchange of knowledge which silently molded public opinion and exerted a tremendous influence for Humanism and higher ideals. The Hieronymian schools, especially those at Deventer and Zwolle, became recognized centers of intellectual interest and Humanism. They were visited by wandering scholars, and the pupils that were trained there strengthened the new learning as teachers in the universities and schools throughout the Netherlands and Germany."[20]

It should be observed that there was a direct contact between Luther and the Hieronymians. It was one of their schools he attended at Magdeburg, mentioned by him as being the school of the Nüll Brethren, another name by which the order was known. Wessel was very highly appreciated by Luther as a theologian, and he says that if he had read Wessel's writings earlier his accusers might have claimed that he had derived his views from him, so much agreement there was between them. Even Erasmus recognized that the spirits of Wessel and Luther were akin, for he says: "Wessel has much in common with Luther."[21] Reuchlin and Erasmus being the contemporaries of Luther, were well known to him, and both made direct contributions to Luther's reformatory work by their Hebrew and Greek scholarship.

THE INVENTION OF PAPER AND PRINTING.—The two greatest aids to the spread of learning and the extension of popular education to the masses which the closing Middle Ages produced, were the discovery of the process of making paper on a large and reasonably cheap scale and the invention of printing by means of a press and movable type. From the earliest times material on which to write and preserve political records and accumulated learning had been a vexing problem. Clay, stone, metal, skins, and papyrus

---
20) *History of Education, Middle Ages*, pp. 146-47.
21) Raumer, *Geschichte der Pädagogik*, vol. I, p. 62.

were used, but all these were expensive and not readily obtained. Furthermore, multiplication of copies of books by hand was a slow and expensive process, and the result was that books were few and costly and learning sealed up as far as the masses were concerned. Consequently there was a lack of incentive to acquire even a rudimentary knowledge of reading and writing. The Arabs early discovered the process of making paper or obtained it from the Chinese. From the Moslems the process became known to the Europeans. The first paper mill was established in Italy in 1276, and the first paper mill in Germany was opened at Mainz in 1320. By the middle of the fifteenth century, when printing was invented, paper was in common use throughout Europe. In 1438 Gutenberg invented printing from movable wooden type, another lost Chinese art, and 12 years later Schaeffer and Faust cast the first metal type. In 1456 the first Latin Bible was printed at Mainz by Gutenberg and Faust. This was the first complete book to be printed. It was bound in two volumes, and a copy of this work was sold in New York in 1911 for $51,000.[22] Soon presses were set up both on the continent and in England, and books began to become both numerous and reasonably cheap. This naturally stimulated the desire for learning among all classes, even the common people becoming interested in learning to read and to write. The two inventions were, therefore, of the utmost significance to the cause of popular education. Says Adams: "One immediate consequence of this invention was that the results of the revival of learning, its new spirit of independence and its methods of criticism could no longer be confined to one country or to those who were being called scholars. They

---

22) Monroe, *History of Education*, p. 255.

spread rapidly throughout Europe, affecting large masses of the people who knew nothing of the classics and became vital forces in that final revolution of which Luther's work forms a part."[23]

OTHER INFLUENCES.—Besides these influences which have been briefly sketched above there were a number of others at work at the close of the fifteenth century. It was on the whole an age of increasing ferment and unrest intellectually, religiously, and socially. It was an age of geographical explorations and new interest in the study of geographical science. Exploration, trade, and industrial expansion followed. Travel increased, new contacts were established, and new worlds were opening up on every hand. The third estate was rapidly rising into power, demanding new rights and privileges, and even the dormant peasant class was beginning to show signs of awakening. The invention of gunpowder tended to lessen the distinction between the trained warrior and the recruit and thus helped the lower classes to rise in the social scale. A new era was about to be ushered in.

III. Schools, Curricula, and Teaching

Having thus sketched briefly the principal movements and influences which affected the theory and practice of education during the Middle Ages, we shall next consider the kinds of schools, their curricula, teachers, and methods of teaching, which were in operation at the close of the fifteenth century.[24]

ELEMENTARY SCHOOLS.—According to the Catholic writer, Johannes Janssen, elementary schools flourished in all parts of Germany at the close of the Middle Ages, in which reading, writing, arithmetic, choir

---
23) *Civilization During the Middle Ages*, p. 370.
24) In addition to general works on history of education, see Monroe, Thomas Platter, *Existing Types of Schools*, pp. 3-18, and Platter's *Autobiography*, pp. 79-227.

singing, the Creed, Commandments, and the Lord's Prayer were taught. A large number of these schools, he claims, were even open to girls both of the nobility and the masses. This is, however, entirely too favorable a description of the status of elementary education at this time.

While it is true that Charlemagne's effort in behalf of more general educational advantages for the common people for a time opened to them the conventual and cathedral schools, yet, as we have already observed, his reformation in this respect was far from being permanent. Here and there throughout the Middle Ages there seems to have been bishops who, like Bishop Theodulf of Orleans, were deeply interested in the education of the people. Yet they were notable exceptions and not the rule.[25] Such elementary instruction as was given by the Church was mainly for choir boys and future priests and also for the sons of nobility. Not for the people generally. An exception in this respect were, however, the chantry schools. They were established by bequests providing first of all for the maintenance of a priest to read masses in perpetuity for the repose of the souls of the donors, and secondly for the instruction of usually a stated number of boys in the rudiments of learning. An English grant of this kind, dated November 8, 1489, has the following provision: "Moreover, I will and ordain that the said chaplain for the time being shall teach and instruct in spelling and reading six of the poorest boys of the town of Aldwincle aforesaid, to be named by me and my wife Elizabeth while we are alive, and after our death three named by the rector of St. Peter's Church at Aldwincle aforesaid, and the other three by the chaplain for the time being, freely with-

---

25) Schmidt, *Geschichte der Pädagogik*, vol. II, p. 150.

out demanding or taking any remuneration from their parents or friends; and the boys, when they have been so instructed and taught, shall say every night in All Saints' Church in Aldwincle aforesaid, at the direction of the chaplain aforesaid for our souls and the souls of all the faithful departed the psalm 'Out of the Deep,' with the prayers 'Incline Thine Ear' and 'God of the Faithful.' "[26]

The elementary education given in the Middle Ages is very well characterized by Cubberly in the following language: "In education proper, in the sense that we understand it, the schools provided were still for a very limited class, and secondary rather than elementary in nature. They were intended to meet the needs of an institution rather than of the people, and to prepare those who studied in them for service to that institution. That institution, too, had concentrated its efforts on preparing its members for life in another world, and not for life or service in this. There were as yet no independent schools or scholars. The monks and the clergy constituted the learned class. Theology was the one professional study. The ability to read and write was not regarded by noble or commoner as of any particular importance, and all book knowledge was in the language which the people did not understand when they heard it and could not read."[27]

As for the education of the girls, which Janssen also contends was well provided for, it cannot be shown that the Middle Ages even made an approach to provide for the general education of girls and women. Their education was very much neglected. During the days of chivalry, however, the girls of nobility did receive quite careful education in household duties and skills, reading, writing, music, and polite manners,

---
26) Cubberly, *Readings in History of Education*, pp. 105-6.
27) *History of Education*, p. 172.

but this education was received not in schools but at home in the castle either under the mother's instruction or by a private teacher. The nunneries also provided a limited number of girls with a meager type of elementary education. The educators who did most to promote the education of girls were the Brethren of the Common Life. Holland appears to have been a pioneer in the establishment of schools for girls. Schmidt mentions a few of these schools both in Holland and Germany but observes that they were exceptional, not general.[28] In Lübeck and Nuremberg, burgher schools were established for girls shortly before the beginning of the Reformation.[29] As to the education of girls Painter says: "During the Middle Ages female education, outside of the knightly order, was generally neglected. Here and there in connection with nunneries, a few women attained distinction by their learning, but these cases were exceptional. Among the knightly class where women were held in high honor, great attention was paid to female culture. Not only were the young women instructed in the feminine arts of sewing, knitting, embroidery, and house-keeping, but they also received an intellectual training which, in addition to reading and writing, often included an extended acquaintance with Latin." [30]

With the rise of the third estate into wealth and power through the expansion of trade and industry came also the first secular schools, the guild or burgher schools. While these were established for the sons of the artisan and merchant classes, the clergy to a very large extent were in control, though in places this control was wrested from them.[31] In these schools

---
28) *Geschichte der Pädagogik*, vol. II, pp. 328-29.
29) Ibid., p. 311.
30) *History of Education*, pp. 129-30.
31) Cubberly, *History of Education*, p. 209, and Schmidt, *Geschichte der Pädagogik*, vol. II, p. 312.

reading, writing, and arithmetic were taught, and they were at first generally called writing schools. They developed from being mere guild schools into city schools in which not only the vernacular but also the Latin was taught, thus combining a sort of secondary school with the elementary.

The teachers in all of these schools, whether church or secular, were mainly from the clerical ranks. In many of the burgher schools, however, vagabond school masters were often employed. These were generally known as bacchantes from their drunken habits and immoral mode of living. They were often accompanied by young boys who received some sort of an elementary instruction in return for begging or stealing food and other necessities for the support of their teachers. These boys were generally known as ABC Schützen, or shooters. One of these ABC shooters, Thomas Platter, who later became quite a distinguished educator himself, has left us an interesting autobiography which sheds a great deal of light upon the character and work of these vagabond teachers and their young companions.[32]

The methods of instruction in vogue in the elementary as in the secondary schools were stiff, formal, and very unpedagogical. The teachers read from the text, made a number of explanations, lectured or dictated to the pupils who learned everything by memory and reproduced the memorized lessons to the teacher. The discipline was severe, even brutal. "The stick and the rod," says Schmidt, "drove the pupils to quietness and order as well as to attention and diligence." [33]

THE CATHEDRAL AND CONVENTUAL SCHOOLS.—The

---
[32] Schmidt, *Geschichte der Pädagogik*, vol. II, p. 316 seq.; Monroe, *Thomas Platter*, pp. 19-39; 79-227.
[33] Ibid., vol. II, p. 312.

development of the so-called song schools, which were maintained especially for the training of choir boys, relieved both the cathedral and the conventual schools from the teaching of reading and writing and they became essentially secondary schools. The cathedral schools were established in connection with the cathedral churches and aimed especially to prepare young men for the priesthood. The course of study embraced the so-called seven liberal arts, the trivium embracing grammar, rhetoric, and dialectic, and the quadrivium, which included arithmetic, geometry, astrology, and music. To these secular subjects was added some instruction in theology of a very narrow range, also some music and singing. The monastic schools, maintained in connection with monasteries, also taught the seven liberal arts. Until the rise of the universities, these were the highest educational institutions of the Middle Ages, the soil out of which grew many of the universities. Not all the conventual and monastic schools embraced both the trivium and the quadrivium in their curricula, most of them limiting themselves to the subjects of the trivium. Regarding the trivium and quadrivium, Haskins says: "The first group was the more rudimentary, but the second was rudimentary enough. The number was fixed and the content standardized during the decadence of ancient learning, and the whole conception reached the Middle Ages chiefly in the book of a certain Martianus Capella written in the early fifth century." [34]

The methods of teaching were of the scholastic type, dry, speculative, lectures and comments on the text read by the teacher, dictation, copying, memorizing, and disputation. Thus there was little intellectual development and virtually no real education.

---

34) *Rise of the Universities*, p. 38.

THE UNIVERSITIES.—The complete universities had four faculties, the faculties of arts, law, medicine, and theology. These faculties offered the following courses of instruction:

Organization of the University [35]

I. Faculty of Arts
  1. Trivium
  2. Quadrivium

II. Faculty of Law
  1. Corpus Juris
  2. Canon Law

III. Faculty of Medicine
  1. Hippocrates
  2. Galen
  3. Arabic and Jewish writers since 7th century

IV. Faculty of Theology
  1. Lombard's Sentences
  2. Summa Theologia
  3. Bible

The curriculum of the Faculty of Arts became considerably enriched by the introduction of the works of Aristotle when these became known to the Europeans through the Moors of Spain in the thirteenth century. Aristotle was at first banned from the University of Paris (1237), and he was first introduced into Oxford during the life of Roger Bacon, who died in 1294.[36] The *Corpus Juris* of the Law Faculty was the compilation of Roman law made at Constantinople under Justinian in 529-533. The book of *Canon Law* was complied by a monk by the name of Gratian in 1142 and generally known as *Decretum Gratiani*. The Faculty of Medicine also used textbooks hoary with age. They used the writings of Hippocrates, the "Fa-

---
35) For fuller statement of courses and books see Norton, *Readings in History of Education; Medieval Universities*, pp. 8-9; Cubberly, *Readings in History of Education*, pp. 168-181.
36) Cubberly, *Readings in History of Education*, pp. 137-8.

ther of Medicine," born in Greece about 430 B. C., and those of Claudius Galen, born at Pergamus in 130 A. D. and died 200. The more recent textbooks were derived from the Moors. The Theological Faculty dealt mainly with the *Sentences* of Peter Lombard (1105-60) and the *Summa Theologia* of Thomas Aquinas (1225-74). While the study of the Bible was supposedly a part of the curriculum, it received very little attention, and the criticism of Roger Bacon in 1392 was equally applicable to the place of the Bible in the universities of the fifteenth century. This criticism of Bacon is very significant. It reads as follows: "Although the principal study of the theologian ought to be the text of Scripture, as I have proved in the former part of this work, yet in the last fifty years theologians have been principally occupied with questions (for debate) as all know in tractates and summae,— horse loads composed by many,—and not at all with the most holy text of God. And accordingly, theologians give a readier reception to a treatise of scholastic questions than they will do to one about the text of Scripture. . . . The greater part of the questions, introduced into theology, with all the modes of disputation and solution, are in the terms of philosophy, as is known to all theologians, who have been well exercised in philosophy before proceeding to theology. Again, other questions which are in use among theologians, though in terms of thelogy, viz., of the Trinity, of the fall, of the incarnation, of sin, of virtue, of the sacraments, etc., are mainly ventilated by authorities, arguments, and solutions drawn from philosophy. And therefore the entire occupation of theologians now-a-days is philosophical both in substance and method." [37]

The Catholic historian, Janssen, referring to the

---

[37] Cubberly, *Readings in History of Education*, pp. 175-176; Norton, *Readings*, p. 77.

EDUCATION IN EUROPE

declaration of Luther that he had not seen a Bible till he was twenty years old, makes the following comment: "While in all the Latin schools, which adhered to the traditional church methods, the study of the Bible was carried on assiduously, it appears that in the schools which Luther attended, if we may believe his own testimony, the ancient classics alone were taught. 'When I was twenty years old I had not yet seen a Bible. I thought there were no other Gospels and Epistles besides those in the Homilies.' These words are the more astonishing, seeing that when he was twenty years of age he had already been for two years a student at the Erfurt University, where there could have been no lack of opportunity for becoming acquainted with the Bible, which had been a recognized subject of study there ever since the middle of the fifteenth century." [38]

It thus appears that, according to Janssen, not only was the Bible well known and thoroughly studied at the universities, but this was also the case in the orthodox Latin schools of the time. The great English authority on medieval universities, Rashdall, however, has a different view of the matter and states his view very emphatically in the following words: "Much astonishment has sometimes been expressed at Luther's 'discovery' of the Bible at the convent library at Erfurt. The real explanation of his previous ignorance of its contents is that Luther entered the order, a Master of Arts who had never studied in a theological faculty. Even the highly educated secular priest was not a theologian, or at least a canonist, was not supposed to know anything of the Bible but what was contained in his Missal and his Breviary. So much party capital has at times been made out of the sup-

---

38) *History of the German People*, vol. III, p. 82.

posed 'religious' character of the medieval universities that it is necessary to assert emphatically that the religious education of a 'bygone Oxford,' in so far as it ever had any existence, was an inheritance not from the Middle Ages but from the Reformation. In Catholic Europe it was the product of the Counter-Reformation. Until that time the Church provided as little professional education for the future priest as it did 'religious instruction' for the ordinary layman. Seminaries for the priests, catechisms, and preparation for the first communion, either at the universities or elsewhere, are the product of the Counter-Reformation, not of the Middle Ages. The whole medieval university system, even the college system, in the developed form which it had attained by the end of the fifteenth century, was about as unlike the modern seminary as anything that can well be imagined." [39]

METHODS OF INSTRUCTION.—The methods of instruction employed at the universities were lecturing and disputation, and the learning was largely memory work. There were two methods of lecturing in vogue, one so slow that the student could take time to write the professor's lectures verbatim, the other so rapid that only hurried notes could be taken. By a decree the former method was prohibited at the University of Paris as early as 1355. That some of the students objected very strenuously to this prohibition is evidenced by the declaration in the decree that "auditors who interfere with the execution of this our statute, by shouting and whistling or raising a din, or by throwing stones, either personally or through their attendants or accomplices, or any other way, we deprive of and cut off from our company for one year,

---

[39] *History of the Medieval Universities*, vol. II, Part II, pp. 701-2.

and for each repetition we increase the penalty to twice and four times the length as above."[40]

The methods of instruction used by the medieval university is well and fully described by **Cubberly** in the following words: "The first step in the instruction was a minute and subtle analysis of the text itself, in which each line was dissected, analyzed, or paraphrased, and the comments on the text by various authors were set forth. Next all passages capable of two interpretations were thrown into the form of a question, pro and contra, after the manner of Abelard. The arguments on each side were advanced, and the lecturer's conclusion set forth and defended. The text was thus worked over day after day in minute details. Having as yet but little to teach, the masters made the most of what they had."[41]

Rashdall gives the following characterization of the medieval university system: "In the older university system of Northern Europe there is the want of selection and the consequent incompetency of teachers, and the excessive youth of the students in arts. In the higher faculties, too, we have encountered the constant effort on the part of the doctors to evade the obligation of teaching without surrendering its emoluments, while the real teaching devolved upon halftrained bachelors. It is indeed in the student-universities that the chairs would appear to have been most competently filled and their duties most efficiently discharged. In medieval times students were more anxious to learn than teachers were to teach."[42]

CONCLUSION.—The foregoing survey of educational movements and influences which affected educational

---
40) Cubberly, *Readings in History of Education*, p. 178; Norton, *Readings*, pp. 114-115.
41) *History of Education*, p. 229. See also Norton, *Readings*, pp. 59 and 75.
42) Op. cit., vol. II, Part II, p. 703.

theory and practice during the Middle Ages and the descriptions given of schools and teaching at the close of the fifteenth century seem to warrant the following conclusions.

1. All education, secular and religious, with the exception of a few of the burgher schools, was under the direct control of the Church and carried on chiefly in its own interest as the organized organ of the Christian religion. The State had as yet no part or interest in the education of the young.

2. While there were many forces which reacted upon educational thought and practice from the days of Charlemagne to the Reformation, schools, curricula and methods of instruction remained essentially the same from the twelfth century to the beginning of the sixteenth, with the following notable exceptions:

- (a) The rise of universities and enrichment of their curricula through Moslem contributions and in a very slight measure by Humanism.
- (b) The rise of guild and burgher schools.
- (c) The schools of the Brethren of the Common Life which stressed the vernacular, cultivation of piety, better methods of teaching and more humane discipline, with the introduction of classical studies toward the close of the period through the efforts of such men as Wessel, Agricola, Reuchlin, and Erasmus.

3. What little there was of elementary education was confined to the teaching of reading, writing, arithmetic, some formal religion, and a little singing, and even this was limited to the few. There was no such thing as popular and general education.

4. Secondary education was generally limited to the trivium, Latin grammar, rhetoric, and dialectics, and at best included in addition the quadrivium with its arithmetic, geometry, astronomy, and music and, towards the close of the period, some instruction in philosophy and the natural sciences, but all on the basis of ancient textbooks.

5. Professional study was limited to the more or less complete mastery of a very few ancient textbooks with such meager contributions as the professors themselves were able to make.

6. All instruction was based upon authority, and free investigation found little or no encouragement but was rather repressed.

7. Various factors were at work socially, politically, intellectually, and religiously. The times were pregnant with new ideas, and new and transforming forces were emerging on every hand. The time was ripe for a leader who could incarnate the spirit of his time and was strong enough and courageous enough to assume the intellectual and religious leadership. Such a man arose in the person of Martin Luther, the son of a poor miner at Mansfeld, Germany.

CHAPTER II

LUTHER'S CHILDHOOD AND EARLY EDUCATION

It is not the purpose of this treatise to present a biographical sketch of Martin Luther, the Great Reformer. He is not in want of biographers, for they are so numerous that their works, from the death of Luther to the present time, constitute a veritable library in themselves. In order, however, to rightly understand and interpret the life and achievements of any historic personage it is necessary to inquire into the particular influences which in home, school, and environment helped to mold his character and shape and develope his views of life and his personal attitude toward life itself, and thus prepared him in a large measure for the part played in the life of thought and action. So it is also with our study of Luther as an educator. What he taught concerning child nurture and education and what he accomplished in behalf of Christian child nurture and a general Christian education were in a large measure directly attributable to the training he himself received and the various influences which in his own early life and youth shaped his views and molded his character.

BIRTH.—Martin Luther was born at Eisleben, a little mining town in Thuringia, Germany, on the tenth day of November, 1483, of the parents Hans and Margaretha Luther. The next day, which was St. Martin's Day, he was baptized in the Church of

LUTHER'S CHILDHOOD

St. Peter and Paul, and given the name Martin in honor of the saint on whose day he was baptized. Martin's surname is found in a number of forms, and did not receive any fixed form until as late as 1519, long after he had begun the work of the Reformation. The following are the most common forms of the name Luther, a name which is supposed to have been derived from the name Lothar: Luder, Ludher, Leuder, Luider, Lüder, and Lyder. At the University of Erfurt he was immatriculated as "Martinus Ludher ex Mansfeld," and later his name was registered as "Martinus Luder." At Wittenberg his name appears both as Lüder and Luder at first.[1] In his earliest correspondence he signs his name both Luder and Luther, and for a time immediately after the posting of the Ninety-five Theses he adopted the name "Eleutherius," from the Greek eleutheros, which means to be free.[2] From the year 1519 on the name appears regularly as Luther.

PARENTAGE.—Luther's parents were of the peasant class, and had shortly before his birth moved from the nearby Möhra, where they had a large number of relatives, to the little town of Eisleben. They did not long remain here, however, for about six months after Martin's birth they removed to the nearby town of Mansfeld. The father came from a strong and sturdy peasant stock. He was a man of strong personality, considerable native ability, and deeply religious. While he was a child of his time and a devoted Catholic, he nevertheless showed considerable independence in his religious thinking. Once when very sick, his priest attending upon him, thinking that he was about

---

1) Köstlin, *Martin Luther, Sein Leben und seine Schriften*, vol. I, p. 21; Graebner, *Dr. M. Luther*, p. 5; Michelet, *Life of Luther*, pp. 4-5. See also Smith, *Luther's Correspondence* and DeWette, *Luthers Briefe*.
2) Smith, *Luther's Correspondence*, vol. I, p. 64 seq.

to die, suggested that he remember the clergy with some of his means, a small amount of which he seems to have accumulated since locating at Mansfeld. To this Hans Luther replied that he had many children and they needed what little he could leave them better than the priests. There were in all at least six children, three sons and three daughters. At another time he commented on what he considered a precious dying confession of one of the counts of Mansfeld, who declared that he placed his trust alone in the blood of Christ and His righteousness and commended his soul into the hands of his Savior. His independence of thought in religious matters is also reflected in his keen disappointment and paternal anger when he learned that his son Martin had become a monk, as he felt there were already too many monks. And yet, like the other miner and peasant folk to whom he belonged, he devotedly joined in the saint worship of the time, especially was he like his towns-people devoted to the patron saint of Mansfeld, St. George, the reputed destroyer of the dragon, St. Anna, and the Virgin Mary. Martin's mother was born a Ziegler, near Eisenach, in which town and vicinity she had a number of relatives. Many Luther biographers incorrectly give her maiden name as Lindemann. She was a quiet, pious, somewhat superstitious, and hardworking woman. When Spalatin met her for the first time in 1522, he was struck at the remarkable resemblance between the Reformer and his mother. Luther's artist-friend, Lucas Cranach, has preserved the likeness of both his parents. Concerning his ancestry, Luther himself says in his *Table Talks*: "I am the son of a peasant; my father, my grandfather, my great-grandfather were all thorough peasants."[3] The parents

---

3) Berger, *Luther in kulturgeschichtlicher Darstellung*, vol. I, p. 1; Michelet, *Life of Luther*, p. 1.

were at first very poor and hard-working, but their conditions improved, so that the family in later years appear to have lived in quite comfortable circumstances. Young Martin's early life was therefore spent in poverty. "My father," he says, "was a poor miner; my mother carried in all the wood on her back; they worked the flesh off their bones to bring us up: no one nowadays would ever have such endurance." [4] Speaking of his early poverty and the sons of poverty in general, Luther later in life said in one of his sermons: "The sons of poor people must work themselves out of the dust; they must suffer much. And because they have nothing to boast and brag of, they learn to trust in God, pinch themselves and remain silent. The poor fear God; therefore God gives them good heads, that they may study and learn well and become learned and intelligent, so that they may teach their wisdom to princes, kings, and emperors." [5]

HOME TRAINING.—Luther's home training was of the severest sort. While his parents loved their children very much, and in turn were loved by them, yet their idea of child training included a liberal application of the rod and the strictest kind of legalism. The least disobedience to either parental or divine law seems to have been immediately followed by very severe discipline. "Theirs, however," says the great Luther scholar, Köstlin, "was not that unloving severity which blunts the spirit of the child, and leads to artfulness and deceit. Their strictness, well intended, and proceeding from a genuine moral earnestness of purpose, furthered in him a strictness and tenderness of conscience, which then and in after years made him deeply and keenly sensitive of every fault committed in the eyes of God; a sensitiveness, indeed, which so

---
4) Köstlin. *Luther*, p. 7.
5) Berger, *Luther*, vol. I, p. 1.

far from relieving him of fear, made him apprehensive on account of sins that existed only in his imagination. It was a later consequence of this discipline, as Luther himself informs us, that he took refuge in a convent." [6] As intimated in the preceding quotation, Luther in later life referred to the severe discipline to which he was subjected in his childhood home, and from these references he also drew some valuable lessons. "One should not whip children too hard," he says in one of his *Table Talks*. "My father once whipped me so severely that I fled from him and it was difficult for him to win me back to himself. I would not willingly strike little Hans (his own little son) much, for if I did he would be shy of me and hate me, than which no greater sorrow could happen to me." [7] Nor was it his father alone who was so severe. He also remembers especially once when he was severely beaten by his mother for taking a nut. Concerning this event in his life he says: "If children are evil and do harm and perpetrate wild tricks, they should be punished, especially when they learn to deceive and steal; nevertheless, in punishment reason must be used. For such childish pranks as taking cherries, apples, pears, and nuts must not be punished the same as when money, clothes, and chests are attacked. My parents were so strict with me that they made me timid. Mother flogged me once on account of a little nut so that the blood flowed, and her stern and severe discipline caused me later to enter a monastery and become a monk, though she meant heartily well by it. She merely failed to distinguish between the different dispositions according to which punishment should be measured. But one should punish in such a way that the apple and

---
6) Köstlin, op. cit., pp. 11-12.
7) Smith and Gallinger, *Conversations with Luther*, p. 1.

LUTHER'S CHILDHOOD

the rod go together."[8] By the statement about the apple and the rod, Luther means that reward and punishment must go hand in hand in child training.

The religious influences which played upon him during those early plastic years were also of the stern type. As both his parents were very religious, prayers and hymns were very common in his home and he early learned some simple prayers and hymns at his mother's knee. But he was taught to regard God and Jesus as stern and exacting judges whose favor must be secured through the intercession of the Virgin Mary and the saints. As Köstlin well says, "he was instructed and trained up from childhood in that narrowing conception of Christianity, and that outward form of religiousness, against which, more than anything, he bore witness as a Reformer."[9]

SCHOOL DAYS AT MANSFELD.—Young Martin was early sent to school. It seems that his father was from the very first determined to give his son the very best education possible. He attended the school at Mansfeld till he was fourteen years old, but he seems to have only painful memories from his school days in this town. Besides learning to read, write, and do simple operations in arithmetic, he was also taught the rudiments of Latin grammar. The methods of instruction were of the worst and the discipline was of the most brutal. Concerning his experiences at this school, he later says: "It is a bad thing if children lose their spirit on account of parents and teachers. There have been many bungling masters who have destroyed splendid talents by their blustering, storming, striking, and pounding, because they deal with children in the same manner as executioners and stock-

---

8) *Luthers Werke*, St. Louis ed., vol. XXII, p. 1785. See also Smith and Gallinger, *Conversations*, pp. 1-2.
9) *Luther*, p. 19.

masters with thieves. Ah, what time we had with the lupus [10] on Fridays and Donatus [11] on Thursdays! They asked strictly of each one to parse 'legeris, legere, legitur, lecti mei ars.' These questions were like a trial for murder. Good method in teaching should note differences of character in pupils. I was one forenoon struck fifteen times at school, for no fault of mine, for I was expected to decline and conjugate what I had yet not learned." [12] In his *Letter to the Councilmen in Behalf of Christian Schools*, he also refers to his experiences at Mansfeld, calling attention to the fact that now the "schools are no longer a hell and a purgatory, in which children are tortured over cases and tenses, and in which with much flogging, trembling, anguish, and wretchedness they learn nothing." [13] He also tells of an interesting incident which shows how frightened the school boys were in his day. Some of them, including himself, had been singing Christmas carols outside the home of a peasant, who upon coming to the door, called to them in a loud, coarse voice and so frightened the singers that they hurriedly ran away. The peasant, however, had only good intentions. He wanted to reward them for their singing by giving them good German sausage.[14]

But his seven or eight years spent in the school at Mansfeld had not been spent altogether in vain, for the young lad had at least learned the fundamental truths of the Christian religion, divorced from life though they had often been, and he had laid, because of his ability and studiousness, rather than because of the instruction given, a good foundation for the

---
10) The lupus, wolf, was the monitor who punished the pupils for not speaking Latin.
11) Donatus, author of the Latin grammar used in the Middle Ages.
12) *Luthers Werke*, St. Louis ed., vol. XXII, p. 1785; Smith and Gallinger, op. cit., pp. 2-3.
13) Painter, *Luther on Education*, p. 198.
14) *Table Talks*. Köstlin, *Luther*, vol. I, p. 33.

use of his native language, which he could use with such singular power and effect, and also a foundation for his later ability to handle the Latin language with ease and freedom. But perhaps the best that he derived from the first school he attended was the training he had received in music and song. His love for music and song and his appreciation of them remained with him throughout life, and exerted a very wholesome influence both upon his life and his work.

SCHOOL DAYS AT MAGDEBURG.—In 1497, when young Martin was fourteen years old, his father decided to send him to a better school than he had hitherto attended. To Magdeburg he was sent, accompanied by his friend, Hans Reinicke, the son of a mine overseer by the name of Peter Reinicke, traveling no doubt on foot, carrying what few belongings they had with them. Hans and Martin remained lifelong friends. According to Mathesius, one of Luther's later pupils as well as a boarder in his home for some time, the school at Magdeburg was at that time "famed above many others." [15] Here he attended a school conducted, as he tells us, by the Nüll Brethren, another name for the Lollards or Brethren of the Common Life.[16] Very little is known of Luther's school life here at Magdeburg, and his stay here was only for a brief space of one year. During this time he supported himself, like so many other school boys in his day, by singing and begging. While staying at Magdeburg he was taken very sick, and his life was for a time in the balance. The story of his illness and recovery is told by his physician, Dr. Ratzeberger.[17] Luther relates one incident from his life here which made a deep and lasting impression on him. "When in my fourteenth

---

15) *Luther*, p. 4.
16) De Wette, *Briefe*, vol. I, p. 390; Köstlin, vol. I, p. 34.
17) Köstlin, vol. I, p. 35.

year," he says, "I went to school at Magdeburg, I saw with my own eyes a prince of Anhalt . . . who went in a friar's cowl on the highways to beg bread, and carried a sack like a donkey, so heavy that he bent under it, but his companion walked by him without a burden; this prince alone might serve as an example of the grisly, shorn holiness of the world. They had so stunned him that he did all the works of the cloister like any other brother, and he had so fasted, watched, and mortified his flesh that he looked like a death's head, mere skin and bones; indeed, he soon after died, for he could no longer bear such a severe life. In short, whoever looked at him had to gasp for pity and must needs be ashamed of his own worldly position." [18] Although he thus strongly reacted against this instance of holiness by means of the severest sort of self-mortification, this sight must have powerfully impressed him in an altogether different way as a boy with such a religious background as he had from childhood, and it may have been one of the many influences which led him later in life to seek holiness by a similar route as a monk. One of the most beneficent influences to which Luther was subjected during his brief stay at Magdeburg was no doubt his acquaintance with Andreas Proles, who was at that time vicar of the Augustinian Congregation at Magdeburg. He was a very pious and upright man, who sought earnestly to better the religious conditions of the times, though he did not go beyond the strictly legalistic monkish conception. Luther mentions this man several times in his writings and in his *Table Talks*.[19]

SCHOOL DAYS AT EISENACH.—The following year Luther was sent by his parents to the School of St.

---

18) Preserved Smith, *Life and Letters of Martin Luther*, p. 4.
19) Köstlin, vol. I, pp. 35-36; Kolde, *Martin Luther*, vol. I, pp. 47, 50, 60.

George at Eisenach. This school he attended for four years. His stay in the beautifully situated city of Eisenach under the very shadows of the Wartburg, which played so important a part in the later life of the Reformer and his work, was one which he loved to look back to in his maturer years. And no wonder, for the years spent there were undoubtedly the happiest and most pleasant years of his life. One reason for sending the lad to Eisenach was no doubt the large number of relatives he had there, especially on his mother's side. But these relatives seem to have been very poor, and therefore unable to give the boy any material assistance. He was therefore obliged at first, here as at Magdeburg, to sing and beg for his food. How long he continued to support himself in this manner is not known. After some time, however, his boyish earnestness and sincerity, clear and beautiful voice, and good manners attracted the attention of a lady of position and means by the name of Ursula Cotta, who opened her house and table to him, so that he for the remainder of his stay at Eisenach was well provided for. But this was not the only advantage he enjoyed on account of the motherly friendship of Frau Cotta. The peasant boy and miner's son, accustomed hitherto only to the coarse and uncouth manners of the common people of his day, whose language and manners he learned so well to understand that he in time became Germany's most popular and effective preacher, now also became introduced into the higher and more refined society, and acquired that facility of speech and polish of manner which, in spite of his natural ruggedness, yea, even coarseness of manner, served both him and his great cause so well in dealing with scholars, the nobility, princes, and even the emperor himself. Not only did he freely enjoy the refined atmosphere of the Cotta household, but through Frau

Cotta, herself a Schalbe, he was also introduced to the little circle of the Schalbe Foundation, a little Franciscan convent, and a number of other prominent men and families, among them Johann Braun, the vicar of Eisenach, for whom the young Luther formed a very tender attachment. When he was about to celebrate his first mass after having been ordained priest, he wrote a very affectionate letter to Father Braun, inviting him to be present on this occasion. He would also, he says, in a postscript attached to this letter, have invited "those excellent men of the Schalbe Foundation," but he fears that they are of too high a rank and order to be troubled with "the wishes of a monk now dead to the world." [20] Referring to his sojourn at Eisenach, Luther says in one of his letters: "Eisenach has almost all of my relatives, and there I am to-day recognized and known to most of them, since I studied there four years, nor does any city know me better." [21] This letter is dated January 14, 1520.

But it was not only because of the large number of relatives they had at Eisenach that his parents sent their promising boy to that city. Hans Luther had great hopes for his boy, and was determined to give him the best educational advantages possible. The School of St. George was far famed, and occupied a rather unique position among the schools of the time. Its principal teacher was Johann Trebonius, who had the strange custom when entering the school room every morning to remove his cap or biretta and bow to the assembled pupils, for as he would say, there might be among them a future mayor, learned doctor, chancellor or ruler. Not only would he do this himself, but he would also insist upon his assistants doing so. What a different attitude this teacher and his as-

20) Smith, *Correspondence*, vol. I, pp. 21-22.
21) Smith, *Correspondence*, vol. I, p. 274.

sistants showed towards their pupils from the attitude shown by Luther's former teachers! But old Trebonius was not only a sentimental eccentric; he was also a scholar and a real teacher. He was interested in the new humanistic studies and tendencies, so that Luther for the first time in his life now comes in contact with that movement which so deeply stirred the intellectual life of his time. Under the direction of Trebonius and another teacher by the name of Wigand, the ambitious and studious young scholar made remarkable progress. For the first time in his experience did the life of a school boy seem joy and pleasure to him. He daily engaged in the study of language, especially Latin, history, literature, and music, and showed great proficiency in the composition and delivery of Latin orations and the writing of Latin poetry. He no doubt had other teachers besides Trebonius and Wigand, but they are not mentioned. It is a fact worthy of notice that Luther always refers to the years spent at Eisenach as though he had only pleasant recollections from his "dear Eisenach," and it always seems a joy for him to revisit, whenever possible, this place of his early happy experiences and associations both in and out of school. He also showed an enduring love for his teachers, helping to secure for his aged teacher Wigand a comfortable place of retreat when he was obliged to retire from active service, because he was his "alter Schulmeister."

CHAPTER III

THE STUDENT AND MONK

Having completed his course of study at Eisenach, young Martin, now eighteen years old, was prepared to enter the university to continue his studies. His father's economic condition had in the meantime improved considerably, so he was now in position to provide adequately for Martin's support at school, which would permit the young student to apply himself undevidedly to his studies. Consequently, in the summer of 1501 we find the young lad on his way to Erfurt, where he was enrolled as "Martinus Ludher ex Mansfeld" at the then famous University of Erfurt.

ERFURT AND ITS UNIVERSITY.—The city of Erfurt was a populous and thrifty city in the very heart of Germany. It ranked high as an industrial and commercial city, and was noted for its wealth, political independence, large number of convents, and, most of all, for its University, which at that time was the foremost university in Germany, although not the oldest. So well was this institution of learning reputed that there was a proverb current which said: "Whoever desires to study in earnest, let him betake himself to Erfurt."[1] Luther himself rated the University very highly and spoke of it as outranking all the other German universities of the time, speaking of them as merely small schools compared with it.[2] The University was founded

---
1) Berger, *Martin Luther*, vol. I, p. 31.
2) *Tischreden, Werke*, Erlangen ed., LXII, p. 287.

in 1392 and had been greatly favored by the Popes. It was under the direct supervision of the Archbishop of Mainz, who was its chancellor, and was thus completely under the sway of the Church, all its professors being bound by oath to teach nothing contrary to the doctrines of the Church. At the beginning of each semester, a special mass was held, which was attended by all the professors and students. Each college also had its regular periods of devotion, and each faculty had its own patron saint, the one of the philosophical faculty, with which Luther took his work, being St. George. While the University as a whole was under the domination of Aristotelian philosophy and Scholastic theology, it represented the more moderate tendencies of these schools, and was to a considerable extent influenced by the Humanism of the day.[3] At the time Luther entered the University, it had a teaching staff of thirteen regular professors and some tutors, and a student body that numbered about one thousand. "Theology and the canonical or ecclesiastical law took the highest rank among the studies pursued there. In the two other learned professions, law and medicine, the old Roman civilians and the Greek medical writers were chiefly studied. In the wide department of philosophy, a sort of encyclopedia of the sciences, as contained in the writings of Aristotle, constituted the course of instruction. The Bible was not studied, and none of the Greek authors above named were read in the original. Neither languages, except the Latin, nor history were taught after the manner which afterward prevailed in the universities. Everything still wore the garb of the Middle Ages. There were no experiments in natural philosophy, no accurate criticism in language or history.

---

3) Raumer, *Geschichte der Pädagogik*, vol. IV, p. 28; Janssen, *History of the German People*, vol. III, pp. 32-44.

Learning was either a matter of memory, or it was a sort of gladiatorial exercise in the art of disputation."[4]

The most famous professors at the University were Luther's principal teachers, Jodocus Trutvetter,[5] professor of logic, and Bartholomew Arnoldi of Usingen, professor of philosophy, both alumni of the University. Trutvetter became rector of the University of Wittenberg in 1507 and dean of the theological faculty there the following year. Because of some disagreement with the other members of the Wittenberg faculty, he returned to Erfurt in 1510. Both became very violent opponents of Luther later, Luther vainly endeavoring to become reconciled to them and justifying his position before them. Trutvetter accused Luther of ignorance of both dialectics and theology, as Luther himself states in a letter to Spalatin under date of May 18, 1518.[5] In the same letter he tells of a conference with both his former professors, in which he without success tried to convince them that he was in the right. In a letter to Trutvetter about a week earlier, Luther wrote: "To explain myself further, I simply believe that it is impossible to reform the Church unless the Canon Law, scholastic theology, philosophy and logic, as they are now taught, are thoroughly rooted out and other studies put in their stead. I am so fixed in this opinion that I daily ask the Lord, as far as now may be, that the pure study of the Bible and the Fathers may be restored. You think I am no logician; perhaps I am not, but I know that I fear no one's logic when I defend this opinion."[7] It

---

[4] Henry Barnard, *German Teachers and Educators*, p. 114. See also Berger, op. cit., vol. I, pp. 30-47; Köstlin, *Martin Luther, Sein Leben und seine Schriften*, vol. I, pp. 39-56.
[5] Janssen calls him Trutseller, *History of the German People*, vol. III, p. 32.
[6] Smith, *Luther's Correspondence*, vol. I, p. 85.
[7] Ibid., pp. 83-84.

is not to be wondered at that Trutvetter and Usingen [8] resented such a bold attack upon their favorite studies and regarded his theology as a poison, but as Luther says, "this is what comes from growing old in wrong opinions." This later attitude of Luther and the statements and actions which it prompted show conclusively how he reacted toward both the subject matter taught and the manner in which it was taught during his stay at the University of Erfurt.

STUDENT LIFE AT ERFURT.—The student life at Erfurt was, like student life generally even at that time, carefree, jolly, and in some cases even voluptuous and dissipating. The students who did not board with the professors or private families lived in the houses maintained by the various colleges, where they also received their board. Luther lived at the House of St. George, being a student in the philosophical department. The students banded themselves together into clubs of various kinds then as now, and while there seems to be no evidence that Luther belonged to any such club, he was at least very closely associated with the members of a club, who called themselves "Poets." These students were interested in the Humanistic studies and sought to cultivate a classical Latin style by writing poetry and reciting this to one another. Many of these young Humanists, as Crotus, Spalatin, Lang, Hess, and Mutianus Rufus, remained Luther's life-long friends. Luther was a jovial companion, and was known among them as the philosopher and musician, for he was so devoted to his philosophy that he took no time to cultivate poetry; besides he was a good singer and had learned to play the lute acceptably at one time while he was laid up on account of having wounded his foot with the sword, which he, ac-

---

8) Janssen complains that they "suffered misfortunes and calumnies of all sorts for their adhesion to the Catholic faith." Op. cit., p. 32.

cording to the student fashion of the time, carried. But although Luther was merry and jolly when in the company of his fellow students, he was a very pious, serious, and studious young man, who began every day with prayers, attended every lecture, conferred and discussed with his teachers, and spent a great deal of his time in the library.[9] Of his student life Smith says: "That it was pure and godly may be inferred from the fact that his enemies never found any reproach in it and because of the absence of self-accusation." [10]

STUDIES AND DEGREES.—It was Hans Luther's greatest ambition to make a jurist of his son Martin, and it was for this purpose that he sent him to the University of Erfurt. It was customary, however, before taking up the study of law to lay a foundation in language, logic, rhetoric, and Aristotelian and Scholastic philosophy, and young Luther followed the regular course. He even seems to have gone further than was usual in pursuit of his philosophical studies before entering upon the study of law, because personally he was more inclined to the study of languages and philosophy than to law. He became thoroughly grounded in the works of Aristotle and learned to hate the "blind heathen" very cordially, so that he later in life did all he could to undo the current worship of Aristotle and his philosophy in the universities, and especially among the theologians. In his letter to the German Nobility in 1520, in speaking of the necessary reforms to be made in the university courses, he states that he would oust entirely Aristotle's "Physicorum, Metaphysicae, de Anima, and Ethicorum, which until now have been regarded as the best," so that valuable time, labor, and expense be no longer wasted in study-

---
9) *Historien*, p. 5.
10) *Life and Letters of Martin Luther*, p. 6.

ing these books from which the students only derive false views concerning both natural and spiritual matters. He would, however, retain his books, "Logica, Rhetorica, Poetica, or reduce them to a briefer form," since they are useful in teaching the young to speak and preach well, but he would do away with all the comments on them.[11] Whether he studied Plato or not is doubtful. He at least knew him, and had very little use for him. He was to him merely a "sophist." The Latin writers, Cicero, Virgil, Livy, Ovid, Terence, Juvenal, and others he became very well acquainted with, and cites them extensively in his later writings and addresses. Virgil was his favorite Latin poet. The greatest part of his time seems to have been devoted to the study of the Scholastic philosophers and theologians. Whether he took up the study of Greek and Hebrew while at Erfurt is still an open question. Grisar, his recent Catholic biographer, contends that he began the study of both of these languages while at Erfurt, and even succeeded in procuring a Hebrew dictionary, a very rare book in those days. According to this writer, his fellow student, later a professor at Wittenberg, Johann Lang, assisted him with his Greek studies.[12] So also Smith[13] and Köstlin.[14]

The greatest discovery Luther made during his four years of study at the University of Erfurt was the accidental finding of a copy of the Bible, the first complete Bible he had ever seen, in the University library. He was surprised to learn that the Bible contained so many more texts than the usual Gospel and Epistle texts read and expounded in the churches and found in the postils. Turning the leaves of the Old Testament, he came across the story of Hannah and

---
11) *Werke*, Erlangen ed., xxi, pp. 344-46.
12) *Luther*, vol. I, p. 28.
13) *Life and Letters of Luther*, pp. 26-27.
14) *Luther*, vol. I, p. 115.

Samuel, a story which seems to have made a deep impression on him. Mathesius, who tells this story, adds that Luther then and there wished that he, too, some day might own a complete copy of the Bible himself, a wish which he later happily realized.[15]

About a year after he entered the University, Luther received his first university degree, that of Bachelor of Philosophy. At that time there were fifty-seven in the class, and Luther ranked thirtieth, so that he had apparently not distinguished himself above the average during his first year of university life. However, when in 1505 he receives his second degree, that of Master of Philosophy, he stands second in a slass of seventeen. The conferring of the master's degree was the occasion for a great celebration, in which the townspeople also took part. A torch-procession went through the streets of the city, and the young master received honors from both fellow-students and the citizenry, so that Luther later in life refers to it as the most joyful of all earthly experiences.[16]

A SUDDEN CHANGE.—After receiving his master's degree, Luther returned to his parents for a brief visit before entering upon the study of law. His father was very proud of him, and showed him even the honor of addressing him in the German polite form, instead of the familiar "du." Returning to Erfurt, he at once took up the study of law, not because he himself wished to do so, but to please his father, whose heart was set on his son becoming a jurist. His father had presented him with the expensive work on law, *Corpus Juris*, and provided him with other necessary books. He had even gone so far as to plan for him a marriage, which would help to give him both social position and honor. But only

---
15) *Historien*, p. 5.
16) *Tischreden, Werke*, Er. ed., lxii., p. 287.

THE STUDENT AND MONK

a few weeks had passed since young Martin began the study of law, when all of a sudden he returns the *Corpus Juris* and the other books on law to the bookseller, gives a farewell party to his astonished friends, and seeks seclusion within the walls of the Augustinian monastery of Erfurt. The recent sudden death of a dear friend, probably by assassination, and a violent thunderstorm in which he was caught on a July day, by which his very life seemed threatened, so overwhelmed him with fear of the divine judgment that he in his deep anguish made the vow that if God spared his life he would enter the cloister and devote himself to making penance for his sins and serving God. The thunderstorm soon passed over, but the spiritual storm within Luther's sensitive soul continued with unabated fury and gave him no peace, even after he had carried out his vow and become a monk. In agreement with Luther's own later confessions, Graebner well says: "Fear of the severity of father and mother, fear of the tyranny of the flogging-master of the school, fear of the zealous wrath of the judge on the heavenly throne succeeded one another in the boy and youth, Martin Luther; now this fear had driven him into the cloister."[17] The one consuming passion of this bright and active youth, forgetful of studies, friends, his bright future, and even the earnest wish of his father, was to atone for his sins and find peace with God. The spiritual struggles which ensued, culminating finally in his acceptance of the vicarious satisfaction of Christ and justification by faith alone, as in fact his whole religious experience in the cloister, were of fundamental significance for his future work as reformer and educator, and enable us to understand the theological views which he championed, the motives which prompted his great zeal

---

17) *Dr. M. Luther*, p. 29.

and unselfish labors, and the objects which he sought to realize both through the Church and the School.

HIS OCCUPATIONS AS A MONK.—Besides the Augustinian monastery there were many other monasteries at Erfurt, so that Luther had an opportunity to choose from among them. That he chose the Augustinian monastery was no doubt due to its high reputation both for order and learning and because of the well-known learning, piety, and ability of the vicar-general of the Augustinian Order, Dr. Johann Staupitz. At any rate, it seems that it was of the greatest significance both to Luther personally and to the cause of the Reformation that he came to this cloister rather than to any of the others. While he, like the other monks, was required to do the most menial sorts of labor, even being humiliated by having to go from house to house and beg for the benefit of his cloister, he was also given a rare opportunity for study, and that especially his favorite studies, the Bible, the Fathers, and some of the Scholastics. He was the most learned as well as the most studious monk in the cloister, and the other monks appear to have been very anxious to humble him and delight in tormenting him on account of his studious habits, for they imposed upon him many trifling and even useless tasks and told him that "by begging and not by studying the cloister was served and enriched."[18] Upon his entry into the cloister, he was given for his own use a complete copy of the Bible, and of this book he made the most diligent use. His university teacher, Usingen, advised him to read the Bible less and the Church Fathers more, while Dr. Staupitz encouraged him in his Bible study, and was of the utmost help to him both in his spiritual struggles and in deepening and extending his knowledge of the Bible. While the

---
18) Mathesius, *Historien*, p. 7.

Bible was Luther's main text-book, he also studied the works of many of the Church Fathers and the leading Scholastics very diligently, becoming familiar with the works of Augustine, Athanasius, Jerome, Occam, Scotus, Anselm, Lombard, Aquinas, Bonaventura, Bernard of Clairvaux, Biel, Gerson, D'Ailly, and others. The studies in theology at the cloister were carried on under the direction of Doctors Von Platz and Johann Nathin, of whom the latter seems to have endeared himself the most to Luther, for he frequently sends greetings to him in letters to Johann Lang and other men connected with the monastery. But the men who influenced Luther most at the monastery were the old preceptor, whom Luther frequently mentions, but whose name is unknown, and the vicar-general, Dr. Johann Staupitz.

On May 2, 1507, Luther was consecrated priest and celebrated his first mass.[19] For this occasion he had invited his father and a number of friends. He had been estranged from his father ever since he entered the cloister, his father having become so angry with his son for giving up the study of law and entering the monastery that he had disowned him. The loss of two sons by an epidemic and the reported death of Martin had, however, softened his heart toward the erring son and at least a partial reconciliation had been effected between father and son. When the two met at Erfurt on this occasion they had not seen each other since Martin left home to enter upon his law studies two years previous. As father and son were seated at the banquet table, Martin said to his father: "Dear father, why were you so opposed to my becoming a

---

[19] Smith in his *Life and Letters of Luther* states that the ordination took place in February, 1507, and that it was only the celebration of the first mass that took place on May 2; but this is not in agreement with other authorities. See Mathesius, *Historien*, p. 7; Köstlin, *Luther*, vol. I, p. 83 seq.

monk and became so angry, and perhaps even now do not like it any too well?" The father replied: "Have you scholars not read in Holy Scriptures that one must honor father and mother? Contrary to this commandment you forsook me and your dear mother in our age, when we should have had comfort and help from you, because we spent so much on your studies, and you went against our will into the cloister." [20] These were hard words on such a joyous occasion and deeply wounded the young priest. When he tried to defend himself by saying that he had become a monk through the terrors from heaven, the father simply replied: "Let us hope it was not illusion and deception." While at the Wartburg Luther wrote a treatise on *Monastic Vows* and dedicated it to his father in a lengthy dedicatory letter in which he relates this story and tells of the keenness with which he at that time felt his father's just reproach.[21]

CONTACT WITH THE OUTSIDE WORLD.—Luther did not become a recluse while in the monastery; his interest went beyond the narrow confines of the cloistral walls. No one was more conscious of this fact than his superior and spiritual adviser, Dr. Staupitz. When he needed an instructor in philosophy at the recently established University of Wittenberg in the fall of 1508, he summoned the young scholar and monk from the monastery at Erfurt to take charge of this work. That he had even further plans for him at Wittenberg became evident later, as we shall see. Luther was called back to Erfurt the following year, but when Dr. Staupitz wanted a man on whom he could depend two years later to undertake a journey to Rome in the interest of the re-organization plan of the Augustinian Order, which he was sponsoring, he

---
20) Köstlin, vol. I, p. 84; Graebner, *Luther*, p. 41.
21) Smith, *Luther's Correspondence*, vol. I, pp. 65-71.

THE STUDENT AND MONK

again turned to Luther. In company with another monk Luther traveled from cloister to cloister until the famous city of Rome was reached. Being a keen observer, Luther learned a great many things which he afterward turned into good use in the promotion of the reforms he undertook to carry out. This journey to Rome and the experience of grappling personally with the various problems involved in his mission materially broadened and ripened Luther as a man and a scholar and in a large measure fitted him for the great work he was about to enter upon as professor of theology at the University of Wittenberg and his subsequent work of religious and educational reformation.

Luther returned from Rome about February, 1512, and was then transferred from the monastery at Erfurt to the Augustinian monastery at Wittenberg, where he shortly afterward was made sub-prior. In 1515 he was made district vicar of his order and had general supervision of all the monasteries within his district. In his administrative dealings with other monks he was sympathetic and considerate, and while faithful to the rules and regulations of his order, he believed in a liberal interpretation of them and opposed harsh and rigorous enforcement of them. His letter discharging Michael Dressel as prior of the monastery at Neustadt is a good example of how Luther dealt in official capacity.[22] He was to many an erring and spiritually troubled monk a wise and sympathetic father and counsellor.

---

22) Smith, *Luther's Correspondence*, vol. I, p. 39.

CHAPTER IV

IN THE PROFESSOR'S CHAIR

Whether Luther had been called on to assist in the work of teaching at the monastery of Erfurt before being summoned to lecture at the University of Wittenberg or not, we do not know. It is not unlikely, however, that he had done some teaching at the cloister and that he had so distinguished himself as a teacher that Dr. Staupitz, who was then connected with the University of Wittenberg, mindful of this fact called Luther to that University to teach. At any rate, Luther's university teaching began with his work at Wittenberg during the school year of 1508-9 and continued almost without interruption until his death, in 1546. From the first he was heavily taxed with duties outside of his university work, first as an administrative officer of his order, after 1517, with shaping and guiding the forces of the Reformation. To the general historian and biographer his work as a university professor is almost entirely eclipsed by his work as a religious reformer, and yet it was as a professor of theology, or as he preferred to style himself, "Doctor of the Bible," that he laid the foundations and reared the superstructure of his reformation in Church, State, and School.

THE UNIVERSITY OF WITTENBERG.—Wittenberg, situated on the Elbe about sixty miles southwest of Berlin, was in Luther's day only a comparatively small town of some three thousand inhabitants, but had for some time served as a capital of the Ernestine Saxony, though the Elector had his main castle at Altenburg. The town had, besides the castle, the Town Church, the Castle Church, and an Augustinian monastery, among the buildings of any importance. When by the Treaty of Leipsic, in 1485, Saxony had been divided between the two brothers, Ernest and Albert, Ernestine Saxony was left without a university, so the Elector's subjects were obliged to go outside the domain to either Leipsic or Erfurt for their university training. In order to provide his people with a university of their own, Elector Frederick the Wise, who was himself a well educated man, established the University of Wittenberg in 1502, securing Dr. Martin Pollich, then at the University of Leipsic, as the first rector, and Dr. Johann Staupitz as the dean of the theological faculty. The Elector depended largely upon the monks located at the Black Cloister in Wittenberg for the teaching work to be done at the new university for the present at least. Dr. Pollich was very friendly toward Humanism, and the bent of the new University was from the very first toward the new learning. In 1507 Dr. Trutvetter of Erfurt was called to Wittenberg, but he remained only till 1510, when he returned to Erfurt. Among the earliest to receive their degrees at Wittenberg were Andreas Carlstadt, who became dean of the theological faculty in 1508, and received the degree Doctor of Theology in 1510, and Nikolaus von Amsdorf, who became a Licentiate in Theology in 1511. Both of these men later became noted for the part they took in the Reformation, the former first as a friend and aid of Luther and later an opponent, and the latter a life-long and intimate friend and co-laborer of Luther. Gradually, the University built up a strong faculty in the various departments and began to attract large numbers of students, but its fame as an institution of learning in the sixteenth century rested mainly upon its two most distinguished professors, Luther and Melanchthon.

FIRST EXPERIENCE AT WITTENBERG.—Luther's first experience as a teacher at the University of Wittenberg began in the fall of 1508. He was then summoned by Dr. Staupitz to give lectures on philosophy, for which he was qualified as a Bachelor and Master of Philosophy from the University of Erfurt. He took up his work of lecturing on the Ethics and Dialectics of Aristotle sometime in November, 1508, and continued for about a year. In a letter to his old friend, Johann Braun, vicar at Eisenach, under date of March 17, 1509, he has the following to say about his work at the University: "Now I am at Wittenberg by God's command or permission. If you wish to know my condition, I am well, thank God, except that my studies are very severe, especially philosophy, which from the first I would willingly have changed for theology; I mean that theology which searches out the meat of the nut, the kernel of the grain, and the marrow of the bones."[1] That it was the plan of Staupitz to have Luther advanced to a theological professorship is evident from the fact that the preliminary steps in that direction had already been taken and the required Doctor's Degree would have been conferred sooner than it was, had not Luther been called back to Erfurt for some academic or monastic reason, not well understood, for already on the ninth day of March, 1509, Luther had received the degree of Baccalaureus Biblicus and he was preparing to take his next degree in theology, that of Baccalaureus Sententiarius, the degree preliminary to the doctorate in theology, when he was suddenly recalled to Erfurt.

---
1) Smith, *Luther's Correspondence*, vol. I, p. 24.

IN THE PROFESSOR'S CHAIR

LECTURES ON LOMBARD'S SENTENCES.—Returning to Erfurt he was called to lecture on the *Sentences* of Peter Lombard, the chief text-book in theology in those days. Here he completed the requirements for Sententiarius, and lectured on Lombard for three semesters. A copy of the volume of Lombard used by Luther during these lectures recently discovered in the library of the Ratsschule at Zwickau contains the marginal notes which he made with his own hand and gives some idea of the manner in which he prepared and delivered his lectures on the Master of Sentences.[2] Grisar, who is ever looking for something in Luther's conduct and work with which to find fault, has discovered that Luther shows himself to be both vain and audacious in these notes, for he dares to criticize such scholars as Duns Scotus and Lombard and to have an opinion of his own. Says Grisar: "The vanity and the audacity of the language used is frequently surprising; for instance, when the young master takes upon himself to speak of the 'buffoonery' of contemporary theologians and philosophers, or of an ostensible 'almost heretical opinion' which he discovers in Venerable Duns Scotus; still more is this the case when he expresses his dislike of the traditional scholastic speculation and logic, alluding to the 'rancid rules of logicians,' to 'those grubs, the philosophers,' to the 'dregs of philosophy,' and to that 'putrid philosopher Aristotle.' "[3] Smith, however, finds these notes "stiff, formal, and timid" as compared with Luther's later lecture notes.[4] Grisar, nevertheless, fails to find any heretical teachings in Luther's early notes, for he declares: "In these glosses we may, however, seek in vain for any trace, even of the faintest of Luther's

---
2) *Werke*, Weimar ed., ix., p. 28 seq.
3) *Luther*, vol. I, p. 23.
4) *Life and Letters of Luther*, p. 22.

81

future teaching. The young theologian still maintains the Church's standpoint, particularly with regard to the doctrines which he was afterwards to call into question." [5] And yet Grisar, apparently unknowingly, admits that Luther already at this time held a view of authority which time and again was challenged by the Catholic theologians and which lay at the very root of his whole reformatory movement. In disagreeing with the schoolmen on some point dealing with the nature of the soul, Luther as quoted by Grisar says: "Though many highly esteemed teachers assert this, yet the fact remains that on their side they have not the Holy Scriptures: but I say that on my side I have the Written Word that the soul is the image of God, and therefore I say with the Apostle, 'though an angel from heaven,' i. e., a Doctor of the Church, preach to you otherwise, 'let him be anathema.'" [6] This gloss shows that even as early as 1510 Luther had found his authority in the Bible alone, and dared to oppose it to the authority of the teachers of the Church. Thus it will be observed that the young professor very early began to manifest an independent and critical spirit, which was very much at variance with the pedantic, parrot-like repetition of the thoughts and expressions of the ancient sages so characteristic of the professors of his day.

FURTHER ADVANCEMENT IN THEOLOGY.—In addition to his many other labors in the interests of his order, Luther began to prepare for the degree of Doctor of Theology at the earnest solicitation of his superior, Dr. Staupitz, and other friends during the summer of 1512. Already on October 4 he was promoted to Licentiate in Theology at the University of Wittenberg to which he had now returned, and two

---
5) Ibid., p. 23.
6) Ibid., p. 23.

weeks later, October 18-19, he received the degree of Doctor of Theology, and made a full professor of theology.

LECTURING ON THE BIBLE.—Luther was assigned to his favorite field, the Bible, and shortly afterward began a series of lectures on the Psalms, which soon attracted considerable attention, filling his lecture room with students. These lectures show very careful preparation, keen insight, and the ability to present truth in a fresh, striking, and interesting manner.[7] As to the manner in which Luther prepared his lectures and delivered them before his students Grisar says: "Luther used for his text the Latin Vulgate, making a very sparing use of his rudimentary Hebrew. The glosses and scholia were, however, intended chiefly for the professor himself; to the students who attended his Biblical lectures Luther was in the habit of giving a short dictation comprising a summary of what he had prepared, and then with the assistance of his glosses and scholia, dilating more fully on the subject. Scholars' notebooks containing such dictations given by Luther in the early days together with fuller explanation are in existence, but have never been printed."[8] Dr. Smith gives a very careful and judicious criticism of these lectures in the following words: "Glancing first at the more external qualities, these lectures and notes evince extreme thoroughness—not a bad quality in a professor, and one for which German professors have ever been justly famous. He not only turned the pages of his books, he read, marked, learned, and inwardly digested them. He criticized his authors and with such acumen that two works attributed to Augustine, the genuineness

---

7) These lectures are given in their Latin form in volumes III and IV of the Weimar edition of *Luther's Works*.
8) *Luther*, vol. I, p. 64.

of which he first disputed, have been proved by modern criticism to be spurious. He sought diligently for the best authorities and the most recent books.—Comparing these lectures with the notes on Lombard (1509-10), a considerable advance in freedom and power is noticeable. The early work is stiff, formal, and timid; in the latter, though the text and authorities are still followed fairly closely, there is more freedom of treatment and more of the subjective element. The new religious ideas, especially that of justification by faith, can be plainly made out, and several opinions which could find no room in the Catholic Church come forward. In fact, as far as we can judge, it was in these lectures, his first on the Bible, that Luther began to formulate his peculiar theology." [9]

Following his lectures on the Psalms, he took up the *Epistle to the Romans*, which he lectured on in 1515 and 1516. In 1516 he also lectured on the Book of Judges, and then began his lectures on the Epistle to the Galatians. His lectures on Romans and Galatians are his masterpieces in Biblical exegesis and homiletical applications. Besides his lectures on the books already named, he lectured on many of the other books of the Bible, both in the Old and the New Testament, and in addition to the more strictly theological exegetical lectures, he also gave a very large number of popular expository lecture-sermons to large congregations. His exegetical works constitute, including his sermons, for they were largely of the expository-didactic type, the major portion of the vast literary remains he has left us, and give voluminous testimony to his great ability and power, both as a professor and preacher.

"He was a simple and most gracious teacher," testifies his student from 1539, Mathesius, who also be-

---
9) Smith, *Life and Letters of Martin Luther*, pp. 22-23.

came his biographer,[10] and when his lectures and sermons are read, one involuntarily arrives at the same conclusion, though it must have been vastly different to sit under his cathedra, or as Mathesius and so many other students did, at his very table, and listen to the familiar discourses which he there delivered, so full of human touches, pointed, pithy, witty, and illuminating, which have been preserved to us in the famous *Table Talks*. The secret of his great success as a professor, in addition to his sympathetic and intelligent appreciation of his students and democratic fellowship with them, was the fact that he knew both what to say and how to say it with clearness, point, and telling effect. There was no floundering about, no dealing in platitudes, no surmises, but a clear cut, definite, intelligible presentation, born out of thorough preparation, constant application to study, personal knowledge, and a profound personal conviction. The peculiar quality of his teaching manner is well characterized by Smith, when he says: "He is interesting. Similes, illustrations, examples from current events, apt translations into German, with careful summaries at the end of each subject, made the lectures a wide departure from the ordinary. The students flocked to him with enthusiasm." [11]

---

10) *Historien*, p. 197.
11) Smith, *Life and Letters of Martin Luther*, p. 25.

CHAPTER V

IN THE FAMILY CIRCLE

Long before Luther himself entered the married state, he had discoursed extensively upon the nature and significance of marriage, family life, and the duty of parents and children from his university cathedra and the various pulpits which he from time to time occupied, as well as in his published tracts and other writings, and had thereby exerted a powerful and wholesome educational influence upon all classes of society. He had lifted the ideals of married life and had pressed home with great vigor and in no uncertain terms the exalted privileges, vast opportunities, and serious responsibilities of parenthood. When he as a ripe man already in middle life became a married man and established his own home and family life, he at once began to exemplify what he had himself taught, re-enforcing his teachings by his own example of a Christian husband and father and building together with his good and faithful wife, Catharina von Bora, an exemplary home and family life. Well does Emanuel Martig say: "Of great significance for Luther's educational work was indeed his family life. In the most intimate relation with his pious and prudent wife, he brought up his children in holy zeal and Christian love, and his beautiful family life, which through the intimate intercourse of his friends and the numerous guests in his home became widely known, formed an illuminating example for other families.

Through his affectionate relations with his own children, he attained a deeper appreciation of child nature as well as of the whole process of education."[1]

MARRIAGE.—Luther's marriage, important as it was for himself personally and for the whole cause of the Reformation, was fraught with many difficulties. Although he had long since laid aside the monk's cowl and had come to the conclusion that the vow of celibacy and chastity taken by monks and nuns was invalid, a view which he boldly proclaimed, advising erstwhile monks and nuns to disregard their vows and marry, yet he hesitated for a long time to take this step himself, and some of his most intimate friends and associates had some misgiving lest he might marry and thereby endanger the evangelical cause. In a letter to his friend, Wolfgang Reissenbusch, a teacher at Lichtenberg, under date of March 27, 1525, Luther writes at length on the question of the validity of monastic vows and the right of one who has taken these vows to marry. Reissenbusch was at the time contemplating marriage, but seems to hesitate on account of the vows and the stir and gossip the breaking of them would occasion, and Luther writes him this letter to assure him that his scruples were unfounded and to encourage him in taking the contemplated step. In this letter, Luther says that "a vow against God and nature is impossible and void" and that to be valid it "must not be against God and the Christian faith," which he holds the monastic vow to be. "I believe, honored sir, that you are convinced of what I say," continues Luther at the conclusion of his argument against the validity of monastic vows, "and that you are not troubled by such scruples, but I fancy that human fear and timidity lie in your way, as it is said that he must be a bold man who dares to

---

1) *Geschichte der Erziehung in ihren Grundzügen*, p. 81.

take a wife. There is then the more need to encourage, counsel, and urge you, making you eager and bold." As a further encouragement, Luther tells him what a splendid example he would set others if he married. "It would also be a fine, noble example if you married," says he; "that would help many feeble ones, broaden their paths and give them more scope, so many others might escape the danger of the flesh and follow you. What harm is it if people say, 'So the Lichtenberg professor has taken a wife, has he?' Is it not a great glory and a Christian virtue that you should thereby become a noble excuse for others doing the same?" [2] That Luther's strong encouragement was effective is evidenced by the fact that Reissenbusch was actually married a month later.

Although it may seem from this letter that Luther had at this time some thought of getting married himself, yet in a letter written to Spalatin on the 16th of April following, he states that he has "no thought at all of marriage." He jestingly remarks, however, that unless Spalatin hurries up, he may still get ahead of him and other "prospective bridegrooms." [3] Being strongly urged by his father to marry, he was nevertheless giving some serious thought to the question of marriage himself, for not long afterward, on May 4, he writes to Johann Ruhel at Mansfeld, concerning the peasant revolt which is daily becoming more threatening and bloody and the dangers which confront Luther himself, since he is largely blamed for this revolt, and incidentally remarks: "If I can do it before I die, I will take my Katie to wife to spite the devil, when I hear they are after me. I hope they will not take away my joy and good spirits." [4]

---

2) Smith, *Correspondence*, vol. II, pp. 299-302.
3) Smith, *Correspondence*, vol. II, pp. 304-6.
4) Ibid., pp. 308-10.

IN THE FAMILY CIRCLE

This threat he actually carried out at a private wedding in his home, the Black Cloister, on the evening of June 13, 1525. Present on this occasion were the city pastor, Bugenhagen, Justus Jonas, Dr. Apel, professor of law at the University, and the artist, Lucas Cranach, and his wife. This step was taken hurriedly and without even consulting his most intimate friends on account of the malicious gossip occasioned by his attentions to Catharina von Bora, an escaped nun. Two days after his marriage, he wrote three of his friends at Mansfeld, mentioning that lords, parsons, and peasants are all against him and threaten him with death, and informing them of his marriage in the following words: "Well, since they (the above mentioned enemies) are so silly and foolish, I shall take care that at my end I shall be found in the state for which God has created me with nothing of my previous papal life about me. I shall do my part if they act still more foolishly up to the last farewell. So now, according to the wish of my dear father, I have married. I did it quickly lest those praters should stop it. Tuesday, eight days hence, the one following the Day of John the Baptist, June 27, it is my intention to have a little celebration and house warming, to which I beg you will come and give your blessings. The land is in such a state that I hardly dare ask you to undertake the journey; however, if you can do so, pray come, along with my dear father and mother, for it would be a special pleasure for me."[5] Letters informing other friends of the step he had taken and inviting them to attend his public wedding celebration were sent in many directions, and it was a large gathering of happy friends and relatives that met for this festivity on June 27, 1525, the happiest among them being Luther's father and mother, for

---
5) Smith, *Correspondence*, vol. II, p. 323.

unlike some of his friends they had no misgiving as to the propriety of the step he had taken.

THE EFFECT OF LUTHER'S MARRIAGE.—Luther's marriage caused alarm and even consternation among his friends, while his enemies rejoiced and gloated over what to them was his greatest fall, for now he had fallen so low that he even disregarded his oath as a monk and a priest and had even married an equally wicked nun. The alarm of his friends is best set forth in a letter written by Melanchthon to Joachim Camerarius on the 16th of June, in which, among other things, he writes: "Since dissimilar reports concerning the marriage of Luther will reach you, I have thought it well to give you my opinion of him. On June 13, Luther unexpectedly and without informing his friends of what he was doing, married Bora; but in the evening, after having invited to supper none but Pomeranus and Lucas the painter and Apel, observed the customary marriage rites. You might be amazed that at this unfortunate time, when good and excellent men everywhere are in distress, he not only does not sympathize with them, but, as it seems, rather waxes wanton and diminishes his reputation, just when Germany has especial need of his judgment and authority. These things have occurred, I think, somewhat in this way: The man is certainly pliable; and the nuns have used their arts against him most successfully; thus probably society with the nuns has softened or even inflamed this noble and high-spirited man. In this way he seems to have fallen into this untimely change of life. The rumor, however, that he had previously dishonored her is manifestly a lie. Now that the deed is done, we must not take it too hard, or reproach him; for I think, indeed, that he was compelled by nature to marry. This mode of life, too, while, indeed, humble (low), is, nevertheless, holy and more pleasing to God than celibacy. When I see Luther in low spirits and disturbed about his change of life, I make my best efforts to console him kindly, since he has done nothing that seems to me worthy of censure or incapable of defence. Besides this, I have unmistakable evidences of his godliness, so that for me to condemn him is impossible." [6] This letter, which Melanchthon wrote in Greek, and in a high state of excitement, shows very clearly how Luther's sudden and unexpected marriage affected many of his friends. Yet while Melanchthon thus strongly expresses himself here, and makes insinuations which reflect upon the character of both Luther and his bride, he was one of the happiest among Luther's friends on the day of the wedding celebration and soon learned to hold the nun, who, as he intimates in this letter, by her cunning art had entangled Luther in the meshes of matrimony, in the highest esteem, as did also Luther's other friends and associates.

To Catholic writers, Luther's marriage has always been a welcome target. To them the relation of Luther and Catharina von Bora was not marriage, but simply a liaison, and hence a low and most contemptible relation. This is especially brought out by such writers as Denifle,[7] Janssen,[8] and O'Hare.[9] The Catholic biographer of Luther, Michelet, gives his verdict in the following words: "The strongest mind could not be expected to resist so many shocks, and Luther had been visibly giving way ever since the crisis in the year 1525. —As the intellectual man grew weaker, the empire of the flesh grew stronger; and, yielding to its impulse, Luther married." [10] What logic! Getting married is

---
6) Smith, ibid., p. 324-27.
7) *Luther und Luthertum.*
8) *History of the German People.*
9) *The Facts About Luther.*
10) *Life of Luther*, pp. 196-7.

an evidence of mental debility! Grisar takes great pains to narrate the worst rumors that were current at the time of Luther's marriage, but must admit that they are historically unfounded. Yet he is careful to leave with his readers the impression that Luther's marriage, though carried out in due form, was illegal, and that his moral character was questionable, closing his account with a quotation from Denifle reflecting on Luther's previous chastity.[11] Such reflections are happily without any foundation in fact, and are simply poison-bombs hurled by Catholic propagandists against the cordially hated Heresiarch.[12]

THE SIGNIFICANCE OF LUTHER'S MARRIAGE.—Luther's marriage was of the greatest significance both to himself and his great cause. Together with a former monk, Brisger, and a servant, he lived at the Black Cloister, poorly taken care of physically. For a whole year before his marriage he slept in a bed that was not made up and became foul from sweat. "But," says he, "I worked all day and was so tired at night that I fell into bed without knowing that anything was amiss." His marriage gave him a well-regulated and comfortable home life and constant and loving care during his periods of illness, for he was subject to severe headaches, and, later, other ailments. He was also prone to become discouraged and despondent at times, for which his cheerless bachelor quarters offered no antidote. Surrounded by his faithful wife, his children, and frequently his friends, he found relief in music and song and also in his gardening. Besides, he found in his wife a trusty and sympathetic companion in whom he could confide and with whom he might consult. He was thus physically cared for as never be-

---
11) *Luther*, vol. II, pp. 173-180.
12) Boehmer, *Luther in the Light of Recent Research*, pp. 217-28; Kaverau, *Luther in katolischer Beleuchtung*, p. 12 seq.

fore since he left his home at Mansfeld and given both spiritual comfort and support, all of which meant a great deal to him personally, but even more to the cause which he championed.

But his marriage has a still deeper and more far-reaching significance in the spiritual and educational effect it had upon home life generally, and particularly in laying the foundation of the Protestant Manse, which has played so important a role in the life and literature of Christian nations ever since. In this respect, too, he appears as the great educator of the people. Says the late Dr. Schaff: "The domestic life of Luther has far more than a private biographical interest. It is one of the factors of modern civilization. Without Luther's reformation, clerical celibacy with all its risks and evil consequences would still be the universal law in all Western churches. There would be no married clergymen and clerical families in which the duties and virtues of conjugal, parental, and filial relations could be practised. It has been proven that a larger proportion of able and useful men and women have been born and raised in households of Protestant pastors during the last three hundred years than in any other class of society. Viewed simply as a husband and father, and as one of the founders of the clerical family, Luther deserves to be esteemed and honored as one of the greatest benefactors of mankind." [13] Bishop Thorold of Rochester, England, says: "It will always be a matter of controversy whether or no he (Luther) helped the Reformation and materially augmented his personal influence by his marriage. It is certain that he thereby vindicated the freedom of marriage of the clergy, and bequeathed an exquisite ideal of conjugal and parental

---

13) *The Critic*, Nov. 10, 1888, quoted by Croll, *Tributes to Luther*, p. 70.

love."[14] In a memorial address delivered at Princeton University on the 400th anniversary of Luther's birth, Dr. Theodore L. Cuyler said about Luther's marriage that "the bravest thing Luther ever did after his defiance of the Papacy, was his marriage to the fugitive nun, Catharina von Bora. When questioned for his reasons, he answered in his racy Saxon fashion: 'I wanted to please my father, to tease the Pope, and to vex the devil.' Without this practical protest against the abominable doctrine of celibacy, he would have left his life-work incomplete."[15] Pfleiderer calls Luther the "founder of the Protestant minister's home" and the "creator of the Protestant morality, in that he freed the temporal moral life in family and vocation, in state and society, from the Catholic blemish of unholiness, and reinstated them in their dignities and rights as God willed."[16] The historical correctness of Pfleiderer's statement becomes apparent when we take into consideration what a blighting effect upon marriage and home life generally the doctrine of celibacy and the low order of family life had. This view that the married life was a low mode of living, as even Melanchthon expresses it in the above quoted letter to Camerarius, was a very common one. "The compulsory rule of celibacy stigmatized the divine institution of marriage," says Bauslin, "and cast reproach upon the dearest domestic relations of fatherhood, motherhood, and childhood, always looking upon such relations as belonging to an inferior condition of sanctity and religion."[17] The significance of Luther's marriage to Christian home life in general is well stated by the recently deceased Lutheran scholar, preacher, and author, J. B. Remensnyder, when he says: "Luther

---

14) *Philadelphia Press*, Nov. 10, 1883, Croll, op. cit., p. 82.
15) Croll, *Tributes to Luther*, p. 201.
16) *The Development of Christianity*, p. 189.
17) *The Lutheran Movement of the Sixteenth Century*, p. 286.

gave us the true ideal of a Christian Home. He protested against the false notion that God could only be served by celibacy and retirement from the world into a cloister. He held matrimony to be God's order and that of nature, and therefore it was 'a holy estate.' Hence he protested against the monks and nuns shutting themselves away from active service of men and living at the expense of the community. He held that it was desirable that the clergy should marry, and be familiar with the cares and duties, and also be recuperated by the pleasures of the domestic sphere. And Luther, himself, set the example of a charming and happy family life. Thus he glorified the Christian Home. And in contending that the humblest peasant could serve God and the Church and society by fidelity in his lowly calling, as well as princes on the throne, he upraised and sanctified the duties of common life." [18]

CATHARINA VON BORA.—The woman who became Luther's wife was born at Lippendorf, near Leipsic, on January 29, 1499, and was thus sixteen years younger than her husband. Her father, Hans von Bora, was a nobleman with a small estate, a portion of which, Zulsdorf, became Luther's property by purchase, for which reason he frequently afterward referred to his wife jestingly as Lady Zulsdorf. Catharina's mother died shortly after her birth, and when her father married again, she was sent as a five year old girl to a Benedictine convent at Brehna. Four years later she was transferred to a Cistercian cloister at Nimschen, as one of her relatives was the abbess and an aunt, Lena, who later became a member of Luther's household, known as Aunt Lena, was a sister at this cloister. Here Catharina received a fairly good education. She was consecrated a nun at the early

---
18) *What the World Owes Luther*, p. 82.

age of sixteen. After Luther had begun his reformatory work, and especially after he had proclaimed the invalidity of monastic vows, there was a general desertion from cloisters by both monks and nuns. Luther became instrumental in freeing many nuns from their cloisters, as they wrote to him and invoked his help. On the night of April 4, 1523, Catharina was delivered from her cloister together with eleven other nuns by the aid of Leonard Coppe of Torgau, his nephew, and another young man. Three of the escaped nuns were received by their relatives, but nine of them, including Catharina, had none to receive them, and were taken to Wittenberg, where Luther provided them with good temporary homes and later with husbands. Catharina was received into the home of a prominent citizen and official of Wittenberg by the name of Reichenbach, where she learned to become a good cook and house-keeper, a training she made good use of in the management of Luther's large and hospitable house when she became his wife. She was an intelligent, pious, capable, and energetic young woman, and especially distinguished herself by her domestic economy, thrift, and activity, sympathetic companionship with and care of her husband, and as a loving, good, and wise mother. Her concern and anxiety for her husband increased with the years as his physical ailments multiplied and he became more and more dependent upon her. During his stay at Eisleben in February, 1546, she was especially worried over him, as well she might, for he did not return to her alive from this city. While we have no letters from her hand covering this period, it is evident from his letters, and he wrote frequently to her during this brief stay, that she was greatly worried over his condition. In one of these letters he addresses her as "Selbstmärtyrin zu Wittenberg" because of her anxiety for him, and in another he jestingly refers to the falling down of the plastering in his bed-room as undoubtedly being due to her excessive worrying about him and his condition. She is often accused of having been proud, stingy, and dominating, and while she may have had these faults, the fact remains that she acquitted herself in an excellent manner in her very difficult position as the house-wife in a house-hold upon which great demands were made, with often very little in money and kind to do with, and a husband whose liberality in giving away whatever he had at hand to such as were in real or pretended need, often left her in an embarrassing situation, and she fully merited the unstinted praises and whole-hearted confidence which her distinguished husband bestowed upon her.

LUTHER AND HIS CHILDREN.—Luther had six children of his own and in addition had the responsibility of bringing up eleven orphaned nephews and nieces. His first child, Johannes, his "Hänschen," little Hans, was born June 7, 1526. On this occasion he wrote to his friend Spalatin: "I am a happy husband, and may God continue to send me happiness, for from the most precious woman, my best of wives, I have received, by the blessing of God, a little son, John Luther, and, by God's wonderful grace, I have become a father."[19] To his little son he was deeply attached, and he watched his physical and psychical development with both a fond father's and an educator's interest. In a letter to Spalatin written when Hans was about seven months old, he writes: "My little Hans sends greetings. He is in his teething month and is beginning to say 'Daddy,' and scold everybody with pleasant insults. Katie also wishes you everything good, especially a little Spalatin to teach you what she declares her little Hans has taught her,

---

[19] Smith, *Correspondence*, vol. II, pp. 373-4.

namely, the fruit and joy of marriage, of which the Pope and all his world was not worthy."[20] In July, 1527, Luther was very sick, and both he and those about him thought surely he was dying. Justus Jonas, who was present with him at his bedside at that time, has given us an interesting and touching account of what then took place. "When hot bags were applied to him," says Jonas, "he began to ask about his son, 'Where is my dear little Hans?' The boy was brought in, smiling at his father, and then he said: 'O you good little boy, I commend my dear Katy and you to my dear good God; you have nothing, but God, who is the Father of the orphan and the Judge of the widow, will protect you and provide for you.'"[21] The following November, little Hans was taken severely ill, and his father mentions him in a letter to Justus Jonas, saying: "My little Hans cannot send his greetings to you on account of illness, but he looks for your prayers for him. It is twelve days since he has eaten any solid food, but now he begins to eat a little. It is wonderful to see how the baby tries to be strong and happy as usual, but cannot because he is so weak."[22] In another letter to this same friend the following January, he sends greetings and a New Year's present to the son of Jonas, and concludes his letter jestingly by saying, "My son sends greetings to your daughter, his future wife."[23] In this case Luther proved to be a poor prophet, however, for his son did not marry the daughter of Jonas, but in 1553 married Elizabeth, the daughter of Casper Cruciger, another of Luther's intimate friends.

During that trying year of the Diet of Augsburg, when the cause of the Reformation was again hang-

---
20) Ibid., p. 391.
21) Ibid., p. 407.
22) Ibid., p. 421.
23) Ibid., p. 429.

ing in the balances, when Luther was himself in great distress physically and spiritually, suffering from physical ailments, grief over the recent death of his father, and anxiety for the evangelical cause, he penned the most delightful letter to his son, a letter which has become the outstanding literary gem of its kind, and one of the best testimonies to Luther's profound understanding of child nature and great ability to adapt himself to it. The letter is written at Coburg, June, 1530, and reads as follows:

"Grace and peace in Christ, my dear little son. It pleases me very much that you are learning well and praying diligently. Continue to do so, my son, and when I come home I will bring you a pretty present.

"I know a lovely, pleasant garden where many children are, they wear golden jackets and gather nice apples under the trees and pears and cherries and purple plums and yellow plums, and sing and run and jump and are happy and have pretty little ponies with golden reins and silver saddles. I asked the man who owns the garden whose children they were. He said: 'They are the children who gladly pray, learn, and are good.' Then said I: 'Dear man, I also have a son, whose name is little Hans Luther; may he not also come into the garden, that he too may eat such lovely apples and pears and ride such fine little ponies and play with these children?' Then the man said: 'If he gladly prays, learns, and is good, he may also come into the garden, Lippus and Jost, too, and if they all come together they shall have whistles and drums and fifes and all kinds of stringed instruments, dance and shoot with little cross-bows.'

"Then he showed me a fine lawn in the garden fixed up for dancing, and there were hanging nothing but golden whistles, drums, and fine silver cross-bows. But as it was early and the children had not finished eating,

I could not wait to see them dance, and I said to the man: 'O my dear sir, I will go right away and write my dear little son Hans about all these things, so that he will pray diligently, learn well, and be good, in order that he too may come into this garden. But he has an Aunt Lena, he must also bring her.' Then the man said: 'All right, go and write him about these things.'

"Therefore, dear little Hans, learn and pray cheerfully, and tell Lippus and Josten, too, that they shall learn and pray; then you will come together into the garden. With this I commend you to God. Greet Aunt Lena and give her a kiss from me. Anno 1530.

Your loving father,
Martin Luther."

When Hans was in his seventh year, his father said of him in one of his *Table Talks*: "My boy Hans is now entering upon his seventh year. Every seven years a person changes; the first period is infancy, the second childhood. At fourteen they begin to see the world and lay the foundation of education, at twenty-one the young men seek marriage, at twenty-eight they are householders and patres-familias, at thirty-five they are magistates in church and state, until forty-two, when they are kings. After that the senses begin to decline. Thus every seven years brings a new condition in body and character, as has happened to me and to us all." [24] From this little talk we learn how closely Luther observed child life and unconsciously

---

Note. This letter is given in Smith's *Life and Letters of Martin Luther*, pp. 351-2, and his translation has been followed in the main, but as it deviates considerably in places from the original, the author has made alterations to conform more closely with the German text as given in the Erlangen edition of *Luther's Works*, vol. LIV, pp. 156-7. Lippus and Josten were the sons of Melanchthon and Justus Jonas, respectively, their right names being Philip and Justus.

24) Smith and Gallinger, *Conversations with Luther*, p. 42.

made a little beginning in the study of modern genetic psychology.

Luther's relation to his son Hans is typical of his relation to all his children. He says that "the youngest children are always loved the most by the parents. My little Martin is my dearest treasure. Hans and Lena can now speak and do not need such care, therefore it is that parents always love the little infants who need their love the most." [25] His other children were Elizabeth, born Dec. 10, 1527; Magdalena, born May 4, 1529; Martin, born Nov. 9, 1531; Paul, born Jan. 28, 1533, and Margaret, born Dec. 17, 1534.

Elizabeth died as an infant, and her parents grieved her loss very deeply. Writing to his friend Nicholaus Hausmann under date of August 5, 1528, the grief-stricken father says: "My little daughter Elizabeth is dead. It is marvelous how sick at heart, how womanish it has left me, so much do I grieve for her. I would never have believed that a father's heart could be so tender for his child." [26] His daughter Magdalena grew into a lovely and sweet-dispositioned girl, and the father lavished his love on her, yet without spoiling her. She died in her fourteenth year, leaving another deep wound in the tender father-heart. The death scene and burial of Magdalena, Luther's "Lenchen," is touchingly told in the *Table Talks*.[27] It seems to have been a sweet consolation for the father to be able to say after her untimely death, that he was unaware of ever having provoked her to anger. A beautiful picture has been preserved of her painted by Cranach.

The other children survived the father. Hans took up the study of law after his father's death, and became a government official. Martin studied theology,

---
25) Smith, *Life and Letters of Luther*, p. 352; *Werke*, Er. ed., vol. LVII, p. 260.
26) Smith, *Correspondence*, vol. II, p. 451.
27) Smith and Gallinger, *Conversations*, pp. 47-8.

but was not strong physically, and never entered the ministry. He died at the early age of thirty-nine. Paul became a famous physician, and the daughter Margaret became the wife of a wealthy nobleman by the name of Georg von Kunheim. Köstlin observes that while only Paul Luther especially distinguished himself, even the searching scrutiny of the Papists and Jesuits has been unable to attach any stain to the life and character of Luther's children,[28] showing that the father's careful and prayerful bringing up of his children, assisted faithfully by their pious and devoted mother, was crowned with success.

LUTHER AT THE TABLE.—Luther as a private man is best known from the many glimpses we get of him at the table with his family, servants, boarders, and guests gathered at the meal hours. Not because he was either a great eater or drinker. Melanchthon testifies that he wondered often how so robust a man could eat and drink so sparingly. It is the picture of the genial, witty, earnest and pious, sometimes even coarse, house-father, with his broad outlook on life, wide human knowledge and sympathies, deep insight into things spiritual, tender as a child and strong as the oak, mildly forgiving, severely denouncing, that we get of the man seated or, at times, standing, at the table, discoursing on a thousand and one subjects, asking and answering questions, giving fatherly counsel, encouragement or reproof. These glimpses of the man in home and private life we obtain from the *Table Talks*, of which further mention will be made in a later chapter.

ANOTHER HOME SCENE.—The most beautiful home scenes from the life of Luther are, however, those which have been immortalized by the artists Spangen-

---
28) *Martin Luther*, vol. II, p. 493.

berg and Koenig, representing Luther surrounded by his wife and children in their sitting room. Koenig's picture is well described by Remensnyder, when he says: "It is Christmas Eve. The tapers on the tree are burning brightly, showing those wonderful angels, stars, trumpets, birds, and dolls which Christmas trees alone can bear. Luther sits in the center, his wife leaning happily on his shoulder, the larger children playing about, the babe with its little night cap, kept up for the scene." [29] The painting by Spangenberg represents Luther as playing the lute, his wife sits close by with the youngest child on her lap, the other four children stand close to the father singing, and Melanchthon sits at the table in the rear, as a spectator and listener. Such happy scenes were not uncommon in this busy man's home, and no doubt left their deep impress on the children that grew up under such influences. To Luther and his wife these were moments of joy and relaxation; to the children they were the sources of enjoyment and inspiration of the most wholesome and effective spiritual and educational value.

LUTHER'S CLOSING DAYS.—Luther's closing days were passed away from the home circle and the scenes which he loved so much. He had gone to Eisleben on a mission of reconciliation. The two brother-counts of Mansfeld were alienated, and Luther as a friend of both was asked to help bring about a reconciliation between them. His three sons were with him on this journey, visiting with their uncle Jakob Luther at Mansfeld, while he was busy at Eisleben. As has already been mentioned, his wife was very much worried over him on this occasion. He wrote her frequently to allay her anxiety, the last letter he ever wrote being

---

29) *What the World Owes Luther,* p. 59.

written to his wife four days before he died. His task was accomplished and a settlement effected between the brothers, when he was suddenly taken severely ill, and died on the night of the 18th of February, surrounded by several of his friends and his sons Martin and Paul, in the city where he had been born sixty-three years before. He was buried at Wittenberg four days later.

In one of the few preserved letters of Luther's wife, we have her estimate of the one who for twenty-one years had been her husband, and her tribute to him. This letter was written to her sister under date of April 2, 1546. Speaking of her loss, she says: "I can easily believe you have hearty sympathy with me and my poor children. Who would not be sorrowful and mourn for so noble a man as was my dear lord, who much served not only one city or a single land, but the whole world? Truly, I am so distressed that I cannot tell my great sorrow to any one, and hardly know what to think or how to feel. I cannot eat nor drink, neither can I sleep. If I had had a principality and an empire, it would never have cost me so much pain to lose them as I have now that our Lord God has taken from me, and not from me only, but from the whole world, this dear and precious man." [30]

Catharina von Bora survived her husband by six years. She died following injuries received in an accident, Dec. 20, 1552, and was buried at Torgau.

---

30) Smith, *Life and Letters of Luther*, p. 424.

CHAPTER VI

LUTHER'S THEOLOGY

Luther's theological views were fundamental to his every attitude and activity as a reformer, and naturally, also, had a determining influence upon his interest in and work in behalf of a broad and general Christian education. Before proceeding to present his educational works and the educational principles set forth in them, we shall, therefore, briefly review his position on the essential points of Christian doctrine. It should be borne in mind that it was in the fields of Christian theology, and the empirical Christian life that Luther rendered his first and greatest service to mankind and made his largest and most significant contributions to the intellectual, political, and religious freedom and happiness of man. In unshackling the human mind from the repressive authority of a strongly entrenched and all-dominant ecclesiastical authority; in enunciating the principle of freedom of conscience, political liberty, and the right of private judgment, even in matters pertaining to religion, and the interpretation of Scripture; in emphasizing personal responsibility, sanctity of secular pursuits, institutions, and ordinances, the individual's personal relation to God, with no mediating person or institution but Jesus Christ and Him alone; and in consistently and persistently teaching and preaching these truths, Luther has made all the world indebted to him for all time as the greatest of educators and human benefactors.

Luther was not a systematic theologian, i. e., he did not formulate a theological system, for as Shedd says: "His power as a theologian did not lie in systematizing but rather in penetrating and deep views of particular truths."[1] He attempted to formulate no theological system, and, therefore, never assembled into one work the various points of his theology. These are found scattered throughout his voluminous works, especially in his sermons, exegetical works, the two catechisms, special treatises like the one on *Freedom of the Will* and the *Liberty of a Christian Man*, and in a very brief form in his own private confession of 1528 and the Smalcald articles. The great systematist of the Reformation was his colleague and intimate associate Melanchthon. But it was Luther who, with his keen and penetrating insight, deep spirituality, and unbounded zeal, mined the truths out of Scripture, verified them by a comparative study of the Scriptures themselves and the Fathers, vitalized these truths in his own personal experiences, set them forth in a popular, gripping, and convincing manner, and defended them against the attacks of his opponents, as well as against the fanatical misconstruction and abuse by some of his erstwhile followers. A progressive unfolding of his theological views is discernible from the time of his stirring experiences at Erfurt throughout his pre-reformation teaching and preaching, but especially so following his open break with the Church of Rome in 1520. The controverted points of doctrine, as those pertaining to Christ, redemption, means of grace, man, sin, the Christian life, and the Church, which he was constantly called upon to defend and therefore also

---

1) *Symposiac of Martin Luther*, p. 27.

LUTHER'S THEOLOGY

all the more stressed in his preaching, teaching, and writing, naturally attained the fullest development. With the publication of his *Private Confession* in 1528 and even before, it may be said that his theological views had been completely rounded out and matured, and though he may state them variously from time to time later on, the substance is always the same.

Köstlin very correctly and splendidly characterizes Luther's theology in the following language: "Luther's doctrine is thus a testimony coming fresh from the life, and designed to influence life in a way in which this can scarcely be said of the theology of any other teacher since the time of the apostles. Although constantly moving amidst the most exalted conceptions, it is never concerned with bare ideas, scholastic categories, abstractions, or even words, but always with facts and with the highest realities themselves; and these appear without any effort upon his part to fall of themselves into their places with inner harmony." [2]

THE BIBLE.—To Luther the Bible was the inspired and infallible Word of God, the only standard rule of faith and life. From it alone may Christian doctrine and guidance for the Christian life be drawn. To this Word of God he constantly appeals and upon it alone he founds his theology, and yet he assumes a hitherto unheard of, and therefore to many, an astoundingly critical attitude towards the canonical books, which drew from his opponents the strongest of criticisms. The antilegomena of the Old Testament, the socalled apocryphal books, he separated completely from the other books of the Old Testament with the declaration that they were useful reading but not like the other books, authoritative in matters pertaining to doctrine and life. The antilegomena of the New Testament,

---

2) *The Theology of Luther*, vol. II, p. 206.

Hebrews, James, II Peter, II and III John, Jude, and Revelation, he also distinguishes from the other New Testament books, though the question of the New Testament canon had virtually been finally settled by the Synod of Carthage in 397, a decision since adhered to by the teachers of the Church. In his introductions to these books in his German Bible, he frankly admits that he does not regard them as of equal authority with the other New Testament books and appeals both to the testimony of the early Church and the internal evidence of the books themselves in support of his position. He makes some distinction, however, between these books themselves in his evaluation of them. Hebrews he places rather high. Jude he regards merely as a repetition of II Peter, and his Epistle, together with James and Revelation, he places very low in value and consequently placed them last in his arrangement of the order of the New Testament books. He also made distinction between the books of the Old and New Testaments which he regarded as canonical, expressing himself very definitely with respect to their value and content. While he placed some of the Old Testament books higher than others in value, there was only one Old Testament book which he would have cast out of the Canon, and that is the Book of Esther, because God is nowhere mentioned in it. The Gospel of John he estimates higher than the Synoptic Gospels, and the Epistles of Paul to the Romans and Galatians he places above the rest of the Epistles, though he is confident that the rest of them are genuine and canonical. While he came to have a better appreciation of both Hebrews and Revelation towards the close of his life than he had earlier expressed, he never came to regard them and the other New Testament antilegomena on a parity with the other books of the New Testament. The great deciding principle as to the canonicity of a book to him was whether it set forth Christ as Savior clearly and definitely or not, though he also took both internal and external evidences into consideration. His theology throughout was Christocentric, and this was also his principle of Biblical criticism. The determination of the authentic books of the Bible was with him a very serious matter, owing to the large place which tradition had had in the development and attempted vindication of Romanish doctrine which he opposed. He was, therefore, at great pains to establish with absolute certainty the authoritative canonical books. When this was established to his own satisfaction, he appealed to these books with never-failing trust and did not, as he himself states, dispute with anyone who did not accept the Bible as the Word of God.[3]

DOCTRINE OF GOD.—The idea of God is always determining in both one's religious thinking and views of life. It also determines, to a very large extent, religious attitudes and relationships, as well as interests and activities in life. So it was also in the case of Luther. To him God was not merely a philosophical and abstract concept, implying a certain unknown and mystical being and force. God was to him a real spiritual being, a divine personality, eternal, holy, omniscient, omnipotent, just, good, loving, and true, who was not only the Maker, Ruler, and Preserver of all things but who also sustains a definite personal relation to all created things, especially to His chief visible creature, man. His doctrine of God is quite fully set forth in his *Small* and *Large Catechisms*, in the explanations of the First Commandment (Augustinian numbering) and the First Article of the Creed. Here he presents Him as a kind, loving, tender, and com-

---

3) Köstlin, *The Theology of Luther*, vol. II, p. 227; *Werke*, Er. ed., vol. XXVIII, p. 840.

passionate heavenly Father who daily and richly provides for man's wants and who has shown His supreme love to man in the gift of His Son, Jesus Christ, to be the Savior of the world. While he recognizes two aspects of God, the hidden and the revealed, he does not trouble himself very much about the hidden aspects of God's being and attributes, but he deals quite fully with God in His manifold revealed aspects both in His relation to the world generally, and in His dealings with man. Of these characteristics of God he especially emphasizes His goodness and mercy. "I think," he says, "we Germans from ancient times designate God more elegantly and appropriately than in any other language by that name from the word 'good' since He is an eternal fountain which gushes forth and overflows with pure good and from which emanates all that is and is called good." [4] This is a far different idea of God from the one he had been taught in his boyhood. He was taught to regard God as a stern and exacting judge whose wrath must be averted and whose favor must be obtained through an intercession of the Church, the Virgin Mary, and the Saints, a view of God which had often frightened and terrified him and which finally drove him into the cloister.

But he did not present merely a one-sided view of God. God was also to him a holy and righteous God who visits His punishment upon the transgressor. Yet in presenting this aspect of God's dealing with man he ever seeks to show that God deals in justice and mercy and that all His dealings with men have a beneficent, pedagogical purpose. In explaining Exodus 20:5-6 in his *Large Catechism*, he says: "Now there is comprehended in these words both a threatening of wrath and a friendly promise, so as not only to terrify

---
4) *Book of Concord*, Jacob's ed., p. 394.

LUTHER'S THEOLOGY

and warn us, but also to induce and encourage us to receive and highly esteem His Word as a matter of divine earnestness, because He Himself declares how much He is in earnest and how rigidly He will enforce it, namely, that He will severely and terribly punish all who despise and transgress His commandments; and again how richly He will reward, bless, and do all good to those who hold them in high esteem, and are glad to act and live according to them." [5]

Such a conception of God, so Scriptural and so lofty, could not but exert a powerful influence upon the man himself and become a potent educational influence in the lives of those who came in contact with him and his teaching. His was not the formal, judicial conception of God, current in his day, nor was it the speculative and rather metaphysical idea of Zwingli. As Klotsche well says: "Luther conceived of God as almighty love and righteousness revealed in Christ; he looked into the heart of Christ, and there found the heart of God. According to Zwingli, God is to be known before Christ. He is the infinite, unchangeable power of all things, absolute causality." [6] Luther conceived of God as revealed in the Son, Jesus Christ.

THE DOCTRINE OF THE PERSON AND WORK OF CHRIST.—As has already been stated, Luther's theology is Christo-centric and it is, therefore, very natural that he should have developed the doctrines of Christology and Soteriology more fully than any other doctrines, laying special emphasis upon them in sermons, lectures, and writings. He does not sharply distinguish these two doctrines but invariably considers them together. About these central doctrines all other points of Christian theology cluster, for upon Christ and His redemptive work alone depends the salvation of

---
5) *Book of Concord,* pp. 435-6.
6) *History of Doctrines,* p. 184.

111

man. "Everything is thus made to depend upon the article concerning Christ, the Son of God sent into the world, who has secured forgiveness of sins and eternal life," says Köstlin. "Whoever has this Christ has all things. The other articles of Christian doctrine, although likewise founded upon Scripture, are not there so urgently insisted upon. In this doctrine is, however, included the truth that we obtain grace, not through our own works, but alone through the Mediator. This article and that upon justification are but one. All errors have arisen wherever this doctrine has been neglected. Whoever, on the contrary, holds it fast, will be preserved by it from heresy, and it will secure for him the Holy Spirit, so that he shall be able to 'differentiate and judge clearly and plainly' in regard also to all other articles." [7]

The significance of Luther's contribution to a fuller understanding and better appreciation of these cardinal doctrines of the Christian religion is clearly indicated by the Reformed theologian Dr. H. R. Mackintosh in his work, *The Doctrine of the Person of Jesus Christ*, in which he says: "With Luther there came into the world a deeper understanding of the person of Christ than had prevailed since the apostolic age. . . . Luther's system of belief rests on and revolves round the person of Jesus Christ. To him faith in God and faith in Christ are one and the same thing. . . . . It was among the rare excellencies of Luther's Christology that he fastened an indissoluble bond, as St. Paul had done, between the person of the Redeemer and His redeeming work. . . . To him the manhood of Christ signified more than to any post-apostolic teacher. . . . Very plain words, accordingly, are used regarding the reality of Jesus' earthly life as one of limitation,

---

7) Op. cit., vol. II, p. 218.

growth, and trial. . . . But if Christ was true man, faith is equally assured that He was not mere man. It is the very corner-stone of Luther's theology that none other than God could avail to atone for human sin. Athanasius himself could not speak more plainly than he as to the absolute centrality of the Godhead of Christ. . . . These two sides, the deity and the humanity, were held or rather fused together by Luther with a kind of passion. . . . Christ as daysman, as Mediator, must by the very constituents of His person have standing-ground on both sides, so binding God and man in unity. . . . By a vitalizing innovation he drew the mind of a whole age back to the historic Christ, declaring with tremendous power that faith possesses its proper object solely in the person of the crucified and exalted Lord. . . . And to this hour the Church is occupied with the problem essentially as it was stated by Martin Luther." [8]

Luther accepted in full the teachings of the Ecumenical creeds, the Apostolic, Nicene, Athanasian, regarding the person and work of Christ as fully in accord with the teachings of Scripture. He regards Jesus Christ as the Son of God and the Son of Man, true God begotten of the Holy Spirit and true man, born of the Virgin Mary. To him the divinity and humanity of Christ were absolute realities supported by the clear testimony of Scripture, required by the fallen state of man for his redemption, and verified in his own personal experiences. He held the two natures in Christ to be inseparable in the one personality, Jesus Christ, yet in such a manner that neither is the true divinity destroyed nor the true humanity. The mystic relationship between the two natures he explained as a communion of attributes (communi-

---

8) Weidner, *Christology*, pp. 193-4.

catio idiomatum), the peculiar relationship of the two natures whereby the properties and attributes of both are ascribed to the one divine, human personality.

In harmony with his conception of the relation between the two natures in Christ, he also taught the ubiquity of the person of Christ, i. e., Christ is everywhere present. The session at the right hand of God he did not regard as a session at the fixed locus or point, a conception held both by Zwingli and Calvin and fundamental to their view of the spiritual presence in the Lord's Supper. Luther, on the other hand, held that "right hand of God" must mean everywhere, for God is omnipresent. Hence Christ also as the second person in the Godhead and one with the Father, is also everywhere. Upon this conception of the ubiquity of Christ rests Luther's doctrine of the real presence in the Lord's Supper.

Luther's doctrine of the work of Christ is throughout a clear and vivid reflection of Paul's doctrine of soteriology as well as of his own personal religious experiences. Jesus Christ, true God and true man, holy, pure, perfect, and sinless, fulfilled in an absolute and perfect manner every demand of God's holy Law and suffered the penalty for the transgression of the Law for us and in our stead and thus made complete satisfaction for all our sins. Thus He fulfilled the Law both in an active and a passive manner, actively by His holy life in perfect obedience to the Law and passively by suffering for man the penalty, spiritual and physical death, for the transgression of the Law, whereby He brought about objectively a full atonement between God and man, in which every sinner may become a partaker by faith in Jesus Christ as his personal Savior and Lord.

The work of Christ is further conceived of in connection with His three-fold office, of prophet, high priest, and king. As prophet He is the teacher and preacher of truth, grace, and life; as high priest He has once for all entered into the Holy of Holies and presented the supreme sacrifice and made atonement for sin; and as king He sits at the right hand of God, having dominion over all things, especially ruling in the lives of his followers in His spiritual kingdom.

THE DOCTRINE OF THE HOLY GHOST.—Luther taught both the reality and the personality of the Holy Ghost as one with the Father and with the Son proceeding from the Father and the Son and of the same divine essence. The work of the Holy Ghost is to make Christ and His redemptive work known to man through the instrumentality of the Church and its ministry by the Means of Grace, calling sinners to Christ, sanctifying and preserving the saints in a true and living faith unto the end. The very essence of his doctrine of the Holy Spirit is briefly but comprehensively set forth in the following words in his explanation of the Third Article in his *Small Catechism.* "I believe that I cannot of my own reason or strength believe in Jesus Christ, my Lord, or come to Him; but the Holy Ghost has called me through the Gospel, enlightened me by His gifts, and sanctified and preserved me in the true faith; in like manner as He calls, gathers, enlightens, and sanctifies the whole Christian Church on earth, and preserves it in union with Jesus Christ in the true faith; in which Christian Church, He daily forgives abundantly all my sins and the sins of all believers, and will raise up me and all the dead in the last day and will grant everlasting life to me and to all who believe in Christ."

THE DOCTRINE OF THE TRINITY.—Luther was thoroughly and consistently Trinitarian in his theology. The fullest and most perfect conception of God is to him made possible only by conceiving of Him as trinity in unity and unity in trinity. The Father can be known only through the Son, and the Son only through the Holy Spirit. "We could never," he says, "attain to the knowledge of the grace and favor of the Father except through the Lord Christ, who is a mirror of the paternal heart, outside of whom we see nothing but an angry and terrible judge. But of Christ we could know nothing except by the revelation of the Holy Ghost." [9] He maintains that the Father, Son, and Holy Ghost are of one essence, three co-eternal, co-equal, and distinct persons and yet he ascribes a certain pre-eminence to the Father, since "the Son and the Spirit nevertheless have what they have and are from the Father." [10] Thus the Father is the source and the origin of the Godhead, the Father, who is of no one, begetting His Son from eternity and the Holy Spirit proceeding from both. When the Father, who is thus the source of the divinity of the Son and the Holy Spirit is mentioned, it must, therefore, be understood that both the Son and the Holy Spirit are included. All three persons of the Godhead share in the external works ascribed to either, as creation to the Father, redemption to the Son, and sanctification to the Holy Spirit.

THE DOCTRINE OF MAN.—Luther teaches that man, created in the image of God, is His chief and best creature, for whose sake all other things were created. In designating man in this manner, he refers to God's visible creatures, for he speaks of the angels as the "most exalted creatures." He generally makes no distinction between "image" and "likeness," though he does make a distinction in degree not in quality in his explanation of Genesis 5:1, holding that "likeness" is the more comprehensive, indicating the completeness

---
9) *Book of Concord*, p. 447.
10) Köstlin, op. cit., vol. II, p. 316.

of the image. Man was originally pure, righteous, innocent, and happy. He possessed a right will and a true knowledge of God and lived in His fellowship. There was the most intimate harmony between his spiritual and physical nature and the world in which he lived. Luther's idea of "original righteousness" involves his whole conception of man's original state, physical as well as spiritual. With man's fall, original sin comes to take the place of original righteousness and man's entire state is naturally most radically changed. To Luther original sin was the fallen, corrupted state of human nature, not sins committed. The committed or actual sins flow from man's sinful state, original sin. Luther's doctrine of original sin is thus briefly stated by the *Formula of Concord*: "Moreover, this Original Sin is called by Luther natural sin, personal sin, essential sin; not that the nature, person, or essence of the man is, without any distinction, itself Original Sin but that, by such words, the distinction might be indicated between Original Sin which inheres in human nature and other sins which are called actual sins. For Original Sin is not a sin which is committed but it inheres in the nature, substance, and essence of man, so that though no wicked thought ever should arise in the heart of corrupt man, nor idle words be spoken, nor wicked deed be done, yet the nature is nevertheless corrupt through Original Sin which is born in us by reason of the sinful seed and is a fountain head of all other actual sins as wicked thoughts, words, and works."[11]

This original sin is transmitted from parent to offspring. Luther rejected the doctrine of creationism and adopted the doctrine of traducianism with respect

---
11) *Book of Corcord*, pp. 495-6.

to the propagation of the soul.[12] It remains in a man after Baptism or regeneration, though the guilt or imputation is removed. The power of original sin is gradually overcome in the regenerate through the process of sanctification.[13]

As to the human will, Luther held that man has considerable liberty in secular matters, being able to choose intelligently and rationally between two or more objects presented for his consideration. But in spiritual matters the will is dead or inclined alone to that which is evil so that it does not will or choose to do that which God wills until moved and inclined by the Holy Spirit. Hence man lacks all ability of himself and by himself to come into the right relation to God, have a "right will" toward God, contribute anything whatsoever to his salvation or in any manner merit salvation. It is only by the work of the Holy Spirit, through the Means of Grace, that man is enabled to accept the proffered grace and become a child of God. The salvation of man is the work of God alone, man not co-operating.

THE DOCTRINE OF FAITH AND JUSTIFICATION.— Faith, according to Luther, is a living, active trust in and appropriation of the grace and mercy of God in Christ, offered through the Gospel. It is wrought in man without any co-operation on his part by the Holy Spirit, through the preached Word. It is thus the gift of God. In his introduction to Paul's Epistle to the Romans he says: "Thus faith is a divine work in

---

12) Creationism is the doctrine that souls are especially created for each human being and united with the embryo shortly after conception. It was held by some of the Church Fathers, among them Jerome, and is the doctrine held by both the Eastern and Roman Catholic Churches. Traducianism is the doctrine that the souls are propagated in the same manner as the body by natural generation. It is sometimes called Mediate Creationism, the soul being the creation of God mediately through the parents. This is the doctrine held by most Lutheran theologians.

13) See *Apology to Augsburg Confession*, ch. I, art. II, *Book of Concord*, pp. 81-83.

us that changes us, of God regenerates us, and puts to death the Old Adam, makes us entirely different men in heart, spirit, mind, and all powers, and confers the Holy Ghost. Oh, it is a living, efficacious, active thing that we have in faith so that it is impossible for it not to do good without intermission. It also does not ask whether good works are to be done; but before the question is asked it has wrought them and is always busy. But he who does not produce such works is a faithless man and gropes and looks about after faith and good works and knows neither what faith nor what good works are, yet meanwhile babbles and prates in many words concerning faith and good works. Justifying faith is a living, firm trust in God's grace, so certain that a man would die a thousand times for it rather than suffer this trust to be wrested from him. And this trust and knowledge of divine grace renders him joyful, fearless, and cheerful with respect to God and all creatures, which joy and joyfulness the Holy Ghost works through faith; and on account of this, man becomes ready and cheerful to do good to everyone and to suffer everything for love and praise to God who has conferred this grace." [14]

It is this faith that justifies the sinner. By means of it he possesses the perfect righteousness of Jesus Christ and stands justified before God. Justification he speaks of essentially as the forgiveness of sins. God makes the sinner righteous by forgiving him for Christ's sake all his sins and imputing to him the righteousness of Christ. Like so many Lutheran theologians and preachers, he also confuses at times justification and regeneration. "Justification," he says, "is a certain, genuine regeneration into newness, as John says: they who believe in His name, etc., are born

---

14) *Book of Concord*, pp. 583-4.

of God." [15] The justified and regenerate man possesses a two-fold righteousness: essential righteousness, the righteousness of faith, which Luther also calls "passive righteousness," and inherent, incipient, actual, or righteousness of life, which he calls "active righteousness." Concerning this second and personal form of righteousness and its relation to essential righteousness, as Luther conceived it, Köstlin says: "To this true righteousness belongs, secondly, our own actual righteousness, which must proceed from that essential righteousness which is from without. This consists of devotion to good works, mortification of the flesh, love to our neighbor, humility, and the fear of God. The first righteousness becomes complete in the second, since the latter is constantly laboring for the mortification of the Old Adam. But the first meanwhile always remains in the believer, whereas the second is subject to interruption." [16]

The doctrine of faith and justification is, like the doctrine of the person and work of Christ, fundamental to Luther's theology. Concerning this doctrine he says in the *Smalcald Articles*: "Of this article nothing can be yielded or surrendered even though heaven and earth and all things should sink to ruin. 'For there is none other name under heaven given among men whereby we must be saved,' says Peter (Acts 4:12). 'And with His stripes we are healed' (Isa. 53:5). And upon this article all things depend which, against the Pope, the devil, and the whole world, we teach and practice. Therefore, we must be sure concerning this doctrine and not doubt; for otherwise all is lost and the Pope and the devil and all things against us gain the victory and the suit." [17]

---
15) Köstlin, op. cit., p. 439.
16) Op. cit., vol. I, p. 286.
17) *Book of Concord*, p. 312.

LUTHER'S THEOLOGY

CHRISTIAN LIFE.—Luther had a very exalted idea of the Christian life, an idea radically different from that which was common in his day. His idea of Christian life is especially set forth in his treatise on *Liberty of a Christian Man*, published in 1520. In this treatise he sets forth, as Kurtz puts it, the following two propositions: "A Christian man is a free lord over all things and subject to no one; and a Christian man is a ministering servant of all things, and subject to everyone. On the one hand, he has the perfect freedom of a king and priest set over all outward things; but on the other hand he yields complete submission in love to his neighbor which, as consideration of the weak, his very freedom demands."[18]

Being justified by faith, the Christian lives in the most intimate and blessed relation and fellowship with God through Jesus Christ his Savior and possesses and enjoys the highest spiritual blessings. While sin still clings to him, he daily repents of his sin and daily receives full forgiveness for all his sin. He walks in holiness and righteousness before God, doing works pleasing and acceptable in His sight. The Holy Spirit sanctifies and preserves the Christian from day to day, so that the believer makes daily progress in the way of sanctification, but perfection is only attained after death, when the believer, glorified, shall be arrayed in full perfection and sinlessness.

Luther had no use for the monkish vows and fastings, though he highly commends voluntary bodily fasting as beneficial and conducive to spiritual growth. To him all legitimate, earthly relations and activities were God's pleasing work, and he held that it was possible to please God even in the most menial earthly occupation, thus removing from non-ecclesiastical oc-

---
18) *Church History*, vol. II, p. 238.

cupations the unholiness and baseness attached to them in his day, and raising them to a position of dignity and sanctity. The three holy orders to him were the ministry, family life, and government, which were all to be pervaded and sanctified by Christian love. While he places the ministry of the Gospel very high, he places the universal priesthood of believers none the less high, blotting out all distinction between clergy and laity except as to the office. Family life he especially extols as the great ordinance of God for the curbing of lust and unchastity, the propagation of the race, the establishment of ordered home life, sheltering, fostering, and training children for service both in Church and State. Matrimony is, therefore, holy and well pleasing to God. As to the Christian's relation to secular government, he held that every Christian owes obedience to it in matters pertaining to secular affairs, but is not subject to it in matters pertaining to things spiritual and to conscience, thus laying down the principle of freedom of conscience and civil and religious liberty. While Luther did not minimize the importance of life after death either as a motivation for the present life or as the culmination of it, he emphasized in a remarkably high degree the significance, joy, blessedness, opportunities, and responsibilities of the present life both in relation to God and fellow man. Hence the zeal with which he sought to promote the highest and broadest type of Christian education fitting the young for a happy and useful life in Church and State.

In his *Private Confession* of 1528, he says about these three orders: "The only holy orders and institutions established of God are these three: The ministerial office, matrimony, temporal government. All who are in the pastoral office or in the service of the Word are in a holy, legitimate, good order and station, one well-pleasing to God, those, namely, who preach, administer the sacraments, have charge of the common treasury, sextons, and messengers or servants who minister unto them, etc. These are indeed holy works before God. So then to be father or mother, to govern the house well, and to train up children for the service of God, is also really a holy state, a holy work and holy order. So too when children or servants are obedient to their parents or masters, this is nothing but holiness, and whoever is found in this state, is a living saint on earth. So too a prince or sovereign, judges, officials, chancellors, clerks, man-servants, maid-servants, and all who serve them and all subjects, all this is nothing but a holy work and holy life before God, because these three institutions or orders are comprehended in God's Word and command. But whatever is comprehended in God's Word must be holy. For the Word of God is holy, and sanctifies everything that comes in contact with it." [19]

THE MEANS OF GRACE.—"It is the Holy Spirit who begets in the believer the new life which we have been contemplating and who, from the very beginning of his religious experience, awakens faith within him. It is precisely also in this faith, wrought by the Holy Spirit, that the Christian possesses, enjoys, and puts into practice the new life, clinging constantly to Christ, the Reconciler, and ever learning to apprehend Him more fully. Christ is now, however, continually presented and the blessings of His redemption imparted in the objective external Word and in the sacraments." [20] This work the Holy Spirit seeks to accomplish through the Means of Grace, the Word and the two sacraments, Baptism and the Lord's Supper.

---
19) Graul, *Distinctive Doctrines*, pp. 36-37.
20) Köstlin, *Theology of Luther*, vol. II, p. 489.

To these Means of Grace Luther also added absolution.

The Word is the chief and principal means of grace, the foundation upon which the others rest and the source from which they derive both their form and efficacy. Through the preached Word the Holy Spirit convicts of sin and convinces of grace, leading the sinner to repentance and faith and the appropriation of the grace offered through Christ. This Word has inherent power and is effective regardless of the personal character of the preacher.

The sacraments are divinely ordained, signs, seals, and vehicles of grace. Their efficacy depends not upon the person who administers them but upon the accompanying words of institution. While efficacious in themselves objectively considered, they do not work *ex opere operato*, as the Catholic Church teaches, i. e., by virtue of application, but their effect is dependent upon the faith of the person who receives them. "Whether it be the Sacrament of the Altar," says he, "or whether it be Baptism, or whether it be the Word in the public assembly, thou truly hast just so much as thou believest." [21]

Baptism was to him the sacrament of regeneration whereby the new spiritual life of faith was implanted in the infant or the one baptized, and all his sins forgiven. The effectiveness of the sacrament in each particular case is, however, dependent upon the faith of the recipient, yet not in such a way that the faith on the part of the recipient makes the sacrament efficacious, for "when the Word is added to the water, Baptism is genuine even though faith be wanting. For my faith does not make Baptism but receives it; and Baptism does not therefore become spurious if it be

---

21) Köstlin, op. cit., vol. II, p. 505; *Werke*, Er. ed., vol. XXI, p. 133; vol. XII, pp. 170, 213.

wrongly received or employed, as it is not bound to our faith but to the Word."[22] Although Baptism removes the guilt of sin, it does not remove concupiscence, or original sin, which remains in the baptized. The effects of Baptism he regarded as being permanent, so that even if there should be a lapse from grace on the part of the baptized, his repentance would but be a return to baptismal grace. "Baptism," he says, "abides forever; and even though someone should fall from it and sin, we nevertheless always have access thereto, that we may again subdue the old man. But we must not again be sprinkled with water; for though we were a hundred times put under the water, it would nevertheless be one Baptism, although the act and significance continue to remain. Repentance, therefore, is nothing else than to return and approach to Baptism, that we return to and practice what had been begun and had been abandoned.[23] The form of Baptism he regarded as immaterial. All he insists on is that water be used in conjunction with the words of institution and applied to the candidate for Baptism. He insists strongly on infant Baptism, holding that such Baptism is pleasing to Christ as shown by His own works and required by the sinful state of the child itself.[24] He taught that infants can believe or receive faith through Baptism, saying: "We bring the child in the purpose and hope that it may believe, and we pray that God may grant it faith: but we do not baptize it upon that, but solely upon the command of God."[25]

Although Luther held that Baptism is necessary to salvation, he admits that God is not so bound to Baptism that He cannot save without it. Hence he

---
22) *Large Cat., Book of Concord*, p. 472.
23) *Large Cat., Book of Concord*, p. 475.
24) Ibid., p. 471-74.
25) Ibid., p. 473.

does not dare to say that children who die unbaptized are lost.

"Through Baptism," says Luther, "we are in the first instance born anew; the Lord's Supper is then a food for souls which nourishes and strengthens the new man." [26]

The Lord's Supper Luther defines as follows in his *Large Catechism*: "It is the true body and blood of our Lord Jesus Christ in and under the bread and wine which we Christians are commanded by the Word of Christ to eat and to drink." [27] He rejected the Catholic doctrine of transubstantiation, i. e., that the substance of the bread is changed into the substance of the body of Christ and that the substance of the wine is changed into the substance of the blood of Christ through the blessings of the priest, so that they no longer are bread and wine except in appearance and taste, but the actual body and blood of Christ. He also rejected Zwingli's idea of mere symbolism and commemoration as well as Calvin's doctrine of mere spiritual presence. He taught the real presence of the body and blood of Christ in, with, and under bread and wine as vehicles or carriers of the heavenly and unseen elements. It is the body of the crucified, risen, and glorified Christ which is truly present and given in the Lord's Supper. This doctrine he defended against his opponents by the words of institution, the doctrine of the inseparability of the two natures in Christ, and the doctrine of the ubiquity of the glorified Christ, even according to His human nature. Through the Lord's Supper forgiveness of sins is received. It is also a pledge and token of God's promise and grace, a food to refresh and strengthen the soul, a testimony to and remembrance of Christ's suffering

---
26) Köstlin, op. cit., vol. II, p. 511.
27) *Book of Concord*, p. 477.

LUTHER'S THEOLOGY

and death and a means of communion and fellowship with Christ and fellow believers.

Luther recognized the possibility of falling away from God as well as subsequent repentance and return. He therefore had a very high regard for private absolution and held it to be the sacrament of forgiveness of sin and restoration. He connects it with Baptism, however, saying in his *Large Catechism*: "Here you perceive that Baptism both in its power and significance comprehends also the third sacrament, which has been called repentance, as it is really nothing else than Baptism." [28] While he rejected the Roman confessional, he insisted that private confession and absolution should be retained by the Church for the relief of penitent and burdened sinners. The confession should, however, be voluntary and free from any coercion whatsoever, even with respect to the enumeration of sins.

THE CHURCH.—The Church was to Luther the communion of believers or saints which possesses the Means of Grace and is recognized by the preaching of the Word and the administration of the sacraments. It also possesses the Power of the Keys or absolution and excommunication. The Means of Grace and the Power of the Keys are to be administered publicly by the regularly called and ordained ministers of the Church. He recognized no priestly order created by the sacrament of ordination, simply the office of the ministry which was to be filled by the calling of properly qualified men from the general priesthood of believers. He regarded ordination merely as the form of calling and induction into office, not a sacrament conferring a special indelible character and priestly power as taught by the Roman Church. In the mat-

---

28) *Book of Concord*, p. 475.

ter of government of the Church, he recognized the rights of the local congregation to self-determination and self-government under its lawfully called pastors and bishops. Only such rites and customs as are useful for order, decency, and spiritual edification and not forbidden in God's Word should be observed. Uniformity of government and church rites is not necessary to the true unity of the Church, which unity is spiritual rather than external. In church government he thus laid down the principles of congregationalism as opposed to the hierarchical principles.

THE STATE.—As we have already seen, Luther regarded the State or government as a divine institution. His ideas of government are clearly set forth in two treatises published in 1520 and 1524.[29] He recognizes clearly the distinction between State and Church both in nature and function and maintains that each has its separate sphere of authority and activity. The State rules in secular matters and the Church in spiritual and neither has the right to intrude upon the other's realm. While he thus maintains the principle of separation of the Church and the State, he nevertheless regards them as inter-related institutions working together for the best interests of man temporally and spiritually and the promotion of the Kingdom of God and His glory. While the State may compel Church attendance, it cannot drive to faith nor inflict the death penalty upon false teachers.[30]

THE LAST THINGS.—Luther accepted the general teachings of the Church with respect to the Last

---

29) *Letter to German Nobility on the Improvement of the Christian Estates* and *Letter to the Councilmen of German Cities in Behalf of Christian Schools.*
30) On Luther's political ideas, see Waring, *The Political Theories of Martin Luther.*

Things which were not found to be contrary to Scripture, but he seems to have been too occupied with the earthly life of the believer to pay a great deal of attention to the life after death and the development of the doctrines pertaining to eschatology. In his *Private Confession* he merely says: "Finally, I believe in the resurrection of all the dead, both of the pious and the wicked, at the last day, so that each shall receive in his body according to his deeds, and thus the pious enjoy everlasting life with Christ, and the wicked suffer everlasting death with the devil and his angels." [31]

Since we cannot enter into details as to Luther's views on the subjects generally considered under eschatology, we conclude with the following words of Köstlin, which will describe Luther's attitude toward and contributions to the doctrine of the Last Things. "Under nearly all the topics embraced in the theology of Luther, we find it difficult to present in concise form the full wealth of his independent ideas and views. It may appear very strange that the case should be so entirely different in regard to the subject of our present chapter—that there should here, on the contrary, be a dearth of positive ideas peculiar to himself, introduced anew by him into Christian theology, or quickened by his energy into fresh vigor. His principal achievement in this sphere was, in fact, chiefly negative in character, i. e., the opposing and rejection of the Roman Catholic doctrine of purgatory, and that, too, upon the basis of the fundamental evangelical doctrine of the plan of salvation, against which the theory of purgatory had arrayed itself. The views which he himself adopts concerning the condition of

---

31) Graul, *Distinctive Doctrines*, p. 44.

departed souls are but slightly developed. In regard to the final state of man and of the world after the Day of Judgment, he makes no attempt to secure new information from the Scriptures, however freshly and vividly he draws upon their resources." [32]

CHAPTER VII

PEDAGOGICAL WORKS

Bible Translation

In this and the three following chapters we shall deal with Luther's pedagogical writings. These were both various and numerous, for Luther was deeply interested in the cause of a broad and general Christian education. He was ever on the alert to speak or write a word that would advance the cause of popular education. Hence, we find that his pedagogical views were expressed both incidentally and specifically. In an incidental manner he sets forth his educational ideas in his sermons, the lectures he delivered to his students, his familiar and free discourses at the table in his own home, the letters to his friends, the introductions he wrote for hymnbooks, tracts, and other writings by his associates, as well as in the introductions to the tracts he himself wrote on a variety of subjects. In his strictly educational tracts and treatises, such as his appeal to the German nobility in behalf of social improvement, the appeal to the German city governments in behalf of Christian education, the so-called sermon on *Sending Children to School* and his two Catechisms, he sets forth his theories on education in a very specific and somewhat detailed manner.

Interesting and valuable as are his incidental remarks on education, found in his sermons, lectures, tracts, table talks, letters, etc., as well as his specific pedagogical writings, his greatest contribution to popular and higher education, as well as to the life of the Christian and the life of the Church generally, was his matchless translation of the Bible into the German language. By this great achievement he gave to his people, and indirectly to other peoples, the Word of God in a popular, readable German language, and laid the foundation for religious, intellectual, social, linguistic, and literary activities, the immediate and remote consequences and significance of which are of such a nature and scope that they defy both attempts at tracing and at limitation. We shall, therefore, first treat of Luther's translation of the Bible.

GERMAN BIBLE TRANSLATIONS BEFORE LUTHER.— Catholic writers, as a rule, never tire of minimizing the value of Luther's Bible translation and point out that there were before Luther's time a number of German translations of the Bible which were widely known and used. They draw very heavily upon the information furnished by Protestant scholars, especially Lutheran, showing that there were many German translations even before Luther began his. Therefore, the translation by Luther was neither called for nor necessary. Furthermore, they endeavor to prove that there was an abundance of copies of the Bible both in Latin and German during the school and student days of Luther, so that his declaration that he had not seen a copy of the whole Bible until he was twenty years old is nothing but pure fabrication and falsehood. It is also claimed that Luther made use of at least one of these German versions as the basis of his own, a claim which O'Hare seeks to substantiate with a quotation from the Protestant writer Vedder.[1]

---

1) *Facts About Luther*, p. 202.

PEDAGOGICAL WORKS

Three important questions are thus raised. 1. Were there German translations of the Bible before Luther's time? If so, what were they and by whom were they published? 2. To what extent were they known to the people and used by them? 3. Did Luther know of these translations? If so, what use, if any, did he make of them?

The first question is easily answered, especially the first part of it. The Gothic version of Ulfilas of the fourth century is generally mentioned as the first German translation of the Bible. From the eighth to the fifteenth century there appeared a number of partial translations, as the Psalter and the Gospels, fragments of which are still extant. From 1466 to 1522[2] there were printed fourteen versions of the whole Bible in High German, four in Low German, twenty-two psalters, and twelve other parts, according to Wilhelm Walther and others.[3]

The second question raised is not so easily answered. According to Catholic writers, the Bible in German translation was widely distributed under Church auspices and well known to the people. O'Hare says: "Proofs without number might easily be adduced to

---

2) Following are the pre-Lutheran German Bible editions according to the generally accepted order and chronology: High German-Strassburg version, printed by Johannes Mentel, c. 1466; Strassburg, Eggestein, c. 1570; Augsburg, Jod. Pflanzmann, c. 1473; Augsburg, Günter Zainer, c. 1473; Basel, 1474; Augsburg, Zainer, 1477; Augsburg, A. Sorg, 1477; Augsburg, A. Sorg, 1480; Nuremberg, A. Koburger, 1483 (Copy in library of Union Theological Seminary, New York); Strassburg, Grüninger, 1485; Augsburg, H. Schönberger, 1487 and 1490; Augsburg, Hans Otmar, 1507; Augsburg, Silvanus Otmar, 1518. All these editions give essentially the same translation, based mainly on a Spanish copy of the Latin Vulgate. Zainer and Koburger made a number of changes in their editions. Only the names of the printers are known: the translator or translators remain concealed, but traces point to Bohemian or Waldensian origin. Low German—Delft, 1477, only Old Testament without Psalms; the Picture Bible of Cologne, c. 1478 or 1479; Lübeck, 1494, original translation to II Kings, chapter vii, the rest being taken from the Cologne Bible; Halberstadt, Ludvig Trutebul, 1522. See E. Nestle, *New Schaff—Herzog Encyclopedia of Religious Knowledge*, vol. II, pp. 144-45; *Realencyk. f. p. Theologie und Kirche*, vol. III, pp. 64-70.

3) *Die deutsche Bibelübersetzung des Mittelalters;* E. Nestle, *Realencyk.*, vol. III, pp. 64-70; X, p. 217; *New Schaff—Herzog*, vol. II, p. 144.

133

show that the Bible was known, read, and distributed with the sanction and authority of the Church in the common language of the people from the seventh to the fourteenth century. . . . The contention of the ignorant and bigoted who would have the simple and unlettered believe that Rome hated the Bible and did her best to keep it a locked and sealed book, is so utterly absurd and stupid that all honest and patient researches of distinguished scholars flatly and openly oppose it by accumulating evidence from the simplest facts of history. . . . When will they, in the presence of the Church's zealous guardianship of the Bible from the beginning, rid themselves of the silly mouthings of the anti-Catholic bigots in declaring that Luther was the very first to give his poor, languishing countrymen the Bible in their own tongue, a book which, as a student at Erfurt, he knew was held in high esteem and which, as a monk and priest, he was obliged by rule to have known, studied, and recited for years. To maintain that Luther knew not and could not find any Bibles except the one he was supposed to discover as librarian of his convent is to brand him as a liar. . . . All along she (the Church) employed her clergy to multiply it in the Greek and Hebrew languages and to translate it into Latin and the common tongues of every Christian nation that all might read and learn and know the Word of God. She and she alone, by her care and loving watchfulness, saved and protected it from total extinction and destruction." [4]

That such extravagant Catholic claims cannot be substantiated by the actual facts of history is patent to everyone somewhat familiar with the history of the Catholic persecution of Bible translators and the laity who possessed and read the Bible. The scope and

---
4) *Facts About Luther*, pp. 195-97.

purpose of this chapter forbid an extended discussion of this mooted question. Suffice it to say that the historic position of the Roman Catholic Church with respect to Bible translation and Bible reading, is clearly indicated by the zealous endeavors on the part of the Popes to prevent the spread of the Bible in translations at the beginning of the last century when Bible societies began to spring up in Europe. Pope Pius VII in 1816 condemned Bible societies as the plague of Christendom and renewed the injunction against Bible translations. The same position was taken by his successor, Leo XII.[5] Whatever vernacular translations of the Bible the people possessed before Luther's day, they possessed in spite of the Church, not because of her friendliness toward and zeal for the spreading of the Bible among the people in a language they could read and understand. The efforts to bring the Bible to the people in their own language were put forth by such "heretics" as the Waldensians, Hussites, and Wiclifites, not by the Church or under her auspices and with her encouragement.

Dr. Dau, who has made a careful study of this question, states his conclusions in the following words: "Whatever knowledge of Scripture the people in the Middle Ages possessed was confined to those who could read Latin. Catholic writers claim this was at that time the universal language of Europe, but they wisely add: 'among the educated.' One of them says: 'Those who could read Latin could read the Bible, and those who could not read Latin could not read anything.' Exactly. And now, to prove the wide diffusion of Bible-knowledge in their Church before Luther, these Catholic writers should give us some exact data as to the extent of the Latin scholarship in that age. Fact

---

5) Kurtz, *Church History*, vol. III, p. 224.

is, the Latin tongue acted as a lock upon the Scriptures to the common people. Hence arose the desire to have the Bible translated into the vernacular of various European countries.

"This desire Rome sought to suppress with brutal rigor. The bloody persecutions of the Waldensians in France, which almost resulted in the extirpation of these peaceful mountain people, of the followers of Wyclif in England, whose remains Rome had exhumed after his death and burned, of the Hussites in Bohemia, were all aimed at translations of the Bible into the languages which the common people understood.

"In July, 1199, Pope Innocent III issued a breve, occasioned by the report that parts of the Bible were found in a French translation in the diocese of Metz. The breve praises in a general way the zeal for Bible-study, but applies to all who are not officially appointed to engage in such study the prohibition in Ex. 19, 12, 13, not to touch the holy mountain of the Law. During the reign of his successor, Honorius III, in 1220, laymen in Germany were forbidden to read the Bible. Under Gregory IX the same prohibition was issued, in 1229, to laymen in Great Britain. In the same year the crusades against the Albigenses were concluded, and the Council of Toulouse issued a severe order, making it a grave offense for a layman to possess a Bible. In 1234, the Synod of Tarragona demanded the immediate surrender of all translations of the Bible for the purpose of having them burned. In 1246, the Synod of Baziers issued a prohibition forbidding laymen any theological books whatsoever, and even enjoining the clergy from owning any theological books written in the vernacular. Eleven years after Luther's death, in 1557, Pope Paul IV published the Roman Index of Forbidden Books, and, with certain exceptions, prohibited laymen from reading the Bible.

Not until the reign of King Edward VI was the 'Act inhibiting the reading of the Old and New Testaments in the English tongue, and the printing, selling, giving, or delivering of any such other books or writings as are therein mentioned and condemned' (namely, in 34 Hen. VIII. Cap. 1) abrogated. The Council of Trent ordered all Catholic publishers to see to it that their editions have the approval of the respective bishop. Not until February 28, 1759, did Pope Clement XIII give permission to translate the Bible into all the languages of the Catholic states. Not until November 17, 1893, did Pope Leo XIII issue an encyclical enjoining upon Catholics the study of the Bible, always, however, in editions approved by the Roman Church. (Kurtz, *Kirchengesch.* II, 94, 217; *Univers. Encycl.*, under title *Bible;* Peter Heylyn, *Ecclesia Restaurata* I, 99; Denzinger, *Enchiridion,* 1429. 1439. 1567. 1607.)

"Catholic writers seek to make a great impression in favor of their Church by enumerating, on the authority of Protestant scholars, the number of German translations of the Bible that are known to have been in existence before Luther. But they omit to inform the public that not a single one of those translations obtained the approbation of the bishop. One cannot view but with a pathetic interest these sacred relics of an age that was hungering for the Word of God. The origin of these early German Bibles has been traced by scholars to Wycliffite and Hussite influences, which Rome never stamped out, though her inquisitors tried their best to do so. The earliest of these Bibles do not state the place nor the year of publication. Can the reader guess why? They were not published at the seat of the German Archbishop, Mainz, but most of them at the free imperial city of Augsburg. Can the reader suggest a reason? Many of them are printed in abnormally small sizes, facilitating quick concealment. Can the reader imagine a cause for this phenomenon? In these old German Bibles particular texts are emphasized, for example, Rom. 8, 18; 1 Cor. 4, 9; 2 Cor. 4, 8; 11, 23; 1 Pet. 2, 19; 4, 16; 5, 9; Acts 5, 18, 41; 8, 1; 12, 4; 14, 19. If the reader will take the trouble to look up these texts, he will find that they warn Christians to be prepared to be persecuted for their faith. Has the reader ever heard of such an officer of the Roman Church as the inquisitor, one of whose duties it was to hunt for Bibles among the people? In places these old German Bibles contain significant marginal glosses, for example, at 1 Tim. 2, 5 one of them has this gloss: 'Ain mitler Christus, ach merk!' that is: One mediator, Christ—note this well!" [6]

Thus while there were German Bibles in existence before Luther, they did not exist with the will and consent of the Church and were neither widely distributed nor generally known among the people, not even among the clergy.

As to the third question there has also been a great deal of discussion. Dr. Nestle states that two directly opposite judgments have been formed on this question. "According to the one he (Luther) did not know them (earlier German versions) at all, according to the other he was a plagiarist of the worst sort. The one is as incorrect as the other." [7] That Luther knew of at least some of these earlier versions is evident from his letter to Amsdorf under date of January 13, 1522, in which he says: "Now I know what translating means and why, so far, no one who undertook it ever put his name to it." [8] This is undoubtedly a

---

6) *Luther Examined and Re-Examined.* p. 64-67.
7) *Realencyk, f. p. Theologie und Kirche,* vol. III, p. 72.
8) Quoted by Grisar, *Luther,* vol. V., p. 495; *Werke,* St. Louis ed., vol. XV, p. 2557.

PEDAGOGICAL WORKS

reference to some of these German translations then in existence as they were anonymous, except for the name of the printer. That he had an appreciation of the work of translating carried on by others is evident from his letter to Johann Lang quoted on page 140 and the following statement in a letter to Link in May, 1527, in which he says: "I do not despise the German translation of the prophets which has just appeared at Worms, except that the German is quite obscure, perhaps because of the dialect used. The translators are diligent, but who can do all things? I am now girt up to translate them myself." [9]

Whichever copies of earlier editions Luther knew and whatever use he made of them, one thing is certain, he took the greatest possible pains, assisted by a few able and faithful helpers, to render the Hebrew and Greek Scriptures into a readable and intelligible German with his usual striking independence and produced a work in a bold contrast to the imperfect and more or less unreadable previous German translations from the Latin Vulgate. His translation of the Bible at once became the most popular as well as the most widely read book of the time and was even used to a considerable extent by his foes. In his treatise on translation, published in 1530 as a defense against the attacks of Emser, he makes mention of the fact that his enemies learned to speak, read, and write German from his Bible translation, which they were not able to do before, yet they give him no credit but continue to heap upon him calumnies and condemnation.[10] Luther's German Bible stands as the best testimony in favor of Luther against all insinuations and accusations of plagiarism on his part. Although his translation was not the first one made into the German

---
9) Smith and Jacobs, *Luther's Correspondence*, vol. II, p. 399.
10) *Werke*, Weimar ed., vol. XXX. 2, p. 633.

language, it was nevertheless the first one made on the basis of the Hebrew and Greek original texts, and this fact alone makes his German Bible translation an event of epoch-making significance.

TRANSLATION OF THE NEW TESTAMENT.—Luther had been repeatedly urged by his friends and associates to undertake the translation of the Bible, and no sooner was he within the confines of the Wartburg before he commenced on the New Testament, using for this purpose the Greek Testament of Erasmus, the second edition of 1518-19. In a letter to Spalatin, dated May 14, 1521, he writes: "I am reading the Bible in Greek and Hebrew."[11] This was preliminary to the work of translation. In a letter to Lang at Erfurt, who was also working on a translation of the New Testament and had already published his translation of the Gospel according to Matthew, under date of Dec. 18, 1521, he says that he shall "lie hidden until Easter." "In the meantime," he continues, "I shall continue to write my Postils and shall translate the New Testament into German, a thing which my friends demand and at which I hear you are also working. Would that every town had its interpreter,[12] and that this book alone might be on the tongues and in the hands, the eyes, the ears, and the hearts of all men."[13] To Amsdorf he writes on the 13th day of the following January: "I shall put the Bible into the German, though in so doing I am taking upon myself a burden beyond my strength. Now I see what translating means, and why, so far, no one who undertook it ever put his name to it. As for the Old Testament, I cannot touch it unless you are here to give your help. Could I find a hiding place with one of you,

---
11) Smith, *Luther's Correspondence*, vol. II, pp. 27-28.
12) Should be translator, the German Dolmetscher as here used meaning one who translates rather than one who merely interprets.
13) Ibid., p. 80.

I would come at once so as to start the work of translating from the outset with your assistance. The result ought to be a translation worthy of being read by all Christians. I hope we shall give our German folk a better one than that which the Latins have. It is a glorious work at which we all toil, for it is a public matter and is meant to serve the common weal."[14] The whole translation of the New Testament was completed in rough draft in the remarkably short period of three months. On the 30th of March, 1522, Luther writes to Spalatin: "I had translated not only the Gospel of John, but the whole New Testament while I was at my Patmos (he left the Wartburg on March 3, and arrived at Wittenberg on March 7), but now Philip and I have begun to polish the whole thing, and (God willing) it will be a worthy piece of work. We shall use your service sometimes in finding right words, so be ready. But remember to give us simple words, not those of the camp or the court, for this book must be adorned with simplicity. I am going to begin now. Please give us the names and the colors of the gems in Revelation xxi; or better yet, get them from the court, and let us have an opportunity to see them."[15]

TRANSLATION OF THE OLD TESTAMENT.—Before

---

14) Quoted by Grisar, *Luther*, v. 495; *Werke*, St. Louis ed., vol. XV, p. 2557.
15) Smith, *Luther's Correspondence*, vol. II., pp. 118-119.

Note. The printing of the New Testament in German was begun in May, 1522, and the first edition appeared off the press in September under the title, *Das Newe Testament. Deutzsch. Vuittemberg*. It was printed by Melchior Lotther, but it bore neither the name of the translator nor the name of the printer. It was printed in an edition of 3,000 copies, and is known as the *September Testament*. Another edition, somewhat revised, appeared the following December, and is known as the *December Testament*. Other revised editions were published in 1526 and 1530. There were no less than sixteen editions and fifty reprints published in Germany before the year 1557, showing the great demand there was for the New Testament in the German language. See Grisar, *Luther*, vol. V., p. 496 seq., and the Weimar edition of Luther's Works, *Deutsche Bibel*, vol. II., p. 200 seq. The latter volume contains a complete list of the editions and reprints of the German New Testament.

the translation of the New Testament had been completed, work was already begun on the Old Testament. Of the many difficulties encountered in rendering the Old Testament into a readable and intelligible German, Luther frequently writes to his friends and co-laborers. Job seems especially to have given the translators trouble. Concerning this book, Luther writes to Spalatin on Feb. 23, 1524, as follows: "We have so much trouble in translating Job on account of the grandeur of his sublime style, that he seems to be much more impatient of our efforts to turn him into German than he was of the consolation of his friends. Either he always wishes to sit on his dunghill, or else he is jealous of the translator who would share with him the credit of writing his book. This keeps the third part of the Bible from being printed." [16] To Wenzel (Wenzeslaus) Link he writes about the difficulties encountered in translating the Prophets under date of June 14, 1528: "We are sweating over the work of putting the Prophets into German. God, how much of it there is, and how hard it is to make these Hebrew writers talk German! They resist us, and do not want to leave their Hebrew and imitate our German barbarism. It is like making a nightingale leave her own sweet song and imitate the monotonous voice of the cuckoo, which she detests." [17] Mathesius quotes him as saying, "I have been sitting with Masters Philip and Aurogallo for fourteen whole days over a single line or word, before it would speak German." [18]

But in spite of the difficulty of making the Hebrew speak a fluent and idiomatic German, the great task was at last completed, and the first edition of the

---
16) Ibid., p. 221.
17) Ibid., p. 445.
18) *Historien*, p. 244.

whole Bible in German came off the press of Hans Luft in 1534, under the title: *Biblia, das ist die gantze Heiliche Schrift*. It carried the name of Luther as translator and the name of Hans Luft as printer. While Luther had received considerable assistance from Aurogallo, professor of Hebrew at Wittenberg, Melanchthon, and a few others, it was nevertheless essentially his own work throughout. He had been chiefly responsible for the successful achievement. Yet he received no compensation for this work, nor in fact for any of his literary work, for he wished the Word to be as free as possible to the people. The printers, however, made good money on Luther's works.[19]

REVISION OF THE BIBLE TRANSLATION.—Not only had Luther taken great pains with the original translation of the Bible, but he also labored very zealously, assisted by a number of scholars, such as Melanchthon, Bugenhagen, Aurogallo, Georg Rörer, Creuziger, Ziegler, Forstemius, and Pommer, to thoroughly revise his translation after it had been completed. Mathesius gives a very full account of the care and deliberation with which this work was undertaken.[20] The minutes of the conferences held by the revisers so well kept by Georg Rörer give us a clear insight into the manner and thoroughness with which this work was prosecuted.[21] No pains were spared, and every available source of information was consulted in order to

---

19) Luther's Bible was well received, and the presses were busy supplying the demand for copies. No less than thirty-four editions and seventy-two reprints were published before 1540. During Luther's lifetime eighty-four original editions and 253 reprints appeared. "According to fairly good authority," says Grisar, "no less than 100,000 complete Bibles left Lotther's press at Wittenberg between 1534 and 1584." *Luther*, vol. V, p. 498. See also *Deutsche Bibel*, Weimar edition, vol. II, p. 545 seq. Both Luther's German New Testament and his German Bible were illustrated with wood cuts prepared by Lucas Cranach.
20) *Historien*, p. 240 seq.
21) Volumes III and IV, *Deutsche Bibel*, Weimar ed. of Luther's *Werke*.

make the German Bible true and faithful to the original. The revision undertaken by Luther and his colleagues was completed in 1542.

THE LANGUAGE AND FAITHFULNESS OF LUTHER'S GERMAN BIBLE.—The excellency of language, faithfulness of rendition, and the tremendous literary and cultural influence of Luther's translation have been extensively commented upon by scholars of many lands and of all denominations. The testimony may vary in minor details, but there is universal unanimity in according to this work of Luther the highest commendation for its scholarly and literary excellency and ascribing to it a very prominent place in the history of the German language.[22] In proof of this statement, the following quotations are taken from Audin and Grisar, two Roman Catholic writers, the one a Frenchman, the other a German, neither one of whom can be accused of any prejudices in favor of Luther, rather than from the numerous statements that might be cited from Protestant scholars.

Writes Audin in his *History of Luther*: "The idiom which Luther employed was admirably adapted for his purpose. It was the Saxon dialect of the German, which possessed at once solid strength and attractive beauty. It was the language of Hermann, and had not yielded to the influence of the conqueror's dialect. It was, perhaps, the only one then spoken capable of reproducing, without much disadvantage, the sacred text: and yet it has grown old and met the lot of all living tongues. The translation of the Bible is, however, a noble monument of literature; a vast enterprise, which seemed to require more than the life of man, but which Luther accomplished in a few years.— The poetic soul finds in this translation evidences of

---

22) Even O'Hare admits this fact, *The Facts About Luther*, p. 204.

genius, and expressions as natural, as beautiful and melodious as in the original languages. Luther's translation sometimes renders the primitive phrase with touching simplicity, invests itself with sublimity and magnificence, and receives all the modifications which he wishes to impart to it. It is simple in the recital of the patriarch, glowing in the predictions of the prophet, and colloquial in the epistles of St. Peter and St. Paul. The imagery of the original is rendered with undeviating fidelity: the translation occasionally approaches the text. Add to this the odor of antiquity which the dialect used by Luther exhaled, and which is as pleasing as the peculiar tint that is found in the engravings of the old German masters. We must not, then, be astonished at the enthusiasm which Saxony felt at the appearance of Luther's version, of which the New Testament was first published. Both Catholics and Protestants regarded it as an honour done to their ancient idiom. The Humanists were especially delighted, for in their eyes this translation elevated the popular language, which might afterwards contend with the classic tongues, the destinies of which seemed fixed." [23]

The more recent writer Grisar, who is also much more prejudiced against Luther than was Audin, is nevertheless even stronger in his commendation of Luther's translation of the Bible than is Audin. Says he: "The excellence of Luther's translation of the Bible from the point of view of the text is unquestionable. For what the author above all aimed at, viz., a popular rendering of the text which should harmonize with the peculiarities of the German language, that he certainly achieved. Through his Bible translation, owing to its general use throughout a large portion

---

23) Pages 213-14.

of the nation, he exerted a greater influence on the upbuilding of the German tongue than by all his other vernacular works. In his other writings, in which he was ever striving to improve his mode of speech, we may often find real models of good German, which consciously or not, had a widespread influence on the language. In the case of the Bible, however, this was far more noticeable, for not only was his language there more polished, but the fact of the text being so frequently committed to memory, quoted from the pulpit and surrounded by that halo which befits the Word of God, helped to extend its sway.

"Not only did he take infinite pains to translate aright such phrases as ring unfamiliar to Western ears, but he was also assisted by his happy gift of observation and his knack of catching the true idiom. His habit of noting the words that fell from the lips of the populace, or as he says, of 'looking into the jaw of the man in the street,' was of the utmost service to him in his choice and use of terms. 'No German talks like that,' 'that is not put "germanice," ' 'the German tongue won't stand for that,' and similar utterances frequently recur in the minutes of the conferences when he is finding fault with the renderings proposed by others or even his own earlier ones." [24]

Speaking of the influence on the German language which Luther's translation of the Bible had, Grisar further says: "In Lutheranism the New High German of the Bible found its way not only into the educated, ecclesiastical circles, but also to the common folk, into whose ears the preachers assiduously dinned countless favorite texts in their new form; it also became familiar to the teachers and the children in the schools. No more powerful lever for the furtherance of New High German could have been found. A cen-

---
24) *Luther,* vol. V, p. 503.

tury after, New High German had become the language of the churches and the schools in the regions subject to Luther's influence, while the South German and Low German dialects had largely lost their hold." [25]

Yet Grisar [26] contends that it is going too far when it is asserted that Luther by his Bible translation actually became the founder or creator of the High German language, and this contention is not altogether unfounded, but it must nevertheless be maintained that Luther breathed new life into the dormant germs of the High German dialect, gave it a fixed form, purity of style, and fluency of expression, and so popularized it that it became not only the language of the learned and the cultured, but also the treasured possession of the common people.

SOME ADVERSE CRITICISM ON THE BIBLE TRANSLATION.—It is only to be expected that so strong a Catholic as Grisar and a Jesuit in training and aims, should find something to criticize Luther adversely for in this translation. He charges him with having permitted his theological bias to lead him to take liberties with rendering the original text into German, too loose views regarding the Bible Canon, and impure motives in undertaking and carrying out the translation.[27] As to the last mentioned indictment he contends that Luther's motive for rendering the Bible into the German tongue was not so much to bring "the holy Word of God" to his fellow Germans as a personal and polemical one, for Luther's chief purpose was through the translation of the Bible to further attack the Pope and the Catholic Church. There can be no doubt that Luther realized that the render-

---
25) Ibid., p. 508.
26) Ibid., p. 509.
27) Ibid., pp. 525-585.

ing of the Bible into the vernacular and placing it in the hands of the people generally would be a powerful weapon against the errors of the Roman Catholic Church, and it so proved to be, but it is doing Luther a gross injustice when it is claimed that his chief motive for translating the Bible was a controversial and polemical one. His chief aim and motive in this great undertaking was to render the Word of God into a readable, intelligible, and idiomatic German in order that even the common people might have direct access to it, be taught and edified by it, and be able to judge for themselves in matters pertaining to Christian life and doctrine. That such was the case is evidenced by many direct statements of Luther himself and the position he took respecting the priesthood of believers and the right of private interpretation of Scripture. Grisar's criticism of Luther's attitude to the Canon is justified by the facts in the case, and Luther's position in this respect has been repudiated by Lutheran theologians from his own day to the present. It should be noted, however, that liberal theologians generally have always pointed to Luther's rather free and seemingly unguarded expressions regarding the authenticity and integrity of certain books of the Bible, as, for example, II Peter, James, Jude, and Revelation, in the New Testament, with a great deal of satisfaction.[28] As to the first objection raised, it may be safely stated in defense of Luther that he did not willfully alter the sense of Scripture in order to suit his own peculiar theological bias. He sincerely endeavored to render the original text into a faithful German equivalent. And yet, no one who has had the least to do with translating works from one language into another, will deny that the

---

28) For a further discussion of this point, see section on "Bible" in chapter VI, p. 107.

personal element enters into the work of translation, for no matter how objective and unbiased a translation one desires to render, the question of personal understanding and interpretation necessarily enter in, especially in the more difficult passages, and it will of necessity be the translator's own understanding of the given passage that will be reflected in the translation. Yet this is not a fault of the translator; it is a factor inherent in and inseparable from the very work of translating itself, for even a translation, be it ever so literal, is nevertheless a form of interpretation. That Luther's translation, like our Authorized and even Standard Revised Version, to say nothing about the various individual translations, as Moffat's, Goodspeed's, and others, should reflect in a greater or lesser degree the translator's personal understanding of particular passages, is not strange, and should not be charged to wilful and conscious effort to deceive. The passage which Grisar and others especially complain of is Romans 3:28, the *sedes doctrinae* of the doctrine of justification by faith. It is claimed that Luther took liberties with this passage in the interests of his own doctrine on justification by faith and against the doctrine on this point in the Roman Catholic Church. This is not, however, a complaint which originates with Grisar; it was urged against Luther's translation in his own day, and has been voiced over and over again, particularly by Catholic writers, ever since. The point of attack is Luther's insertion of the word "allein" in his German rendering, since this word is found neither in the Greek original nor in the Latin Vulgate. The insertion of this word is very ably defended by Luther himself in his *Sendbrief vom Dolmetschen*, written as early as in 1530. He declares that he is fully aware of the fact that this little objectionable word is not found in either the Greek original or the Latin Vulgate, but denies the charge that it was inserted to strengthen his own doctrinal position. In order not to weaken the effect of the defense by venturing a translation, it is given in Luther's own characteristic language. "Ich hab mich des geflissen ym dolmetzen, das ich rein und klar teutsch geben möchte. Das ist aber die art unser deutschen sprache, wenn sie ein rede begiebt von zweien dingen der man eins bekennet, und das andre verneinet, so braucht man des wort 'solum' (allein) neben dem wort 'nicht' und 'kein.' Als wenn man sagt: der Baur bringt allein korn und kein geldt, Nein, ich hab warlich jytzt nicht geldt, sondern allein korn. Ich hab allein gessen und noch nicht getrunken."[29] No one familiar with the idiom of the German language can deny the validity of Luther's argument in his own defense on this point. Hence, we have here not a case of theological bias, but the question of how the German would say exactly the same thing as the great apostle said on this important matter.

O'Hare makes a good deal of the attack which Jerome Emser made upon Luther's translation. Says he: "Jerome Emser, a learned doctor of Leipsic, made a critical examination of Luther's translation when it appeared and detected more than a thousand glaring faults. He was the first who undertook to show the falseness of the translation and to correct its errors."[30] On this whole controversy it is very profitable to read Luther's defense, *Sendbrief vom Dolmet-*

---

29) *Werke*, Weimar ed., vol. XXX. 2, pp. 636-7.
For the benefit of those who do not read the German language, we also give this passage in our own English translation: I have taken pains in translating to present the original in a pure and clear German. It is, however, the peculiar trait of our German language, when speaking of two things, one of which is asserted, the other denied, that the word "solum," *alone*, is used as a co-relative with *"not"* and *"none."* As, for instance, when we say: "The farmer brings *only* grain, and *not* money;" "No, truly, I have now *no* money, but *only* grain;" "I have *only* eaten, and *not* yet drunk."
30) *The Facts About Luther*, p. 205.

schen. Emser was the most violent and persistent of Luther's literary opponents, and in 1527 published what purported to be a correction of Luther's German New Testament. Luther frequently mentions this man and his attacks upon him in his letters, and in the treatise on translation mentioned above, he refers to him as "the dauber of Dresden," who has mastered Luther's New Testament, reproduced it virtually word by word, removed Luther's introduction, explanations, and name, and inserted his own instead, so that Luther's New Testament was actually being sold with some modifications under the name of Emser to the Catholics![31]

---

31) *Werke,* op. cit., p. 634.

CHAPTER VIII

PEDAGOGICAL WORKS

THREE STIRRING APPEALS

Three of the most stirring appeals that Luther ever sent forth properly belong to the category of pedagogical writings. These were the *Address to the German Nobility* in 1520, the *Letter to the German Councilmen in behalf of Christian Schools* in 1524, and the *Sermon on Sending Children to School* in 1530. We shall deal with each one of these tracts in the order named.

I. *Address to the German Nobility* [1]

The full title of this masterly and comprehensive tract is *The Address to the Christian Nobility of the German Nation on the Improvement of the Christian Estates.*

WHEN WRITTEN.—This tract was written during the late spring of 1520. In a letter to Spalatin under date of June 8 of that year Luther writes: "I have the intention of publishing a broadside to Charles and the whole German nobility against the tyranny and wickedness of the Roman court." [2] This "broadside" of which he here speaks was already completed, so that he wrote the preface to it on June 23 following. To Link he writes on June 20: "I have in press a book in the vernacular against the Pope: *To the No-*

---
1) *Werke*, Weimar ed., vol. VI, pp. 381-469.
2) Smith, *Luther's Correspondence*, vol. I, p. 329.

bility of Germany on Reforming the Christian Estates. It will mightily offend Rome by exposing her impious arts and usurped powers." [3] On August 5, he wrote to Spalatin concerning this tract as follows: "Even if my trumpet-blast will meet the approval of none, yet it must meet my approval as a necessary attack on the tyranny of the Roman Anti-Christ who destroys the souls of the whole world. It is very sharp and vehement, so that I hope it will make even those languid little evil-speakers gasp." [4] Not long after this, the booklet was off press and a new and revised edition was planned, for Luther writes to Spalatin again under date of Aug. 23, saying: "The additions to the book will be put in the second edition which Lotther is bringing out. The book will also be corrected." [5] The first edition thus came off the press during the latter part of July and a new and revised edition was already in preparation a month later.

ITS RECEPTION.—The address to the German nobility produced a mighty stir, and laid both the social and the religious foundation for the great reformer's work. Many of his friends were both astonished and frightened at his audacity, and his enemies flew into a fit of rage. Melanchthon gave vent to his mingled feelings in a letter to Lang in which he says: "At first I rather did not disapprove than approve the plan for writing an epistle to the German nobility, for our friend was urged to do so by some whose opinion we must both respect. Moreover, the thing itself being of God, I would not try to obstruct. I would not rashly hinder Martin's spirit in this cause, to which he seems to have been called by Providence. Besides, the book is now printed and distributed and cannot

---
3) Ibid., pp. 341-42.
4) Ibid., p. 344.
5) Ibid., p. 347.

be recalled."[6] Many of the nobility were pleased and found food for thought. Thus Elector Friedrich of Saxony, in sending a copy of the book to his brother Duke Johann, writes: "Herewith I send you a book written by Dr. Martin Luther in which you will find many wonderful things. God Almighty grant that it turn out well, for truly things are coming to light which many people conceal; may God Almighty vouchsafe to us poor sinners that we be improved and not made worse thereby."[7] Luther's enemies, on the other hand, severely attacked the tract and its author. This was especially the case with Eck and Emser, who issued fiery countertracts. Meanwhile edition upon edition of Luther's tract went forth from the Lotther press at Wittenberg, and reprints were produced elsewhere. This tract of Luther has been regarded by many as his masterpiece,[8] and there can be no question but that it is a most comprehensive and vivid portrayal of the social and religious conditions prevailing in Germany at the time and presents a wise, constructive plan for their improvement.

CONTENTS.—The tract opens with a special greeting to Luther's friend and intimate associate Amsdorf, pastor at Magdeburg, in which he declares that the time for silence has ceased and the time to speak has come. Since it does not seem possible to bring about reforms through the ministry of the Church, he says he is going to make an appeal direct to the princes in the hope that some definite improvements may result. Then follows a very polite and humble salutation addressed to the emperor and the Christian nobility of the German nation. In the first part

---

6) Ibid., p. 347.
7) Ibid., pp. 347-348.
8) "Luther's greatest work," says Smith, ibid., p. 342, and Leopold von Ranke, the great German historian, speaks of it as an epochmaking work, *Werke*, op. cit., p. 397.

of the body of his tract he shows that the ecclesiastical power of Rome has entrenched itself by the erection of three great walls: (1) The doctrine that the spiritual power is above the worldly power in all matters; (2) the Pope alone can interpret Scripture; (3) the Pope alone has power to summon church councils. The first wall Luther overthrows by holding forth the doctrine of the spiritual priesthood of believers and the sacredness of all legitimate occupations. The second wall crumbles under his argument that it is the right and privilege of all members of the spiritual priesthood of believers themselves to read and interpret Scripture. The third wall, he declares, will fall wherever the first two have fallen, the Pope himself becoming amenable, not superior, to church councils.

Having thus laid the foundation, he proceeds to set forth in twenty-eight pointed sections the abuses taught and practiced by the Church of Rome and the social, moral, intellectual, and religious conditions that prevail throughout the German nation, in each case indicating a constructive program for the correction of the abuses and the improvement of the conditions prevailing among the people. Section 25 deals especially with reform in the schools from the universities down.

II. *Letter to the Councilmen of the German Cities.*[9]

The complete title of this tract is, *To the Councilmen of All the Cities of Germany That They Shall Establish and Maintain Schools* (*An die Rathherren aller Städte deutsches Lands dass sie Christliche Schulen aufrichten und halten sollen*). Under the above given title appear the words of Jesus, "Suffer the little children and forbid them not to come to me"

---

9) *Werke*, Weimar ed., vol. XV, pp. 9-53; English trans., Painter, *Luther on Education*, pp. 169-209.

(Matt. 19:14), as a motto. The "Letter" was written in December, 1523, or early in January, 1524. Michael Hummelberg of Ravensburg mentions it in a letter to a friend under date of February 28, 1524, which indicates that it was already off the press and distributed by that time.[10]

OCCASION.—The writing of this tract was primarily occasioned by the conditions that prevailed in Germany at the time with respect to education. In the first place the old cathedral and conventual schools had fallen into disuse where the Lutheran Reformation had taken hold, as their purposes, means, and methods did not fit into the new order of things and they were not readily adjusted to meet the new requirements. This adjustment was not an easy matter to accomplish, nor could it be hastily done. The old schools had been supported by enforced contributions. This could now no longer be done, for the people who were used to the ecclesiastical domination and exactions were naturally glad to be relieved of the burdens imposed, and were neither ready nor willing at once to assume the burdens involved in the support of schools voluntarily. The churches of the Reformation were as yet not sufficiently organized to take over the support and management of schools. Hence the appeal to the city governments.

In the next place there was a rising tide of super-spiritualism as the result of the views and activities of such radical reformers as Münzer and Carlstadt. These super-spirituals regarded learning with suspicion and even hostility. Their slogan was "Gelehrte sind Verkehrte," the learned are perverse or wrongheaded. As a result of Carlstadt's activities, the city schools of Wittenberg were discontinued in 1522, but were opened again under Bugenhagen with

---
10) *Werke*, ibid., p. 9.

Luther's assistance the following year. Another school which suffered greatly from the influences of these fanatical spirits was the one at Erfurt. It was, therefore, not strange that men like Eobanus Hess and other scholars should fear that the new theology would prove destructive to learning. Replying to the complaint of Hess in regard to this matter, Luther writes on March 29, 1523: "Do not be disturbed by the fears which you express that our theology will make us Germans more barbarous in letters than ever we have been; some people often have their fears when there is nothing to fear. I am persuaded that without knowledge of literature, pure theology cannot at all endure, just as heretofore when letters have declined and lain prostrate theology, too, has wretchedly fallen and lain prostrate."[11] In order to counteract this fanatical opposition to learning and the acquisition of languages, Luther devotes a considerable portion of this tract, throughout which he makes a very strong apology for learning in general, not only for the use of the Church but also for the State.

Finally, the rising tide of industry and commerce brought about by enlarging intercourse among peoples and new discoveries led many to take advantage of the opportunities offered to acquire wealth in industrial and commercial enterprises. For trade and industry, learning was not considered essential, and the chances for making money were good, inducing many fathers to refuse to send their boys to school, directing them into industrial and commercial activities instead. The new state of things in the Church seemed not to offer the secure ecclesiastical positions for the boys as under the old system, and therefore the inducement to send the boys to school and fit them for service in the Church was not so strong as formerly. Cog-

---
11) Smith, *Luther's Correspondence*, vol. II, p. 176.

nizant of this situation, Luther shows the need as well as opportunities for educated men and women both for the Church and the State, and appeals to the city governments to take the necessary steps to establish schools, to secure properly educated citizens in general, and specially trained leaders in Church and State.

CONTENTS.—Luther's introduction begins with the Apostolic salutation and is couched in the most polite and humble language. It breathes forth the spirit of the true patriot who seeks not his own, but his country's welfare. "Having three years ago," he says, "been put under the ban and outlawed, I should have kept silent had I regarded the command of men more than that of God. Many persons in Germany both of high and low estate assail my discoveries and writings on that account, and shed much blood over them. But God who has opened my mouth and bidden me speak, stands firmly by me, and without any counsel or effort of mine strengthens and extends my cause the more, the more they rage, and seems, as the second Psalm says, to 'have them in derision.' By this alone any one not blinded by prejudice may see that the work is of God; for it exhibits the divine method, according to which God's cause spreads most rapidly when men exert themselves most to oppose and suppress it." [12]

After briefly describing the conditions prevailing in Germany at the time as a fitting background for his appeal he pleads: "Therefore I beg you all, in the name of God and of our neglected youth, not to think of this subject lightly, as many do who see not what the prince of this world intends. For the right instruction of youth is a matter in which Christ and all the world are concerned. Thereby are we all aided. And

---
12) Painter, *Luther on Education*, p. 169.

consider that great Christian zeal is needed to overcome the silent, secret, and artful machinations of the devil. If we must annually expend large sums on muskets, roads, bridges, dams, and the like, in order that the city may have temporal peace and comfort, why should we not apply as much to our poor, neglected youth, in order that we may have a skillful schoolmaster or two?"[13] This appeal he supports by reciting the reasons why the city councils should establish public schools to provide for the education of the young: (1) because the people have been relieved of the "exactions and robbery" of the Church in the form of indulgences, masses, vigils, and endowments and should show their gratitude to God for this favor by supporting free public schools for their children; (2) because "Almighty God has truly granted us Germans a gracious visitation and favored us with a golden opportunity. We now have excellent and learned young men, adorned with every science and art, who, after they are employed, could be of great service as teachers;"[14] (3) because it is a divine command that children should be given a good Christian education.

But the city officials might object: "All that you say is addressed to parents; what does it concern the members of the city council."[15] The reason why it applies to the city councilmen, Luther replies, is that parents generally neglect this duty, wherefore it desolves upon the city councils as the guardians of the people's spiritual and temporal welfare to make the necessary provisions. Parents neglect this duty either because they lack piety and uprightness and could not train the children properly even if they would; or be-

---
13) Ibid., pp. 173-74.
14) Ibid., pp. 174-75.
15) Ibid., p. 179.

cause the majority of parents are not qualified to do it themselves even if they would; or, even if they are both willing and qualified, they are so occupied with their daily work as to find insufficient time to properly educate their children. Therefore necessity demands that there be either public schools or that each family keep a private tutor, something most families could not afford. Hence he concludes: "Therefore it will be the duty of the mayors and council to exercise the greatest care over the young. For since the happiness, honor, and life of the city are committed to their hands, they would be held recreant before God and the world, if they did not, day and night, with all their power, seek its welfare and improvement. Now the welfare of a city does not consist alone in great treasures, firm walls, beautiful houses, and munitions of war; indeed, where all these are found, and reckless fools come into power, the city sustains the greater injury. But the highest welfare, safety, and power of a city consists in able, learned, wise, upright, cultivated citizens, who can secure, preserve, and utilize every treasure and advantage."[16] The sense of this duty, he then seeks to bring home by pointing out that society in general stands in great need of an intelligent and well educated body of citizens, both for the maintenance of the best and most efficient government and the promotion of the general welfare, happiness, and prosperity of the people. "Since then," he continues, "a city must have well trained people, and since the greatest need, lack, and lament is that such are not to be found, we must not wait till they grow up of themselves; neither can they be hewed out of stones nor cut out of wood; nor will God work miracles, so long as men can attain their object through

---

16) Ibid., pp. 180-81.

means within their reach. Therefore we must see to it, and spare no trouble and expense to educate and form them ourselves." [17]

Because of the fanatical opposition on the part of the radical reformers against the acquisition and the use of other languages than the German, he makes out a strong case for the teaching and learning of languages, showing their great importance both in understanding and interpreting Scripture and in carrying on civil government and secular affairs. After stating the objection raised against the acquiring of languages and laying the foundation for his argument, he makes a lengthy plea in behalf of the study of languages and other liberal arts, in the course of which he says: "But, you say again, if we shall and must have schools, what is the use to teach Latin, Greek, Hebrew, and the other liberal arts? Is it not enough to teach the Scriptures, which are necessary to salvation, in the mother tongue? To which I answer: I know, alas! that we Germans must always remain irrational brutes, as we are deservedly called by surrounding nations. But I wonder why we do not also say: Of what use to us are silk, wine, spices, and other foreign articles, since we ourselves have an abundance of wine, corn, wool, flax, wood, and stone in the German states, not only for our necessities, but also for embellishment and ornament? The languages and other liberal arts, which are not only harmless, but even a greater ornament, benefit, and honor than these things, both for understanding the Holy Scriptures and carrying on the civil government, we are disposed to despise; and the foreign articles which are neither necessary nor useful, and which besides greatly impoverish us, we are unwilling

---

17) Ibid., pp. 181-82.

to dispense with. Are we not rightly called German dunces and brutes?"[18]

Having in the foregoing especially stressed the importance of learning for the spiritual interests of man, he now returns to the consideration of the value of learning for the civil and secular affairs, saying: "So much for the utility and necessity of the languages, and of Christian schools for our spiritual interests and the salvation of the soul. Let us now consider the body and inquire: though there were no soul, nor heaven, nor hell, but only the civil government, would not this require good schools and learned men more than do our spiritual interests? Hitherto the Papists have taken no interest in civil government, and have conducted the schools so entirely in the interests of the priesthood, that it has become a matter of reproach for a learned man to marry, and he has been forced to hear remarks like this: 'Behold, he has become a man of the world, and cares nothing for the clerical state,' just as if the priestly order were alone acceptable to God, and the secular classes, as they are called, belonged to Satan, and were unchristian."[19] In this section he pleads for the establishment of public schools on the ground that "even if there were no soul and men did not need schools and languages for the sake of Christianity and the Scriptures, still, for the establishment of the best schools everywhere, both for boys and girls, this consideration is of itself sufficient, namely, that society, for the maintenance of civil order and the proper regulation of the household, needs accomplished and well-trained men and women."[20] The type of education for boys and girls generally, which he advocates, is

18) Ibid., p. 183.
19) Ibid., pp. 194-95.
20) Ibid., p. 196.

a broad and practical Christian education which will fit them for the various common stations in life. The brighter and more promising pupils he would have receive special training in order that the State and Church may benefit from their superior abilities and training. This part of his argument he closes with the following earnest plea: "Therefore, dear Sirs, take to heart this work, which God so urgently requires at your hands, which pertains to your office, which is necessary for the young, and which neither the world nor the Spirit can do without. We have, alas! lived and degenerated long enough in darkness; we have remained German brutes too long. Let us use our reason, that God may observe in us gratitude for His mercies, and that other lands may see that we are human beings, capable both of learning and teaching, in order that through us, also, the world may be made better. I have done my part; I have desired to benefit the German states, although some have despised me and set my counsel at naught as knowing better themselves,—to all which I must submit. I know indeed that others could have accomplished it better; but because they were silent, I have done the best I could. It is better to have spoken, even though imperfectly, than to have remained silent." [21]

Finally he makes a plea for the establishment of public libraries and indicates the general character of books to be collected, for such libraries, covering language, literature, history, law, medicine, arts, science, and theology.

His conclusion is a real rhetorical gem. It breathes forth the earnestness and sincerity of purpose and the unselfish motive which prompted him to write and publish this tract and pleads with his readers to give due consideration to the matters presented, not for

---

21) Ibid., p. 202.

his sake, but for the sake of Germany and her best interests.

THE EFFECT.—The effect of this stirring plea of Luther is well indicated by the following words of Dr. O. Albrecht, who has edited this tract for the Weimar edition of Luther's works and written the critical introduction to it: "Luther's rousing call was not in vain. Already in the year 1524 certain significant evangelical school reforms took place which must be regarded as the fruit of the efforts of the reformers and, especially, of Luther's tract addressed to the councilmen, such as in Magdeburg, Nordhausen, Halberstadt, and Gotha. In 1525 Eisleben followed and Nuremberg in 1526. During the following decade there was manifest a growing zeal for founding and remodeling city Latin schools throughout the entire Germany and, indeed, it prevailed until well into the middle of the sixteenth century in the Protestant territories." [22]

III. *Sermon on Sending Children to School.*[23]

Although Luther called this writing a sermon, it is in reality not a sermon at all but a treatise on schools and schooling and parental and governmental responsibility with respect to the education of children and young people. The title in full is *A Sermon on Keeping Children in School*, or more literally, *A Sermon That Children Be Kept in School* (*Eine Predigt dass man Kinder zur Schulen halten sollen*).

OCCASION.—Luther was very much concerned about the general neglect of parental duty towards the children, particularly with respect to their Christian nurture and education. This parental neglect he had

---
22) *Werke*, Weimar ed., vol. XV, p. 15.
23) *Werke*, Weimar ed., vol. XXX. 2, pp. 508-88; English trans., Painter, *Luther on Education*, pp. 210-71.

PEDAGOGICAL WORKS

already frequently mentioned in his sermons and catechetical writings as well as in some of his exegetical works. He expresses himself at some length on this subject in his characteristically plain and forceful manner in the introduction he wrote to the book of Justus Menius on *The Christian Home*.[24] In concluding this introduction, he gives notice that he has in mind a special treatise on this subject which he hopes to publish in due time, and in which he will deal more fully with this important matter. This was in 1529, a year before the promised treatise appeared. In the meantime it was taking shape, many of the thoughts presented having appeared in his sermons at Wittenberg from time to time. Yet it was not until his sojourn at the Castle of Coburg, during the time the Diet of Augsburg was in session, that he actually composed this educational document. He had evidently at first planned only a brief discourse on the subject, but as he worked on it, it grew into the proportions of a little book. In his letter of inscription to Lazarus Spengler, he says: "It has so grown on my hands as to become, in fact, a book, though I have been obliged to restrain myself lest it become too large. So rich and fruitful is the subject." [25]

He mentions this writing to Melanchthon in a letter dated July 5, 1530.[26] Shortly afterwards the manuscript must have left his hands for the printer, for on August 15 he appends a postscript to a letter written to his wife, in which he expresses both surprise and impatience at the delay in printing his book. He sent the copy, he declares, in order to get it published, not to have it stored away. If he wanted it to lie idle he might as well have kept it himself. He directs his wife

---

24) See p. 207.
25) Painter, op. cit., p. 210.
26) *Werke*, Weimar ed., vol. XXX. 2, p. 509; St. Louis ed., vol. XVI, p. 914.

to take the manuscript from the printer Schirlenz and hand it to another printer that its publication may be expedited.[27] However, he was soon put at ease, for a number of printed copies arrived by special messenger, and he at once proceeded to send them out to his associates. In sending a copy to Melanchthon he writes under date of August 24, "I enclose the treatise on the schools—a real Lutheran document, whose prolixity even its author cannot deny. It is my nature."[28]

PURPOSE.—The purpose of this treatise is clearly stated by Luther himself in his inscription to Spengler when he says: "I have prepared a sermon to preachers, who are scattered here and there, on the duty of admonishing their people to send children to school. . . . Although I can well believe that your preachers are active enough and that they, as highly favored of God, recognize and further this interest so that—thanks be to God—they do not need my admonition and instruction; yet it does no harm that many agree in this matter and thus present a stronger front to the devil."[29] In his introductory address to the pastors, the purpose is also made very clear. He aims to appeal to the pastors to do their full duty with respect to Christian education and impress upon their parishioners the vital significance of a broad and Christian education. His treatise is, therefore, very much in the nature of a pastoral or episcopal letter to the clergy.

CONTENTS.—The "Sermon" contains three introductions, two main divisions and a brief conclusion.

The first introduction is addressed to Lazarus Spengler, councilor of Nuremberg, to whom the tract

---
27) Currie, *Letters of Martin Luther*, p. 241: St. Louis ed., vol. XXI. a, pp. 1541-42.
28) Currie, op. cit., p. 242.
29) Painter, op. cit., pp. 210-11.

was dedicated. The reason for inscribing the tract to Spengler, Luther gives in the following words: "I have sent it forth under your name with no other purpose than that it might thereby attract more attention and be read, if it is worthy, among your citizens."[30] He commends Nuremberg and its councilmen for the excellent school which has been established there, an institution, Luther says, which is "an ornament to your city and is widely celebrated like the wise council who, in its establishment, showed a Christian regard for their subjects, and provided not only for their eternal weal but also further temporal needs and honor."[31] But other parts of Germany are not so fortunate, for there is a sad and wide-spread neglect of the children, and many parents are content when their children have only a little knowledge of arithmetic and the reading of German. But this is not sufficient, Luther contends. "For a congregation, and especially a large city, must have not only merchants, but also people who know more than arithmetic and reading in German books. German books are made especially for the common man to read at home. But for preaching, governing, and directing, both in the spiritual and the secular sphere, all the sciences and languages of the world are insufficient, let alone the German, particularly at this time when we have to speak with more people than neighbor Jack. But these devotees of Mammon do not think of government, nor consider that without preaching and ruling they would not be able to serve their idol for an hour."[32] The inscription to Spengler closes with a commendation of him and the work which he has al-

---
30) Ibid., p. 210.
31) Ibid., pp. 211-12.
32) Ibid., p. 213.

ready done and pleads with him "to help forward the cause."

The second introduction is addressed to the pastors in general. In this address he calls attention to parental negligence, the increasing temptations to the service of Mammon, and the duty and opportunity of pastors with respect to Christian education. "Since now as pastors we are to watch against these and other wicked devices, we must not sleep, but advise, urge, and admonish, with all might, industry, and care, that the common people may not allow themselves to be deceived and led astray by the devil. Therefore let every one take heed to himself and to his office that he may not sleep and thus let the devil become god and lord; for if we are silent and sleep, so that the youth are neglected and our descendants become Tartars or wild beasts, we will have to bear the responsibility and render a heavy account. . . . Much depends truly upon us, since we see that some who are even called ministers, go about the matter as if they wished to let all schools, discipline, and doctrine perish, or even to help to destroy them, since they cannot, as hitherto, lead the wanton life to which Satan impels them."[33]

The third introduction belongs to the "Sermon" proper and sets forth the reason for the tract and the manner in which the subject will be discussed. He complains "that the common people are placing themselves in opposition to the schools, and that they wish to bring up their children without other instruction than that pertaining to their bodily wants," and expresses the hope that there may be some who will heed his plea for the proper education of the children and young people "after contemplating the advantages

---
33) Ibid., pp. 217-18.

and disadvantages of education."[34] The subject is to be discussed under two heads, first, its spiritual or eternal aspects, and secondly in its temporal and secular relations.

In the first part, he discusses very fully and in a convincing and appealing manner the nature and functions of the pastoral and teaching offices and their necessity for the spiritual well-being of the people. He also shows that the fears held by the people generally that, since the passing of the Catholic priesthood and monastic life, with the assured provision for the support of both priests and monks, there was little demand for pastoral service and no certain assurance that if their sons should engage in the ministerial work they would be adequately provided for, were entirely unfounded. "Consider," he says, "for yourselves how many pastorates, schools, and other offices are daily becoming vacant. That fact assures your son of a support before he needs it or has earned it.—I should like to know where in three years we are to get pastors, teachers, and sextons? If we remain idle, and if the princes in particular do not see to it that both preparatory schools and universities are properly maintained, there will be such want of educated persons, that three or four cities will have to be assigned to one pastor, and ten villages to one chaplain, if perchance the ministers can be found at all."[35]

The second part is a masterly plea for a broad and general Christian education considered purely from the secular and temporal point of view. While Luther places the ministerial office highest and regards it as the most necessary, he places the office of government a very close second, for it is "a beautiful

---
34) Ibid., p. 218.
35) Painter, op. cit., pp. 238-9.

and divine ordinance, an excellent gift of God, who ordained it, and who wishes to have it maintained as indispensable to human welfare; without it men could not live together in society, but would devour one another like the irrational animals.—It protects every one in body, so that he may not be injured; it protects every one in family, so that the members may not be wronged; it protects every one in house, lands, cattle, property, so that they may not be attacked, injured, or stolen." [36] He contends that for the maintenance of good government education is necessary, for "in civil government it is the jurists and scholars who uphold this law, and thereby maintain secular authority; and just as a pious theologian or sincere preacher in the kingdom of Christ is called a messenger of God, a savior, a prophet, priest, steward, and teacher, in like manner a pious jurist or a faithful scholar in the government of the emperor might be called a prophet, priest, messenger, and savior." [37] Under the term "jurist" he means not only the lawyers in general, but "the whole body of civil officers—chancellors, secretaries, judges, advocates, notaries, and whatever else belongs to the civil administration." [38] For such positions the sons of all may qualify by becoming properly educated. "Such great works your son can do, and such a useful person can he become, if you direct him to the civil service and send him to school," he says. "And if you can become a sharer in this honor, and make such good use of your money, ought it not be a great pleasure and glory to you?" [39] Furthermore, he speaks of the men that are needed in the medical and other professions and the personal satisfaction which a good edu-

---
36) Ibid., p. 243.
37) Ibid., pp. 245-6.
38) Ibid., p. 246.
39) Ibid., p. 247.

cation gives to its possessor, aside from the wider and more efficient service it enables him to render. Finally, he maintains that the government has the right to compel the people to send their children to school just as well as it has the right to compel the citizens to serve in the army and perform such other duties as are required of citizens.[40]

EFFECT.—It is impossible to trace and measure the effect of this appeal. Some effects were immediate, others remote, but the most outstanding effects were the lifting of the vision of the people generally, the deepening and enlarging of the consciousness of responsibility and opportunity on the part of pastors, parents, and governmental officials, and the crystallizing of the suggestions offered into the very groundwork of German popular education with its world-wide ramifications. Says Schmidt: "Luther aroused with his voice of admonition the feelings and disposition of the family, leading to the introduction of Christian child nurture. He inspired magistrates and princes to establish schools, permeated by the spirit of the Reformation, and even made it their duty to introduce compulsory education." [41]

---

40) Ibid., pp. 263-4.
41) *Geschichte der Pädagogik*, vol. I, p. 46.

CHAPTER IX

PEDAGOGICAL WORKS

The Two Catechisms

Among the strictly pedagogical works of Luther, his two Catechisms naturally hold first place. This is especially true of his *Small Catechism*, which has been the basic text-book of elementary religious instruction in the Lutheran Church for four centuries. "Next to the Bible, Luther's *Small Catechism* has proved itself the greatest religious text-book ever written," says Dr. A. R. Wentz.[1] "In issuing the *Small Catechism*, Luther gave the Church a book of singular, superlative importance. Its great significance is found (1) in the fact that it is the crowning consummation of the evangelical endeavors put forth by the Church during the course of fifteen centuries; (2) in the deeply evangelical interpretation of its constituent parts, which issues from the article on justification; (3) in its great pedagogic excellence: its consummate linguistic form, the absence of all polemics, the refraining from combining the Five Chief Parts into a systematic whole and the restriction to the essentials of Christian faith and life."[2]

So popular has this little pedagogical volume of Luther become that it is often referred to as the "Layman's Bible," a title not at all inappropriate, for it contains in systematic, simple, and teachable form the very gist of the Bible. In his charming little

---
1) *Lutheran World Almanac* for 1928, p. 64.
2) Dr. Reu, *Lutheran World Almanac* for 1928, p. 58.

book on the Catechism, the author's colleague, Dr. Tanner, well says: "It is the Catechism that has enabled the Lutheran Church to impart concentrated, definite knowledge in a form that could be repeated without a change. In the simple words of the Catechism we have in a permanent form a brief summary of all the essential teachings of the Bible." [3]

The literature on the history, character, pedagogical value, exposition, and use of the Catechisms of Luther, especially the *Small Catechism*, is simply enormous, showing the great value and significance attached to these pedagogical classics and the deep and extensive interest taken in them by scholars of the foremost rank.[4]

CATECHISMS BEFORE LUTHER.—Catechetical instruction was, of course, given in the Church from the earliest time, but no textbooks on the catechetical material existed until well into the Middle Ages. There were expositions of the Lord's Prayer, the Creed, and the Ave Maria in lecture form, and these were generally used in connection with penance and confirmation. From the eleventh century on, books begin to appear to which the term catechism may rightly be applied, as, for instance, the books of instruction prepared by Notker, a monk at St. Gall, Bruno, bishop of Würzburg, and Gerson. These, however, were not written in the question and answer form. The question and answer form of the catechism was first introduced by the Waldensians. Catechisms were also prepared by the Bohemian Brethren and the English forerunner of the Reformation, Wiclif. There were

---
3) *Ten Studies in the Catechism*, p. 20.
4) See *Werke*, Weimar ed., vol. XXX. 1, texts and critical introductions: Cohrs, *Die evangelischen Katechismus-Versuche vor Luthers Enchiridion*, 5 vols.; *Katechismen Luthers und Katechismen und Katechismusunterricht* in Realencyk. f. p. Theologie u. Kirche; Reu: *Quellen zur Geschichte des kirchlichen Unterrichts im evangelischen Deutschland*, 6 vols. on Catechism and one on Bible History; Cohrs, *Catechisms*, New Schaff-Herzog Enc. of Rel. Knowledge, vol. II, pp. 442-49.

also catechisms prepared by some of Luther's own contemporaries, as Bugenhagen, Melanchthon, Brentz, Althammer, Lachmann, Agricola, and others. That Luther was not dependent upon any of these catechisms, although he undoubtedly knew many of them, is evidenced by his own independent treatment and arrangement of its subject matter.

THE SOURCES OF LUTHER'S CATECHISMS.—The ultimate source of Luther's Catechisms is the Bible; the immediate his own works, extending from his preaching on the Commandments in 1516, through his brief exposition of the Commandments, the Creed, and the Lord's Prayer in 1520, his Catechism Sermons from time to time till 1528, and finally three series of such sermons which he preached during the year 1528. Between these two sources we may point to the essentials of Christian instruction employed by the Church from the earliest times to Luther's own, either in the form of oral instruction, tables, brief expositions of the Ten Commandments, the Creed, and the Lord's Prayer for the use of the clergy and the teachers, and the instruction books in question and answer form in use by the Bohemian Brethren and the Waldensians. That Luther acknowledged his indebtedness to the past is evident from a number of his testimonies, as his reference to the three parts of the catechism instruction in *Deutsche Messe* and in the introduction to the *Large Catechism*, where he specifically says that these three parts have been in the Church from of old, although often sadly neglected.[5] Speaking of the claim advanced by some Lutheran writers that Luther was not indebted to the past for the subject matter and arrangement of his Catechisms, Grisar says: "The directness and con-

---

5) *Werke*, Weimar ed., vol. XXX. 1, p. 130; *Book of Concord*, Pop. ed., p. 387.

ciseness of his style must, however, always commend themselves to the reader, even to those who regret that in his work he tampered with the doctrine of the olden Church. But as regards the divisions, the work rests on a foundation hallowed by centuries of ecclesiastical usage." [6] To prove that this fact was even admitted by Luther himself, Grisar quotes from Luther's letter to the people of Frankfurt in 1533, in which he says: "This we have received even from the first beginnings of Christianity. For there we see that the Creed, the Our Father, and the Ten Commandments were summarized as a short form of doctrine for the young and the simple, and were, even from the first, termed Catechism."[7]

PREPARATION AND PUBLICATION OF CATECHISMS.—It thus appears that the preparation of these Catechisms was not undertaken suddenly and in haste. They were the outgrowth of many years of labor in study, preaching, and writing. Hardeland traces the Catechisms through Luther's works from 1515 to 1529.[8] The immediate occasion, however, for the preparation and publication of the Catechisms was the visitation of the churches in Saxony, in which Luther for a time himself took part towards the close of the year 1528. On this visitation he observed a sad state of affairs in the various churches visited with respect to the Christian training and education of the children, due to carelessness, indifference, and ignorance on the part of both parents and pastors. In his introduction to the *Small Catechism*, he says: "The deplorable condition in which I found religious affairs during the recent visitation of the congrega-

---

6) Grisar, *Luther*, vol. V, p. 493; *Werke*, Weimar ed., vol. XXX. 3, p. 567.
7) Ibid., p. 494.
8) *Luthers Katechismusgedanken in ihrer Entwickelung bis zum Jahre* 1529.

tions impelled me to publish this Catechism, or statement of Christian doctrine, after having prepared it in very brief and simple form."[9] Immediately upon his return from his visitation he seems to have taken hold of the task of writing the Catechisms in real earnest, and they were soon ready for publication. The *Small Catechism* appeared in wall-chart form as early as Jan. 20, 1529, and a second edition in the same form appeared in March the same year. The *Large Catechism* was off the press by April 23, and the *Small Catechism* followed in book form on the 16th of the following month.[10] The original title of the *Large Catechism* was *Deutsch Catechismus* with a subtitle, *Der Grosze Katechismus*, in parenthesis. The title of the *Small Catechism* was *Der Kleine Catechismus für die gemeine Pfarherr und Prediger*. The original High German copy of this book has been lost, but Marburg and Erfurt reprints are extant. The standard text of the *Small Catechism* is the Wittenberg edition of 1531, the last revision which was made by Luther himself.[11]

THE CONTENTS AND FORM OF THE CATECHISMS.— Both the Catechisms are divided into five parts and follow the same order of arrangement. 1. The Ten Commandments. 2. The Creed. 3. The Lord's Prayer. 4. The Sacrament of Baptism. 5. The Sacrament of the Altar, or the Lord's Supper. In the introduction to the *Large Catechism*, Luther presents in the very briefest form all five parts of what he calls "the entire Christian doctrine, which should be constantly prac-

---

9) *Werke*, op. cit., vol. XXX. 1, p. 346; *Book of Concord*, p. 359.
10) Cohrs, *Encyklopädie f. prot. Theol. u. Kirche*, X, pp. 130-35; Reu, *Kirchliche Zeitschrift*, Aug., 1926, p. 632.
11) Reu, *A New English Translation of Luther's Small Catechism*, *Kirchliche Zeitschrift*, Aug., 1926, p. 632; *Werke*, op. cit., pp. 846 and 669, seq. Since the above was written the excellent articles on Luther's Small Catechism by Dr. Reu in *Kirchliche Zeitschrift* for Nov. and Dec., 1927, and in *Lutheran World Almanac* for 1928 have appeared, to which the reader is referred.

tised and required and heard recited word for word.[12] Then in the body of the work, he gives very full and simple expositions in a conversational lecture-style of each of the Commandments, each article of the Creed, the seven petitions of the Lord's Prayer, together with introduction and conclusion, and the two sacraments, Baptism and the Lord's Supper. The erotematic form is not used at all in the *Large Catechism*. In the *Small Catechism*, the question and answer form of instruction is followed throughout. In response to a very simple and direct question an equally simple and direct answer is given. There is only a single question on each of the Commandments and on each article of the Creed, one or two on each petition of the Lord's Prayer, seven on Baptism, and five on the Lord's Supper, and the whole presentation is characterized by brevity, simplicity, conciseness, and comprehensiveness. Between Parts Four and Five is a brief instruction in a formula for confession, setting forth the Lutheran conception of confession and its relation to partaking of the Lord's Supper. After Part Five follow three additions or appendixes, one on morning and evening prayers, one on table prayers, and a Table of Duties, setting forth the Christian duties of men, women, and children in the various social stations of life.

PURPOSE AND PEDAGOGICAL VALUE OF CATECHISMS. —Both of Luther's Catechisms were intended for the use of pastors, teachers, and parents to assist them in the religious instruction of the children, not as text-books to be placed in the hands of the pupils. While we now generally apply the term "catechism" to a book of religious instruction employing the erotematic method, that was not the conception of the term in Luther's day, nor was that his own conception, for

---
12) *Book of Concord*, p. 390; *Werke*, op. cit., p. 132.

he used it in the generally accepted sense in the Church from the earliest times as the essential subject matter of elementary Christian instruction and to some extent the manner of imparting it. The application of the term to a particular book is of post-reformation origin. Hence, when Luther speaks of himself daily reciting the Catechism, he does not have reference to the Catechism as a book composed by himself, but the subject-matter of that book, the rudimentary and fundamental points of Christian doctrine. So also when he insists on the learning of the Catechism, it is not the book, but again the essential points of Christian truth.[13]

Luther's idea of catechetical instruction was not what has passed for catechetical instruction in some quarters since his day, and is something far different from what modern educational writers in ignorance caricature and pass off as catechetical instruction and as a fit object of "scholarly" jibes and ridicule. The term is derived from the Greek κατηχεω, which means to sound towards, to sound down upon, from ἤχος, sound, from which comes our word echo, ἠχέω to sound, and κατα, down or toward. The meaning of the word is well defined by Gerberding in the following words: "Classically it was used of the sounding down of the rushing water, of the sound of music falling from the ship on the sea. Then it came to signify the sounding down of a word or words of command or instruction from a superior to an inferior, from a teacher to a pupil. The preposition κατα strengthens the meaning, bringing out more emphatically the back or return sound, the echo, the answer. Thus it came to mean instruction by word of mouth, familiar,

---

13) *Werke*, op. cit., p. 448: Cohrs, *Katechismus und Katechismusunterricht, Encyk. f. prot. Theol. u. Kirche*, vol. X, pp. 135-64; also art. on *Katechese* in same volume; Richard and Painter, *Christian Worship*, pp. 184-5; *Lutheran World Almanac*, p. 62.

conversational instruction, a free, informal discussion between teacher and pupil."[14] The term is used a number of times in the New Testament, but very seldom by classical writers. It is used in the sense of oral information or instruction, particularly with reference to oral instruction in the elements of the Christian doctrine.[15] It is in this sense that Luther uses the term. In his *Deutsche Messe* he advocates the introduction of "a good, short Catechism on the Creed, Ten Commandments, and the Lord's Prayer" into the divine service, following the administration of Baptism or the Lord's Supper, by which he means to say, the giving of a brief, elementary instruction orally in the fundamentals of Christian truth as a part of the order of service.[16] In the same work, he also states that this catechetical instruction, whether at church or at home, is not only to be conducted in such a manner "that they learn to repeat the words by heart, as has happened hitherto, but question them from article to article, and let them answer what each means and how they understand it."[17] Then he proceeds to show how this catechisation may be carried on by giving some examples of questions and answers, and suggests that the children may be interested by being led to think they have two purses, one, a golden, called a faith purse, in which is to be placed all that is taught concerning faith, and another, a silver one, called the love purse, in which all that is taught concerning the love and service to fellow-man and personal suffering and endurance for the sake of Christ and His cause is to be placed. "And let no man think himself too wise," he says, "and despise such child's

---

14) *The Lutheran Catechist*, p. 21.
15) *Luke* 1:4; *Acts* 18:25; 21-24, 24; *Rom.* 2:18; 1 *Cor.* 14:19; *Gal.* 6:6; Sachsse, *Die Lehre von der kirchlichen Erziehung*, p. 301, seq.; Reu, *Catechetics*, p. 3, seq.
16) *Christian Worship*, op. cit., p. 184.
17) *Christian Worship*, op. cit., p. 185.

play. Christ, when He wished to draw men, was obliged to become man. If we are to draw children, then we must become children with them." [18]

This same idea of catechism and catechisation found expression in the numerous amplifications of the *Small Catechism*, which were produced in all parts of Germany during the sixteenth century, following the publication of Luther's Catechisms. Some of these followed the informal lecture plan of the *Large Catechism*, resulting in a number of works on *Katechismuspredigten* (catechetical sermons) or *Kinderpredigten* (children's sermons) as the Nuremberg Catechism of 1533 by Ossiander and Sleupner,[19] or the question and answer form, as in Bucer's Catechism of 1534.[20] From the large collection of catechisms of the sixteenth century assembled by Reu in his monumental work to which reference has already been made, it is apparent that the question and answer or erotematic form was the most popular. It is also the form which has most generally persisted to the present day. These so-called catechisms were all based upon Luther's work, and were in reality only amplifications or explanations of it.

ARRANGEMENT OF SUBJECT MATTER.—The order of arrangement in Luther's Catechisms has often been attacked on pedagogical grounds, it being contended that in the elementary instruction of the child one should rather begin with Baptism or the Creed, than with the Mosaic Law. The principal objection is that the little child should not be compelled to begin his Christian training with the legalistic conceptions of the Old Testament, but rather with the evangelical conceptions of the New. Luther nowhere intimates

---
18) Ibid., pp. 185-188.
19) Reu, *Quellen*, vol. I, pp. 462-564.
20) Ibid., pp. 23-66.

that his Catechisms set forth a specific and rigid theological and pedagogical system as far as the order of arrangement is concerned. He followed the traditional order of Commandments, Creed, Prayer, as he had done in his work of 1520, in which he especially had confession in mind, for which purpose this was the natural and logical order, the Law leading to conviction of sin, the Gospel convincing of grace, which in turn leads to the approach to God in prayer. But as to the order of these parts, though he generally followed the one in common vogue, he also frequently varied it, as he does even in the introduction to his *Small Catechism*, where his order is, Prayer, Creed, Commandments. In his letter to the people at Frankfurt in 1533, he has two variations of the order, the one as given above from the introduction to the *Small Catechism*, and the other, Creed, Prayer, and Commandments. The position generally taken by Lutheran writers on Catechetics is as stated by Gerberding: "They believe it was Luther's idea that each part should be taught by itself, without regard to a supposed relation to the other parts."[21] The strongest opponent of this view is Zezschwitz,[22] but he has been ably answered by Achelis,[23] Reu,[24] Gerberding,[25] and others.[26]

With respect to the order to be followed, the practice has varied among Lutheran catechists. Even as early as 1534 Bucer's explanation of Luther's *Small Catechism* appeared with a different order from the one given by Luther. The order followed here is, Creed, Baptism, Supper, Commandments, and Prayer.[27]

---

21) *Lutheran Catechist*, p. 99.
22) *System der christlichen Katechetik*, vol. I, p. 2, 34.
23) *Praktische Theologie*, vol. II, p. 63 seq.
24) *Catechetics*, pp. 105-126; 342 seq.
25) *Lutheran Catechist*, p. 95 seq.
26) *Werke*, Weimar ed., vol. XXX. 1, p. 416 seq.
27) Reu, *Quellen*, vol. I, pp. 23-66.

The order recommended in one of the best of the latest German catechetics is Creed, Commandments, Prayer, Baptism, Supper.[28] Another order of treatment which has much in its favor pedagogically is, Baptism, Creed, Prayer, Commandments, Supper.[29] But even if the order be followed as given by Luther, no psychological or pedagogical laws need to be violated, because of the thoroughly evangelical treatment of the Christian life which Luther gives in his explanations of the Ten Commandments.[30]

PEDAGOGICAL VALUE OF SMALL CATECHISM.—The intrinsic value of the *Small Catechism*, which has become the great text-book of Christian instruction in the Lutheran Church, considered from the standpoint of language, comprehensiveness, simplicity, adaptability, psychology, pedagogy, and Christian experience, has always been placed very high by Christian educators and scholars from Luther's time to our own, whether within or without the Lutheran Church. Mathesius, after speaking of the *Small Catechism* and the service it had rendered the cause of Christian elementary education in his day, declares that even if Luther had not accomplished more than to give to the world his two Catechisms, the world could never fully thank him for it.[31] It is, of course, only to be expected that Lutheran scholars would have a very high conception of the value of this book, hence no further citation is adduced from the numerous ones that might be cited from the works of Lutheran writers,[32] but we shall let Philip Schaff and McGiffert speak for the Reformed and Grisar for the Roman

---

28) Sachsse, *Die Lehre v. d. k. Erziehung*, pp. 337-364.
29) Lokensgaard, *Outlines of the Catechism; Kateketik*.
30) Gerberding, *The Lutheran Catechist*, p. 100 seq.; *Way of Salvation in the Lutheran Church*, pp. 79-80; F. B., *Der Religionsunterricht in der modernen Pädagogik*, Lehre und Wehre, July-Aug., 1899.
31) *Historien*, pp. 88-94.
32) Gerberding, *Lutheran Catechist*, p. 89 seq.

Catholic Church. Says Dr. Schaff: "Luther's *Small Catechism* is truly a great little book, with as many thoughts as words, and every word telling and sticking to the heart as well as to the memory. It bears the stamp of the religious genius of Luther, who was both its father and its pupil. It exhibits his almost apostolic gift of expressing the deepest things in the plainest language for the common people. It is strong food for a man, and yet as simple as a child. It marks an epoch in the history of religious instruction: it purged it from popish superstitions, and brought it back to Scriptural purity and simplicity."[33] It is also interesting to note the illuminating and discriminating comparison this well known Presbyterian scholar makes between the three great catechisms of Protestantism: Luther's *Small Catechism*, the *Heidelberg Catechism*, and the *Shorter Westminster Catechism*. They are alike in having a two-fold character, that of books of religious instruction and creedal symbols, he states. "But they are alike evangelical in spirit and aim; they lead directly to Christ as the one and all-sufficient Savior, and to the Word of God as the only infallible rule of the Christian's faith and life." "The *Heidelberg Catechism* stands mediating between" the two. Pedagogically, he considers Luther's and the *Heidelberg Catechism* the best, for "they are subjective, and address the catechumen as a church member, who answers from his real or prospective personal experience; while the *Westminster Catechism* is objective and impersonal, and states the answers in an abstract proposition. They use the warm and direct language of life, the Westminster the scholastic language of dogma; hence the former two are less definite but more expansive and suggestive than the Presbyterian formulary, which on the other

---

33) *Creeds of Christendom*, vol. I, p. 250.

hand far surpasses them in brevity, terseness, and accuracy of definition. — The *Heidelberg Catechism* differs from that of Luther by its fulness and thoroughness, and hence is better adapted to a maturer age; while that of Luther has the advantage of brevity and childlike simplicity, and adaptation to early youth." He also makes some other distinction between these two Catechisms with respect to the order and arrangement of the Decalog, Luther's Catechism following the Augustinian order, combining into one commandment Ex. 20:3-6 and separating verse 17 into two commandments, while the *Heidelberg Catechism* follows the Greek order, separating Ex. 20:3-6 into two commandments and counting verse 17 as one commandment.[34]

McGiffert calls Luther's *Small Catechism* "the little gem of the Reformation." "It contains," says he, "a most beautiful summary of Christian faith and duty, wholly devoid of polemics of every kind, and so simple and concise as to be easily understood and memorized by every child. It has formed the basis of the religious education of German youth ever since. Though preceded by other catechisms from the pen of this or that disciple, it speedily displaced them all, not simply because of its authorship, but because of its superlative merit, and has alone maintained itself in general use. The versatility of the Reformer in adapting himself with such success to the needs of the young and immature is no less than extraordinary. Such a little book as this it is that reveals most clearly the genius of the man." [35]

We have already quoted Grisar on the Catechism, but in addition to the commendation already given on pages 174-5, the following statement should also be

---

34) *Creeds of Christendom*, op. cit., pp. 543-4.
35) *Life of Luther*, p. 316.

cited: "The language, more particularly of the *Shorter Catechism*, is throughout a model of simplicity and clearness." He also commends it very highly for being devoid of all polemics.[36]

Whatever friend or foe of Luther's *Small Catechism* and the catechetical method of instruction may have to say in commendation or criticism, the fact nevertheless remains that both have demonstrated their value and usefulness for a continuous period of four hundred years in producing men and women of the highest and noblest Christian character, whose lives have borne rich fruition in all the various walks of life, lives that have been an honor to both State and Church and rendered most valuable service to both.

TRANSLATION OF THE SMALL CATECHISM.—The *Small Catechism* has been translated into a large number of languages and dialects.[37] Wherever the Lutheran missionaries have gone forth to proclaim the Gospel of Jesus Christ, there the *Small Catechism* has followed, done into the vernacular of the people to whom the missionaries have ministered. It was translated as early as in 1532 into the Danish language, even before the Reformation had been introduced into Denmark.[38] In 1537 another translation appeared, and the following year, Palladius produced no less than three versions of it.[39] As Norway and Denmark were united under one government at the time, the Danish translations were also used in Norway. The first translation into the Swedish language was made in 1548.[40] Catechetical sermons and explanations of the Catechism soon followed. The explanation of Lu-

---

36) *Luther*, op. cit., p. 486.
37) For a very full presentation of the history of the translation of Luther's *Small Catechism*, see the articles of Dr. Reu mentioned in the reference on page 176.
38) Bang, *Den lutherske Katekismus' Historie*, vol. I, pp. 98-132.
39) Ibid., pp. 133-344.
40) Ibid., p. 1 seq.

ther's *Small Catechism* which has exerted the greatest influence among the Danish and Norwegian Lutherans, particularly among the latter, is the one by Erik Ludvigssen Pontoppidan, published in 1737, the year following the introduction of the rite of confirmation into the Dano-Norwegian church.[41] While Luther's *Small Catechism* was not as a book translated into the English language until in 1749, when a translation was made by a German and a Swedish pastor in America, Peter Brunnholtz and Peter Koch, Cranmer had a translation made of the so-called *Nuremberg Catechism*, a book which has already been noted (see page 180) in 1548, under the title "Catechismus; That is to say a shorte Introduction into the Christian Religion for the syngular commoditie and profyte of childre and yong people. Set forth by the moste reverende father in God Thomas Archbyshop of Canterbury, Primate of all England and Metropolitane."[42] The English text which has been used most generally in this country since the middle of last century is the one by Dr. C. F. Schaeffer of 1854, as revised by a committee appointed by the General Synod, but there have also been many other translations, resulting in a lack of uniformity in the text by the various branches of the Lutheran Church in America. At the invitation of the Board of Elementary Christian Education of the Norwegian Lutheran Church in America, of which Board the writer has the honor of being a member, a joint translation committee representing all the various Lutheran bodies in this country, excepting those belonging to the Synodical Conference, was formed in 1926, to prepare a uniform English text to be used by the Lutheran bodies represented.

---

41) Bang, *Den Norske Kirkes Historie*, pp. 417-18.
42) Reu, *Kirchliche Zeitschrift*, Aug., 1926, p. 627; Jacobs, *The Lutheran Movement in England*, pp. 314-324.

This translation has already appeared in a provisional edition. It will be ultimately published as a joint jubilee edition commemorating the 400th anniversary of the publication of Luther's *Small Catechism* in 1929.[43]

It is an interesting historic fact that Luther's *Small Catechism* was the first book to be translated into the native American language, being translated into the language of the Delaware Indians in the year 1648 by Rev. John Campanius, a Swedish pastor in the Swedish settlement in Delaware and early Lutheran missionary among the Indians. It was not, however, published until 1696, eleven years after the publication at Cambridge of Eliot's translation of the Bible into the Indian language, which therefore has the honor of being the first book printed in the Indian language, although the *Small Catechism* had existed in that language in manuscript form since completed by the Swedish pastor. It was published at Stockholm and contains both the Swedish and Indian texts in alternating paragraphs. It is a booklet about 4 x 7 inches and contains 160 pages. The introduction of fourteen pages in the Swedish gives a brief account of the Swedish settlements, the work of Campanius, and an interesting account of the discovery of America by the Norsemen in 996. It also quotes William Penn. In the one quotation, Penn commends the Swedes for their just and considerate treatment of the Indians, and in another he speaks very highly of the Swedes as friends and neighbors. The book also contains a map of New Sweden by P. Lindström, dating from 1655, and two Indian-Swed-

---

43) Reu, *A New English Translation, Kirchliche Zeitschrift*, Aug., 1926, p. 626 seq.; *Luther's Small Catechism*, Uniform Text, Newly Revised and Edited by an Inter-Synodical Committee. A Jubilee Offering for the Four Hundredth Anniversary of the Original Publication of the *Small Catechism*, 1529—1929. Provisional Edition.

ish glossaries, one in the Delaware language and one in the related Massachusetts dialect. The former, which is the principal and most complete, is called *Vocabularium Barbaro-Virginiorum* and the latter referred to as of the "Mahukuasser" language. This little book is one of the most precious monuments of American Lutheranism.

CHAPTER X

PEDAGOGICAL WORKS

Miscellaneous Writings

Luther was a prolific writer. His pen seems to have moved almost incessantly. Busy as he was, burdened heavily with a multiplicity of cares, often suffering from physical ailments, it is a marvel that he was able to produce such a vast and varied literary heritage to transmit to posterity. It fills one with amazement to pore over quarto volume upon quarto volume containing the products of his pen at the voluminousness of his writings and the versatility of his mind. In the preceding chapters we have noticed his more outstandding and specific pedagogical writings. In the present chapter, we shall deal briefly with a number of his writings that while not specifically of a pedagogical nature, nevertheless contain much concerning his pedagogical ideas and show his pedagogical interest and insight. It is obvious that no detailed and exhaustive presentation can be given of these miscellaneous writings.

Exegetical Works.—The very foundation of all Luther's reformatory work was his Bible study. From it he drew his principles, his inspiration, and his guidance. As a young professor of theology he at once centered his labors on the study and exposition of Scripture, beginning with the Psalms and Romans, and gradually extending the scope of his studies to the books of the whole Bible. His exegetical works embrace all the books of both the Old and the New Testament, either in the form of more or less complete and exhaustive expositions of entire books, marginal notes, or introductions to individual books. He gave particular attention to the Pentateuch, especially Genesis, to Judges, Samuel, Job, Psalms, Ecclesiastes, Canticles, Isaiah, Daniel, and the minor prophets of the Old Testament, and Matthew, Luke, John, Acts, Romans, I Corinthians, Galatians, Ephesians, I Timothy, Titus, I and II Peter, Jude, and I John of the New Testament. His most complete commentaries are the ones on Genesis, the Psalms, Isaiah, and Galatians.

The services Luther rendered in the field of Biblical exegesis is inestimable. In this respect he was also a bold pioneer and a keen, far-sighted and influential educator. He laid down principles of exegesis which made possible a better and more intelligent understanding and appreciation of the Bible, and opened to lay and learned the rich spiritual treasures of the Bible as never before. Speaking of Luther's place in the history of Biblical exegesis, the distinguished English scholar and churchman, Canon Farrar, says: "God endows His chosen instruments with such gifts as they especially need. It required a personality far different from that of Erasmus to bring about that emancipation of Christendom from sacerdotal tyranny and false exegesis which was the essence of the Reformation. Revolutions have usually been wrought by men whose sympathies were all the more intense and concentrated from their very narrowness, not by men of delicate refinement and many sided powers of appreciation. The genius of Erasmus and the learning of Melanchthon would have produced but small results without the Titanic force of Luther, the sovereign good sense of Zwingli, the remorseless logic of Calvin;—and of these three the greatest was Martin Luther. . . . And he not only gave them (the Germans) the open Bible, but taught them and all the world how best it might be interpreted. His *Commentary on the Galatians* was his only complete and continuous contribution to the exegesis of the New Testament, yet that single work would have proved to be a blessing to millions had it produced no other effect than to lead (as it did) to the enlightenment of John Bunyan and John Wesley. But Luther's German Bible is more than a translation. It forms also an admirable commentary, and in his Prefaces and in all his other works he enunciated rules to which the complete revolution of exegetic methods in modern times has been principally due."[1]

Luther placed the authority of the Scriptures over against the authority of ecclesiasticism, for to him the authority of Scripture was supreme and final. He rejected the traditional four-fold sense in Biblical exegesis, as well as the principle of allegorical interpretation. He asserted the sufficiency and perspicuity of Scripture, and laid down the principle of the right of private judgment and interpretation on the part of every Christian, a principle which has been most sadly abused, it is true, yet absolutely essential to true Christian liberty and freedom from ecclesiastical tyranny. Says Farrar: "In accordance with these principles Luther, in his preface to Isaiah (1528) and in other parts of his writings, lays down what he conceives to be the true rules of Scripture interpretation. He insists (1) on the necessity for grammatical knowledge; (2) on the importance of taking into consideration times, circumstances, and conditions; (3) on the observance of the context; (4) on

---
1) *History of Interpretation*, pp. 322-24.

the need of faith and spiritual illumination; (5) on keeping what he called 'the proportion of faith'; and (6) on the reference of all Scripture to Christ." [2]

But Luther's exegetical works are not only valuable because of their contribution to exegetical principles and practice and the better understanding and appreciation of the Bible, but also because they contain a vast amount of strictly pedagogical material. Luther never permitted an opportunity to go by to stress the importance of Christian child nurture and the means and methods to be employed in bringing up children when expounding Scripture. Consequently we find scattered throughout his expositions of Scripture, observations on child life, the responsibilities and opportunities of parents, teachers, and pastors and the manner in which children should be dealt with and trained. His *Summarium* of the Proverbs in poetic form is also an excellent example of his pedagogic interest and insight.

SERMONS. — Luther was a great preacher and preached extensively. It is difficult to distinguish between his so-called exegetical works and his sermons, for much of his exegetical work was in reality series upon series of expository lectures-sermons on whole books or parts of books. Furthermore, his sermons were for the most part of the expository type, even when he preached upon specific themes to meet certain demands or counteract certain abuses and false conceptions.

Speaking of him as a teacher, Ker, a Presbyterian scholar, says: "Preaching was the center and spring of his power; by preaching he moved Germany and then Europe till he shook the Papal throne. Melanchthon was a scholar and theologian, Calvin was a theologian and an exegete, Cranmer was a religious states-

---
[2] Ibid., pp. 331-32.

PEDAGOGICAL WORKS

man; Luther was great in all those respects, but still greater as a preacher. In this he and John Knox had much in common; Knox also being statesman and educationist but principally preacher. . . . The preaching of Luther soon excited movement. Wittenberg on the Elbe, the university of Gesenius and Tholuck and Julius Müller, was the chief seat of learning in the north of Germany, and students, as well as townsmen, flocked to hear him. They felt the newness and boldness of his style and even of his doctrine. His sermons did not treat of ceremonies and fasts, but addressed the moral and spiritual nature of his hearers with unmistakable meaning and directness. He was taking aim at the heart, with arrows that reached their mark; and men love this in preachers." [3] Another writer on the history of preaching, Dargan, a Baptist, has the following to say about Luther as a preacher: "As a preacher Luther stands in the first rank of those who by the ministry of God's Word have molded the characters and destinies of men. Among all his other offices and achievements—as scholar, theologian, author, and leader—we must not forget that, first of all and chiefly, he was a preacher. At first he could hardly be persuaded to preach, but when he once got at it nothing could stop him." [4] And again: "The tone and spirit of Luther's preaching were what his character and views would lead us to expect. He believed and therefore he spoke—out of his experience and convictions—out of his sense of duty—out of love to God and men, and without the fear of man before his eyes." [5]

In concluding his presentation of Luther as a preacher, Ker draws the following lessons from Lu-

---
3) *History of Preaching*, pp. 149-51.
4) *History of Preaching*, vol. I, p. 389.
5) Ibid., p. 391.

ther as a preacher for preachers of today: "Luther is above our reach in almost everything. But there are many things which, as preachers, we all can learn from him: to be laying up stores of knowledge on all subjects, especially by the study of human nature; to seek a thorough acquaintance with the Bible, the book of the preacher, the sword that nothing can withstand; to have sympathy with men and a single desire to do them good; to aim at a clear, natural, direct style of speech; and to grasp the grand doctrine of Justification by Faith and hold it up as the standard of the Church of Christ, and the source of comfort and strength and holiness in the Christian life." [6]

Being the kind of preacher that he was, it is not strange that Luther, by his preaching, exerted such a tremendous influence upon the people of his day. His sermons were powerful and moving, direct and appealing. They convinced of sin and convinced of grace, they lifted ideals, created a sense of personal responsibility, and brought home lessons on life, duty, and service which compelled attention and impelled to action. Educationally, they therefore naturally wielded a powerful influence, and since they contain many of Luther's observations on Christian education, and the duties and privileges of parents, teachers, and pastors, they constitute a rich source material for the study of Luther's educational ideas and principles. But even those sermons which do not deal with pedagogics directly are rich in the educational element, for this element was always very prominent in his sermons and he tried to live up to the rule of simplicity which he sought to impress upon his students, so that all might understand what was said. Mathesius tells us that Luther emphasized the importance of using a simple, intelligible language in the

---
6) Op. cit., pp. 164-65.

PEDAGOGICAL WORKS

pulpit that everyone, regardless of age or learning, might understand. "The common man," says Mathesius, quoting his great master in substance, "one should not teach with high, difficult, and veiled words, for he can not grasp them. Into the church come little children, maidens, old women and old men, to whom high learning is of no use, because they understand nothing of it. Even if they should beautifully say, 'Oh, but he said some precious things!' and you should ask them, 'What, for instance?' they would have to reply, 'I don't know.'" Then by the way of illustration Luther referred to Christ becoming flesh, in order that He might teach in all simplicity, using the familiar parables of farming, harvest, vintage, and sheep, and continued: "You have large congregations for which you are accountable unto God; be diligent, therefore, to teach simply, faithfully, and plainly."[7] An excellent principle of pedagogy as well as homiletics.

There are two principal collections of Luther's sermons, one known as the Church-Postil (Kirchenpostille) and the other as the House-Postil (Hauspostille). The former contains sermons preached by Luther in the pulpit on the Gospel and Epistle lessons of the Church year. It appears in two parts, the one containing the sermons on the Gospel lessons and the other those on the Epistle lessons. The *House-Postil* contains sermons which Luther preached in his own home to his family and household on Sundays and holidays when he was unable to preach in the church on account of illness. They were delivered extempore by Luther and taken down by two of his co-laborers, Veit Dietrich and Georg Rörer. Dietrich published his collection with a foreword by Luther himself in 1544. In 1559, after Rörer's death, his collection was published at Jena by Andreas Poach. Thus two

---
7) *Historien*, pp. 196-7.

dissimilar versions of his *House-Postil* arose. Besides these two collections there are a large number of sermons by Luther on various Scripture texts and themes. In the *House-Postil* the sermons on the 12th, 15th, and 16th Sundays in Trinity and the one on St. Michael's Day deal largely with child training. In the *Church-Postil* the sermons on the Fourth Sunday after Trinity and the one on Good Works are especially worthy of mention. Pedagogical observations, however, also appear very frequently in many of his other sermons.

LETTERS.—Luther carried on an enormous correspondence, and a large number of these letters deal with questions pertaining to education. Among these letters the following should especially be mentioned:

1. A letter to Margrave Georg of Brandenburg under date of July 18, 1529. In this letter he calls upon the margrave to establish one or two universities within his domain, for "from these schools learned men should be got as preachers, pastors, secretaries, councilors, etc., for the whole principality." To establish and maintain these universities the old monasteries and foundations may be used, he says. The faculty should consist of at least two professors in theology, two in law, one in medicine, one for mathematics, and one "for logic, rhetoric, etc., four or five men." He also suggests that "it is well that in all towns and villages good primary schools should be established out of which could be picked and chosen those who were fit for the universities, out of which the men can then be taken who are to serve your land and people." "If the towns or their citizens cannot do this," he goes on to say, "then it would be well to establish new stipends for the support of a few bright fellows in the deserted monasteries, so that every town might have one or two students. In the course

of time, when the common people see that their sons become pastors and preachers, and get other offices, many of those who now think that a scholar cannot get a living will again keep their sons in school."[8]

2. A letter to Elector Johann of Saxony under date Nov. 22, 1526. In this letter he calls attention to the fact that the compulsory power of the Church having been removed, the people do as they please about sending their children to school and providing themselves with pastors. He shows that it is the duty of the rulers in particular to see to it that schools are maintained, the children sent to school, and the people provided with suitable pastors to care for their spiritual needs. "But because all of us, and especially the rulers," he says, "are commanded to care for the poor children who are born every day and are growing up, and to keep them in the fear of God and under discipline, we must have schools and pastors and preachers. If the older people do not want them, they may go to the devil; but if the young people are neglected and are not trained, it is the fault of the rulers, and the land will be filled with wild, loose-living people. Thus not only God's command, but our own necessity compels us to find some way out of the difficulty." He realizes that there are a number of difficulties that must be overcome, but the importance of education, considered even from a purely secular standpoint, is so great that the power of the government must, if necessary, be invoked to compel the establishment and maintenance of schools, and the old monastic properties may be turned over to be used for this purpose. "If there is a town or a village which cannot do it," he continues, "your Grace has the power to compel it to support schools, preaching places, and parishes. If they are unwilling to do this or to

---

8) Smith, *Luther's Correspondence*, vol. II, pp. 486-8.

consider it for their own salvation's sake, then your Grace is the supreme guardian of the youth and of all who need his guardianship, and ought to hold them to it by force, so that they must do it. It is just like compelling them by force to contribute and to work for the building of bridges and roads or any other of the country's needs. What the country needs and must have ought to be given and helped along by those who use and enjoy the country. Now there is no more necessary thing than the education of the people who are to come after us and be the rulers. But if they cannot do it and are overburdened with other things, there are the monastic properties which were established chiefly for the purpose of relieving the common man, and ought still to be used for that purpose." [9]

3. A letter to Eoban Hess, who taught Latin at Erfurt and who was later professor at Marburg. Hess appears to have expressed some fears that the new theology would have a bad effect upon the knowledge of letters generally, for Luther says: "Do not be disturbed by the fears which you express, that our theology will make us Germans more barbarous in letters than ever we have been; some people often have their fears when there is nothing to fear. I am persuaded that without the knowledge of literature, pure theology cannot at all endure, just as heretofore, when letters have declined and lain prostrate, theology, too, has wretchedly fallen and lain prostrate; nay, I see that there has never been a great revelation of the Word of God unless He has first prepared the way by the rise and prosperity of languages and letters, as though they were John the Baptist. There is, indeed, nothing that I have less wish to see done against our young people than that they should omit

---

9) Ibid., vol. II, pp. 383-4.

to study poetry and rhetoric. Certainly it is my desire that there shall be as many poets and rhetoricians as possible, because I see that by these studies, as by no other means, people are wonderfully fitted for the grasping of sacred truth and for handling it skilfully and happily." [10]

4. A letter to Elector Johann of Saxony, dated May 20, 1530, in which he speaks of his joy over the progress which has been made in the religious education of the children.[11] Schumann includes another letter, addressed to Elector Johann Friedrich of Saxony, under date of July 9, 1535, as being of pedagogical content, but in this letter Luther merely speaks in a humorous vein of the rumored epidemic which was threatening, intimating that it was only a feigned illness on the part of the pupils to get away from their studies and enjoy a vacation.[12]

Luther wrote a number of other letters which make mention of children and their training and the establishment of schools and universities, as one to Spalatin under date of April 16, 1525, in which he tells that he is setting out for Eisleben with Melanchthon and Agricola to establish a Christian school there, and that other schools are to be established in Nuremberg, Magdeburg, and Danzig;[13] or his letter to Elector Johann Friedrich on May 20th the same year, in which he pleads for the strengthening of the faculty at Wittenberg, as so many of its professors were being called away to other fields of service, thereby weakening the university.[14] But to make mention of all these letters would be impossible in this study. Sufficient reference has been made to Luther's letters

---

10) Ibid., pp. 176-77.
11) De Wette, *Briefe*, vol. IV, p. 20; *Werke*, Erlangen ed., vol. LIV, p. 146.
12) *Pädagogische Schriften*, p. 350; *Werke*, Ibid., vol. LV, p. 95.
13) Smith, op. cit., p. 304.
14) Ibid., p. 317.

to show that they contain valuable source material for the study of Luther's educational theories and activities.[15]

TABLE TALKS.—Luther's so-called *Table Talks* were free and spontaneous discourses which he delivered in the course of conversations and discussions at his table in his home, the Black Cloister, surrounded by his family, students at the University of Wittenberg, who were his regular boarders, not infrequently members of the faculty, and often notable visitors from all over Germany, and even from outside countries. Luther and his wife kept an open and hospitable house, and table guests were very common. Mathesius, Luther's biographer, was one of the students who boarded at Luther's table, and he tells many interesting things from his year at the Black Cloister.[16] He took notes of Luther's discourses in 1540, while he daily sat at Luther's table, and his notes constitute one of the sources of Luther's now famous *Table Talks*. He was not, however, the first student to engage in this practice, for it was long before he arrived that Luther's students had gotten into the habit of getting out their pencils and notebooks when their professor and host began his discourses, prompted by some question, some incident that had happened, or some remark made or report given by one of the guests, in order that they might take down for future reference the words of wisdom or humor that fell from the lips of the much reverenced teacher. The first one

---

15) There are many collections of Luther's letters. The latest and most complete is the collection begun by E. L. Enders and completed by Gustav Kaverau. This collection embraces no less than eighteen volumes. The first volume appeared in 1884 and the last in 1923. The best English collection is the one by Smith and Jacobs, two volumes of which are published, a third being in press. The two volumes so far published contain Luther's correspondence to the spring of 1530. Another very good English collection is the one by Margaret A. Currie. It contains selections from 1507—1546.
16) *Historien*, p. 208 seq.

PEDAGOGICAL WORKS

to begin this practice was an Austrian by the name Conrad Cordatus, who was seven years older than Luther, and for many years a regular boarder at the Black Cloister. He began taking notes in 1531 or 1532 and was soon followed by others, from Veit Dietrich to Johannes Aurifaber, who was with Luther at the time of his death, and who was thus the last one to take notes, but he was the first one to publish the *Table Talks*, based on his own and the notes of others. He published his collection in 1566. Preserved Smith in his *Critical Study of Luther's Table Talks*, gives the following list of contributors, with the dates of their stay at Wittenberg opposite their names:

1. Conrad Cordatus, 1524-1537
2. Veit Dietrich, 1529-1535
3. Johann Schlaginhaufen, 1531-1532
4. Anton Lauterbach, 1531-1539
5. Hieronymus Weller, 1527-1538
6. Antonius Corvinus, 1532
7. Johannes Mathesius, 1540
8. Kaspar Heydenreich, 1541-1543
9. Hieronymus Besold, 1541-1546
10. Magister Plato, 1540-1541
11. Johannes Stolz, 1542-46
12. Johannes Aurifaber, 1545-1546 [17]

In addition to the names given by Smith, the following are given in the introduction to the collection of *Tischreden* in the Erlangen edition of Luther's Works, vol. LVII, v-viii; Georg Rörer, Jacob Weber, Ferdinand a Maugis, an Austrian, Johann Sachse of Holstein, Wolfgang Severus, and Dr. Heinicke of Austria.

It is these copious notes of what Luther said at his

---

17) Page 16.

own table from time to time from the establishment of his own household, in 1525, to his death in 1546, made by these men that constitute what we know as Luther's *Table Talks*. These talks cover a remarkably wide range of topics, showing the versatility of Luther, his broad interest, and extensive knowledge. They give us many glimpses into the home life and the character of the man, and many of his sayings, when divorced from the situations out of which they arose and taken without due regard to their origin and nature, may give a very incorrect and misleading view of the life and character of the man, whose statements they are reported to have been. While the notes were certainly taken with his knowledge, yet there is no intimation that they were taken with his approval or ever submitted to him for correction and verification. Both for the biographer and the student of Luther's contributions to education these *Tischreden* are of the greatest value, when due regard is taken of the fact that they are merely secondary testimonies, not primary records made by himself.[18]

Schumann[19] has collected no less than fifty-four talks from the *Tischreden* of educational content, setting forth Luther's ideas of children and their education, teachers, methods of teaching, and schools of various grades. In their brief collection of sayings from Luther's *Table Talks*, Smith and Gallinger have seen fit to give only a few extracts dealing with edu-

---

18) The best and most complete collection of the *Tischreden* is the Weimar edition of Luther's Works, embracing six quarto volumes. The translation into English of a selection of the *Tischreden* by William Haslitt, *The Table Talks or Familiar Discourses of Martin Luther*, published in London in 1848 and reprinted in 1857, with a biography of Luther by Alexander Chalmers, is still the best English collection. The little delightful volume of Smith and Gallinger, *Conversations with Luther*, contains interesting extracts on thirty-six different subjects. The doctorate thesis of Preserved Smith, Columbia University, on *Luther's Table Talks*, is a very valuable contribution to the study of Luther's *Table Talks* in the English language.

19) *Luthers Pädagogische Schriften*, pp. 268-300.

cation, but have given quite a number of his sayings about home and family life and his observations on children.[20]

As examples of Luther's remarks on educational topics in his *Tischreden*, the excerpts made by Smith and Gallinger are reproduced in full below:

"When schools flourish, then things go well and the Church is secure. Let us have more learned men and teachers! The youth furnish recruits for the Church, they are the source of its well-being. If there were no schools, who would there be to take our places when we die? In the Church we are forced to have schools. God has preserved the Church through schools, they are its conservatories. They have no fine exterior, but within they are most useful. In schools the children have learned the Lord's Prayer and the creed; in the little schools the Church has been most wonderfully preserved."

"Schoolmasters become bold and learn how to expound the Bible by teaching school. Nowadays young men want to be ordained at once and avoid school work. If one taught school ten years he might retire with a good conscience, for the work is heavy and little honored. In a city a schoolmaster has as much responsibility as a minister. We can take magistrates, princes, and nobles as we find them, but not schools, for schools rule the world. We see that there is no ruler today who is not of necessity governed by a lawyer or a minister. The princes know nothing of themselves and are ashamed to learn, so they have to apply to the schools. Were I not a preacher there is no profession on earth I would sooner follow. One must not regard how the world esteems and pays it, but how God glorifies it every day."

"It is my opinion that on the last day an honest

---

20) *Conversations with Luther*, pp. 41-65.

schoolmaster will be more honored than all the Popes." [21]

TRANSLATION OF AESOP'S FABLES.—It may seem strange that Luther, the theologian and reformer, busy as he was with so many things, and often hard pressed both by his work and his bodily ailments, should take any interest in fables. Yet, there seemed to be nothing either human or divine in which he did not take an interest, especially if he could find something of value to train the child or sweeten, ennoble, and enrich life. Therefore he was deeply interested in folk-lore, folk-song, folk-proverbs, fairy-tales, and fables, for he was able to put all of these to good use in his preaching, his writing, and his private discourse. Since Luther was under the ban of the empire, and therefore technically an outlaw, he could not be present at the Diet of Augsburg in 1530, but was obliged to remain at some distance from the seat of the Diet, at the Castle of Coburg. Here he was from the very first day busy with a number of things. In a letter to Melanchthon written the same day he arrived, April 22, 1530, he says: "We have at last reached our Sinai, my dear Herr Philip, but out of this Sinai we shall make a Zion and build three tabernacles: one to the Psalter, one to the Prophets, and one to Æsop. But time is needed for this." [22]

We soon find him at work on all three. His stay at Coburg was very trying for him, for he was severely troubled with head-aches, spiritual trials, great anxiety for the cause of the Reformation, and was also deeply grieved over the loss of his father, who died on May 29, and yet he accomplished a great deal while he was there. Besides the work on the Psalms and the Prophets, and a number of other literary

---

21) *Conversations with Luther*, pp. 96-97.
22) Currie, *Letters of Martin Luther*, p. 208.

PEDAGOGICAL WORKS

works, he also managed to translate thirteen of *Aesop's Fables*. It was his intention to translate all of them, purging them from any objectionable features they might contain, and publish them. This work he did not accomplish, however, but he did publish, with an introduction setting forth the nature and value of these fables, the thirteen he translated while at Coburg, in the year 1538. It was especially the moral and educational value of the fables that appealed to Luther. In the introduction to his translation of *Aesop's Fables*, he gives an example of how they should be used in the home, saying that the father, when his family and servants are gathered about the table, may ask them what this or that fable might mean. This would bring out both the story and the meaning, and result in both entertainment and instruction. In his *Tischreden* he also speaks of the value of *Aesop's Fables* and draws many lessons from them.[23]

INTRODUCTIONS TO VARIOUS BOOKS.—Luther wrote a large number of introductions or forewords to books written by his friends and associates as well as to his own. In many of these he takes occasion to set forth some of his views on educational matters, making even many of his introductions source material for a study of his educational views. Thus in his introduction to Johann Walther's hymnbook of 1525, he makes a special appeal to the young as well as in behalf of the young. He recognizes the love which children and young people have for music and song and states that one of the objects of providing this collection of songs, set to four-part music, was to furnish the young with wholesome and instructive songs to draw them away from the influence of "amorous and carnal songs." He closes his introduction by saying: "The world is,

---

23) Schumann, *Pädagogische Schriften*, pp. 181 seq.; Mathesius, *Historien*, pp. 154-167.

alas, not so mindful and diligent to train and teach our poor youth, wherefore we ought to be forward to promote the same." [24]

In his rather lengthy introduction to a collection of funeral hymns published at Wittenberg in 1542, he presents his lofty views of the Christian life, and sets forth the evangelical Christian's view of death, pointing out how funeral services should be conducted in harmony with such views, saying among other things: "St. Paul writes to the Thessalonians that they should not sorrow for the dead as others that have no hope, but should comfort one another with God's Word, as those who have a sure hope of life and of the resurrection of the dead. . . . Accordingly we have, in our churches, abolished, done away with, and out and out made an end of the popish horrors, such as wakes, masses for the soul, obsequies, purgatory, and all other mummeries for the dead, and will no longer have our churches turned into wailing places and houses of mourning, but, as the primitive fathers called them, cemeteries, that is, resting and sleeping places. . . . We sing, withal, beside our dead and over their graves, no dirges or lamentations, but comforting songs of the forgiveness of sins, of rest, sleep, life, and resurrection of the departed believers, for the strengthening of our faith, and the stirring up of the people to a true devotion." [25] He closes his introduction with a free rendering of *Nunc Dimittis*, Luke 2:29-32, into German and gives some suggestions as to the type of hymns suitable for Christian funerals, mentioning among them his own hymn, "In Peace and Joy I Now Depart," of which the first two verses read thus:

---

24) Lambert, *Hymns of Luther*, p. 13; *Werke*, vol. XXXV, pp. 474-5.
25) Lambert, *Hymns of Luther*, p. 13; *Werke*, Weimar ed., vol. XXXV, pp. 478-483.

In peace and joy I now depart,
  At God's disposing;
For full of comfort is my heart,
  Soft reposing.
So the Lord hath promis'd me,
And death is but a slumber.

'Tis Christ that wrought this work for me,
  The faithful Savior,
Whom Thou hast made mine eyes to see
  By Thy favor.
In Him I behold my life,
My help in need and dying.[26]

In 1529 Justus Menius, pastor at Erfurt, published a book on the Christian home and family life entitled, *Oeconomia Christiana*. It was a book with whose contents Luther was very well pleased, as it set forth very clearly the evangelical view of marriage and home life. It was dedicated to Duchess Sibylla, the young wife of Duke Johann Friedrich of Saxony. In his introduction to this book Luther especially dwells upon the sacredness of the marriage relation, the significance of the Christian home, and the importance of Christian child nurture in the home.[27]

Another introduction which should also be mentioned in this connection is the one he wrote for the History of the Duke of Mailand by Galeatius Capella, in which he deals especially with the value of historians and history considered from an educational point of view. After discussing at some length the task of the historian and the service rendered by him, he says: "Therefore historians are most useful people and most excellent teachers, whom we can never

---

26) Lambert, *Hymns of Luther*, p. 62.
27) *Werke*, Ibid., vol. XXX. 2, pp. 4-63.

sufficiently honor, praise, and thank, and it should be a care of our great lords, as emperors and kings, to have histories of their times written and preserved in libraries, and they should spare no expense to procure persons capable of teaching. . . . But it requires a superior man to write history, a man with a lionheart, who dares without fear to speak the truth. For most men write in such a way that, according to the wishes of their rulers or friends, they pass over the vices or degeneracy of their times, or put the best construction upon them; on the other hand, through partiality for their fatherland and hostility to foreigners, they unduly magnify insignificant virtues, and eulogize or defame according to their preferences or prejudices. In this way histories become beyond measure untrustworthy, and God's work is obscured. Since history describes nothing else than the ways of God, that is, grace and anger, which we should believe as if they stood in Scripture, it ought to be written with extreme care, fidelity, and truth." [28]

The introduction to many of his own works, such as the two Catechisms and *Deutsche Messe*, are especially excellent source material for Luther's educational views.

OTHER EDUCATIONAL WRITINGS.—There are a number of other writings by Luther which are of educational value, though they do not directly deal with the subject of education. Among these may be mentioned his liturgical writings, such as his *Prayer Book* (*Betbüchlein*) of 1522, the *Baptismal Book* (*Taufbüchlein*) of 1523, the *Latin Order of Service* (*Formula Missae*) of 1524, the *German Order of Service* (*Deutsche Messe*) of 1526, and the *Wedding Book* (*Traubüchlein*) of 1529. These will be considered in

---

28) Painter, *Luther on Education*, pp. 161-62; *Werke*, Erlangen ed., vol. LXIII, pp. 353-7.

Chapter XII. His hymns might also be mentioned because of their great educational and devotional value, but these will also be considered in Chapter XII.

A writing of special interest must not be overlooked. It is the so-called *Visitation Instructions* of 1528 and 1538. This tract was prepared by Melanchthon and approved by Luther. It was first published in 1528, with an introduction by Luther. In 1538 Luther published a new and revised edition of this booklet himself. The *Visitation Instructions* contains the first Lutheran school plan that was published.[29] What the relation of this school plan was to the one mentioned by Luther in his letter to Spalatin on Oct. 17, 1524, we do not know, no copy of Luther's school plan mentioned in this letter being known. It is interesting to note, however, that as early as 1524, Luther had a definite school plan to propose. In this letter to Spalatin, he says: "I am sending you back your booklet, dear Spalatin, and also the school plan, which should be presented to the princes, not with any great hope, but an attempt must be made in the name of the Lord."[30] Raumer expresses the opinion in a foot note that Melanchthon's plan was very much in agreement with this earlier plan of Luther.[31] It is very probable that the original basis of the school plan for which many writers give Melanchthon the whole credit was Luther's school plan of four years earlier.

Another tract of special educational interest is Luther's *Letter on Translation* (*Sendbrief vom Dolmetschen*) of 1530. This tract was addressed to W. Link, pastor at Nuremberg, and was occasioned by the attacks made upon Luther and his translation of the Bible by his enemies, especially Jerome Emser of Dres-

---
29) Weber, *Melanchthons ev. Kirchen u. Schulordnung*, pp. 1-38.
30) *Werke*, St. Louis ed., vol. XXa, p. 653.
31) *Geschichte der Pädagogik*, vol. I, p. 135.

den. Luther very stoutly and ably defends his work and sets forth the principles of translation according to which he pursued his Bible translation. It is therefore of the greatest value in connection with the history of Luther's German Bible.[32]

Mention may also be made of the other two great reformation tracts of the eventful year 1520, *The Liberty of a Christian Man* and *The Babylonian Captivity of the Church*, for these tracts also exerted a tremendous awakening and educating influence.

---

32) *Werke*, Weimar ed., vol. XXX. 2, pp. 626-646.

CHAPTER XI
PEDAGOGICAL PRINCIPLES

In this chapter we shall endeavor to present briefly the fundamental educational ideas of Luther. His educational ideas cover a wide range, and the literature we have from his pen dealing with the various phases of education is, as we have seen in the preceding chapter, very extensive; hence no full and exhaustive treatment of this subject can be given in this treatise. It will be sufficient for our present purpose to present in brief outline the most salient points of the pedagogical principles which he advocated and so consistently and successfully practised.

THE IMPORTANCE OF CHRISTIAN EDUCATION.—Luther had a keen conception of the vital significance of Christian education, not only as viewed from the standpoint of the temporal and eternal spiritual wellbeing of man, but also as considered from a purely humanitarian point of view. In his introductions to both the Large and the Small Catechism, he stresses particularly the spiritual importance of Christian education. So also in both his *Letter to the Councilmen* and the *Sermon on Sending Children to School.* The reason for a thorough Christian education was to him the uppermost; hence he also lays such emphasis upon the maintenance of schools for the purpose of training pious and well-qualified pastors and teachers, for "an upright pastor serves mankind in body and soul, in estate and honor. But above that, consider how he serves God, and what splendid sacrifices and services he renders: for through his office and word, the kingdom of God is maintained in the world, the honor, the name, the glory of God, a right faith and apprehension of Christ, the fruit of the suffering, and blood, and death of Christ, the gifts, works, and power of the Holy Spirit, the proper use of Baptism and the Lord's Supper, the pure doctrine of the Gospel, the proper manner of chastening and crucifying the flesh, and similar blessings."[1] But "even if there were no soul and men did not need schools and the languages for the sake of Christianity and the Scriptures, still for the establishment of the best schools everywhere, both for boys and girls, this consideration is of itself sufficient, namely, that society, for the maintenance of civil order and the proper regulation of the househould, needs accomplished and well-trained men and women. Now such men are to come from boys and such women from girls; hence it is necessary that boys and girls be properly taught and brought up."[2] Again he says: "There can be no greater injury done to Christendom than to neglect the children. Therefore, if Christendom is again to be helped, the beginning must indeed be made with the children."[3] "That the condition in Christendom at present is so evil is due to the fact that no one concerns himself with the youth, and if it is again to be brought back into a good course, we must indeed start with the children."[4]

THE AIM OF CHRISTIAN EDUCATION.—Luther regards the process of training and education as the normal method of evangelization, by means of which the Kingdom of God is to be peopled and extended.

---

1) Painter, *Luther on Education*, p. 229.
2) Ibid., p. 196.
3) Lindemann, *Luther als Erzieher*, p. 18.
4) Ibid., p. 22.

He begins with the baptized child as a member of the Kingdom of God. This child is to be unfolded and trained for the fullest possible participation in God's Kingdom. Therefore he says: "See to it, that you above all have your children instructed in spiritual things, that you first give them to God; then to secular pursuits."[5] He lays particular emphasis on this parental obligation, "above everything else to bring up their children in the fear and knowledge of God."[6] This is to Luther the fundamental aim, the aim which conditions and makes possible the attainment of all secondary aims, such as training for maintaining right relations with fellowman, carrying on the various secular pursuits in a Christian manner, and serving God and one's fellows to the fullest possible extent and in the most upright and efficient manner.[7]

THE DUTY OF PARENTS.—Luther held a very lofty conception of the marriage relation and held the family in the very highest esteem. "That," he says, "is indeed a very beautiful and happy marriage relation, which has inscribed both on the table and the bed: 'Here is God's favor, will, and most gracious pleasure. Here are the real and immeasurably great blessings and riches.'"[8] A truly Christian home and family life is a "real church, an elect cloister, yea, a paradise, for the father and mother here become like God, because they are rulers, bishops, pope, doctor, pastor, preacher, schoolmaster, judge, and lord."[9] Parents are singularly blessed, for children are the gift of God, but they also have great responsibilities, for they stand in the place of God in their relation to

---
5) Schiller, *Luther über chr. Kinderzucht,* p. 18.
6) Ibid., p. 20.
7) See *Letter to the Councilmen on Sending Children to School,* Painter, op. cit., pp. 169-270; *Werke,* Weimar ed., vol. XV, p. 9 seq. and vol. XXX. 2, p. 508 seq.
8) Lindemann, op. cit., p. 2.
9) Ibid., p. 2.

the children, since in them is "beautifully reflected the divine and fatherly heart toward us. For in father and mother we may sense and experience how God is minded toward man." [10] Therefore, he was also very insistent in urging upon parents to take their parental privileges and duties seriously. "Married people," says he, "should know that they can perform no better and more useful work for God, Christianity, the world, themselves, and their children, than by bringing up their children well. Pilgrimages to Rome and to Jerusalem, building churches, providing for masses, or whatever else the work may be called, is nothing in comparison with the right training of children, for that is the straight road to heaven; and it cannot be more easily attained in any other way. It is the peculiar work of parents, and when they do not attend to it, there is a perversion of nature, as when fire does not burn or water moisten. On the other hand, hell can be no more easily deserved, and no more hurtful work can be done than by neglecting children, letting them swear, learn shameful words and songs, and do as they please." [11] But if parents are to be able to bring up their children rightly, they must themselves be intelligent Christians. "No one should be a father unless he is able to instruct his children in the Ten Commandments and in the Gospel, so that he may bring up true Christians," says he. "But many enter the estate of holy matrimony who can not say the Lord's Prayer, and knowing nothing themselves, they are utterly incompetent to instruct their children. Children should be brought up in the fear of God. If the Kingdom of God is to come in power, we must begin with the children, and teach them from the cradle." [12] In his explanation of the Fourth Command-

---
10) Ibid., p. 2.
11) Painter, op. cit., p. 117.
12) Ibid., pp. 119-20.

ment (Fifth, Reformed), he speaks very plainly to parents concerning their duties toward their children. God "does not wish to have in this office and government knaves and tyrants," he says; "nor does He assign to them this honor, viz., power and authority to govern, and allow themselves to be worshipped; but that they should consider that they are under obligations of obedience to God; and that first of all they are earnestly and faithfully to discharge the duties of their office, not only to support and provide for the bodily necessities of their children, servants, subjects, etc., but especially train them to the honor and praise of God. Therefore do not think that this is appointed for thy pleasure and arbitrary will; but that it is a strict command and institution of God, to whom thou also must give account of the matter.—Let every one know, therefore, that above all things it is his duty, or otherwise he will lose the divine favor, to bring up his children in the fear and knowledge of God; and if they have talents, to give them also opportunity to learn and study, that they may be able to avail themselves of that for which there is need."[13]

THE CHARACTER OF HOME TRAINING.—Luther was a lover of children and a keen observer of them, facts which are well attested in his writings generally, but especially so in his recorded *Table Talks*, in which he often referred to them, their plays, their little quarrels and immediate reconciliations, their sorrows and joys, their implicit trust and confidence. He complains, as noted in Chapter II, of the severity with which he was brought up by his parents and the effect such bringing up had produced on him. Therefore, he

---
13) *Book of Concord*, pp. 414-15. The concluding clause of the last sentence quoted above has a different reading, which is clearer, namely: "and, if they have talents, to have them instructed and trained in a liberal education, that men may be able to have their aid in government and in whatever is necessary." *Book of Concord*, p. 415; *Werke*, Weimar ed., vol. XXX, 1, p. 156.

was also so insistent in urging upon parents the importance of understanding their children and suiting the training and discipline to their age and dispositions. In his exposition of the twelfth chapter of Ecclesiastes, he brings out very strongly that it is the nature of children and youth to run and play and to be busy with something, as well as to associate with other people. Since Solomon realized this fact, and did not forbid the young to rejoice in their youth, Luther says of him: "Therefore Solomon is a real royal schoolmaster. He did not forbid the youth to be with other people, or to enjoy themselves, as the monks do their pupils." [14] It is dangerous to isolate the children and young people from others, he declares. "Therefore the young people should be permitted to hear and see and experience everything, yet so that they be held to honor and discipline. Nothing is gained by monkish coercion. It is well that young people are permitted to associate with others, but they must be earnestly brought up to propriety and virtue, and kept away from vices. To young people such tyrannical, monkish coercion is injurious, for they are as much in need of pleasure and enjoyment as food and drink, for it also keeps them in better health." [15] Nor must the parents rule their children by threats and blows. In his exposition of the Ten Commandments in 1520, Luther gives a very excellent explanation and application of Paul's words to the Ephesians: "And ye fathers, provoke not your children to wrath; but nurture them in the chastening and admonition of the Lord." [16] What Paul warns against here, he states, is the bringing up of the children through severe and harsh discipline to either develope a hatred toward

---

14) Lindemann, *Luther als Erzieher*, p. 65.
15) Lindemann, op. cit., p. 66.
16) *Eph.* 6:4.

parents and all authority, or to make them fainthearted and dejected, so that they are compelled to go through life with an easily frightened and dejected spirit. "A child," says he, "that has once become shy and dejected is for all things incapable and easily discouraged, so that he always is afraid when he is about to do or undertake something. And what is still worse, when such fear has been developed in a man in his childhood, it is a very difficult matter to weed it out during the rest of his life. Since, because they were made to tremble at every word uttered by father or mother, they are frightened throughout life by the mere rustling of a leaf. Likewise, one must not permit the women who take care of the children, to frighten them with severe discipline or buffoonery, especially at night. One should rather see to it that the children are brought up to have a proper fear, fearing the things that are to be feared, and not simply make them easily frightened, something which harms them all their life." [17] "Therefore government of the father over his children on earth is not to be cross and unfriendly. He who rules in anger makes evil worse.— Through love much more will be accomplished than through slavish fear and coercion." [18] And yet he warns against the undue softness and indulgence of so many parents, whereby they spoil their children. Luther believed in the truth and wisdom of the words of Proverbs: "He that spareth his rod hateth his child; but he that loveth him, chasteneth him betimes." "Foolishness is bound up in the heart of a child; but the rod of correction shall drive it far from him." "Withhold not correction from the child; for if thou beat him with the rod, he will not die. Thou

---
17) Lindemann, op. cit., p. 67.
18) Ibid., p. 67.

shalt beat him with the rod and shalt deliver his soul from Sheol."[19] "The parents are generally the cause of the children being spoiled," says Luther. "They err commonly in either of these two ways: either through too much pampering and overindulgence, or through too great severity and embittering. One must keep within bounds on either side."[20]

The home training should also include the instruction in the rudiments of the Christian religion, at least the first three parts of the Catechism and the prayers for morning and evening and at meals provided in the appendix to the *Small Catechism*. "It is the duty of every father of a family at least once a week," he says in his short preface to the *Large Catechism*, "to examine his children and servants, and to ascertain what they know of it, or have learned, and if they be not familiar with it, to keep them faithfully at it."[21] In his *Table Talks* as well as in his writings and sermons, he stressed the importance of learning the Catechism as containing the basic truths of the Christian religion, and pointed out the splendid results which especially the diligent and proper instruction, recitation, and examination in the homes would bring about.[22] But the religious instruction the children may receive at home is insufficient, and well equipped teachers and schools are therefore necessary. "The great majority of parents," he says, "are unqualified for it, and do not understand how children should be brought up and taught. For they have learned nothing but to provide for their bodily wants; and in order to teach and train the children thoroughly, a separate class is needed. Even if parents were qual-

---

19) *Prov.* 13:24; 22:15; 23:13-14.
20) Lindemann, op. cit., p. 74.
21) *Book of Concord*, p. 387.
22) *Tischreden on Catechism, Werke*, Erlangen ed., vol. LVIII, pp. 239-268.

ified and willing to do it themselves, yet on account of other employments and household duties they have no time for it, so that necessity requires us to have teachers for public schools, unless each parent employ a private instructor." [23] In this connection, Luther has, of course, not only religious education, but also the general education of the child in mind.

THE DUTY OF PASTORS.—Luther made heavy demands on the pastor and the pastoral office, but he did not place greater demands on others than he was willing himself to endeavor to measure up to, nor did he make demands in excess of those which Scripture itself imposes. He reminded his fellow-pastors that the pastoral office was now something different from what it had been under the Papacy. "Our office," says he, in the introduction to the *Small Catechism*, "has now assumed a very different character from that which it bore under the Pope; it is now of a very grave nature, and is very salutary in its influence. It consequently subjects us to far greater burdens and labors, while it brings with it an inconsiderable reward and very little gratitude in the world. But Christ will be our reward if we labor with fidelity." [24] The new meaning of the ministerial office involves that it "pays attention to preaching and the ministration of the Word and sacraments; imparts the Holy Spirit and salvation—blessings not to be obtained by means of music and display; includes the duties of pastor, teacher, preacher, reader, chaplain, sexton, and schoolmaster; and is highly praised and extolled in the Scriptures." [25] As to the services rendered by the pastor, he says: "He comforts the sorrowing, gives counsel, settles difficulties, calms disturbed consciences,

---
23) Painter, *Luther on Education*, pp. 179-80.
24) *Book of Concord*, p. 363.
25) Painter, op. cit., pp. 219-20.

helps to maintain peace, to appease, to reconcile, and similar duties without number; for a preacher confirms, strengthens, and supports all authority, all temporal peace, governs the seditious, teaches obedience, morality, discipline, and honor, and gives instruction in the duties pertaining to fathers, mothers, children, servants, and in a word to all other secular relations of life." [26] With this conception of the pastoral office, it is only natural to expect that Luther would place upon it the greatest responsibility for the proper Christian training and education of the children, and so he does. "Let it be your great aim," he says, "to urge magistrates and parents to rule wisely and to educate the children, admonishing them at the same time that such duties are imposed upon them, and showing them how grievously they sin if they neglect them." [27] The *Sermon on Sending Children to School* was addressed to the pastors, and it was through them largely that he looked for results from this appeal in behalf of the Christian education of the children. "Although I know that many of you, without my admonition, attend to this matter faithfully, yet if some perchance forget it, or wish to follow my example in laboring at it more diligently," he says in this appeal, "I send you this sermon, which I have more than once delivered to our people here, that you may see that I strive earnestly with you, and that we thus everywhere do our duty and in our office are justified before God." [28]

DUTY OF THE STATE.—Although Luther made a sharp distinction between the functions of the Church and the State, he did not regard them as non-related institutions. The State as the body politic was to

---
26) Ibid., p. 228.
27) *Book of Concord*, p. 362.
28) Painter, op. cit., p. 217.

PEDAGOGICAL PRINCIPLES

him naturally represented in its organ of control, the government, whether in the more or less democratic government of the free cities or the hereditary and monarchical provincial government by the nobility and the imperial government by the emperor. He generally therefore refers to the State under the terms government, princes, nobles, and emperor. As the institution invested by divine authority with the power of the sword, the government was also in virtue of this power the supreme guardian of the people's intellectual, moral, and religious well-being, as well as the protector of their life, honor, and property, and the maintainer of law and order. It was this conception of the relation between Church and State and the function of the State that prompted Luther to send forth his masterly social and religious appeal to the German princes, known as *The Address to the Christian Nobility of the German Nation on the Improvement of the Christian Estates*, which he sent forth in August, 1520, and in which he calls attention to social and religious conditions prevailing in the German provinces and urgently requests the rulers to take the necessary steps to improve them.[29] It was this same view of the function of the State which led him four years later to issue his strong appeal for the establishment and advancement of Christian schools, known as *The Letter to the Councilmen of all the German Cities in Behalf of Christian Schools*.[30] His views regarding the powers and functions of government have already been indicated by references made to his letters to Margrave Georg of Brandenburg and Elector Johann of Saxony.[31] These same views are also expressed in the documents of 1520 and 1524 mentioned above, as

---

29) See chapter VIII, pp. 152-55.
30) Ibid., pp. 155-64.
31) See chapter X, pp. 196-98.

well as in *The Sermon on Sending Children to School*,[32] and a number of other writings. To provide for the education of the young, Luther considered to be one of the chief functions of the State, for it alone had the power to compel the people to establish, maintain, and support schools, and send their children to school. "Therefore it will be the duty of the mayors and the council to exercise the greatest care over the young," he says. "For since the happiness, honor, and life of the city are committed to their hands, they would be held recreant before God and the world if they did not day and night, with all their power, seek its welfare and improvement. Now the welfare of a city does not consist alone in great treasures, firm walls, beautiful houses, and munitions of war; indeed, where all these are found, and reckless people come into power, the city sustains the greater injury. But the highest welfare, safety, and power of a city consists in able, learned, wise, upright, cultivated citizens, who can secure, preserve, and utilize every treasure and advantage."[33] But the rulers may feel that it is none of their business to make provisions for the education of the children; that is a matter for the parents themselves to look after. To such an objection, Luther replies: "We see indeed how it goes with this teaching and training. And where it is carried to the highest point, and is attended with success, it results in nothing more than that the learners, in some measure, acquire a forced external propriety of manner; in other respects they remain dunces, know nothing, and are incapable of giving aid and advice. But were they instructed in schools by thoroughly qualified male or female teachers, who taught the languages, other arts, and history, then the pupils would hear the history

---

32) See chapter VIII, pp. 164-71.
33) Painter, op. cit., p. 180.

and maxims of the world, and see how things went with each city, kingdom, prince, man, and woman; and thus in a short time, they would be able to comprehend, as in a mirror, the character, the life, counsels, undertakings, successes, and failures, of the whole world from the beginning. From this knowledge they could regulate their views, and order their course of life in the fear of God, having become wise in judging what is to be sought and what avoided in this outward life, and capable of advising and directing others." [34] Hence, from whichever point of view the whole matter is considered, there is no escape, in Luther's mind, from the conclusion that the State must make ample provisions for the liberal education of the young or itself suffer the consequences from such neglect. Therefore, he concludes the whole matter by saying: "I maintain that the civil authorities are under obligation to compel the people to send their children to school, especially such as are promising, as has elsewhere been said. For our rulers are certainly bound to maintain the spiritual and secular offices and callings, so that there may always be preachers, jurists, pastors, scribes, school-masters, and the like; for these cannot be dispensed with. If the government can compel such citizens as are fit for military services to bear spear and rifle, to mount ramparts, and perform other martial duties in time of war; how much more has it a right to compel the people to send their children to school, because in this case we are warring with the devil, whose object it is secretly to exhaust our cities and principalities of strong men, to destroy the kernel, and leave a shell of ignorant and helpless people, whom he can sport and juggle with at pleasure. That is starving out a city or country, destroying it without a struggle, and without its knowledge. The

---

84) Painter, op. cit., p. 197.

Turk does far differently, and takes every third child in his empire to educate for whatever he pleases. How much more should our rulers require children to be sent to school, who, however, are not taken from their parents, but are educated for their own and general good, in an office where they have an adequate support."[35]

We have in these statements of Luther the crystallization of the tendencies that were gaining ground in his day, looking toward a broader foundation, function, and purpose of education. The beginnings of these tendencies are found in part in the rise of the universities, the influences of the Renaissance, the rapid rise of industrial and commercial enterprises, with the elevation of the social status of the middle class, and, in part, of the peasant class, but the moving power which forged the way and compelled action was the Lutheran Reformation, which brought about the crumbling of the power of the Roman Church, religiously, politically, and educationally, the passing of the old form of church schools, and the demands for a new system of popular education in the interests not only of the Church as such, but also in the interests and for the benefit of the State and society in general. The success of such a system must ultimately rest upon the power of the State to initiate, foster, and carry out a scheme for general education and compel the parents, for the benefit of the children as well as the State, to send their children to school. We have, therefore, in the teachings of Luther regarding the educational and cultural functions and powers of the State the foundation principles upon which rests our present highly developed and efficiently operating public school system, with its unexcelled opportunities for primary, secondary, and

---
35) Painter, op. cit., pp. 269-270.

higher education for all, regardless of rank or station in life, color, race, or sex, with a minimum standard of attendance requirement, and the application of compulsory measures for the attainment of that standard.

GENERAL AND SPECIALIZED EDUCATION.—Luther's educational scheme provided for a general elementary education accessible to all, both boys and girls, and which all should be compelled to take advantage of, and, furthermore, ample provisions, both as to school facilities and stipends, which would permit the specially gifted to prepare themselves for the professions, such as teaching, preaching, law, medicine, and other specialized services in Church and State. After discussing the provisions to be made for the general education of all children, in his Letter to the Councilmen, Luther says: "But the brightest pupils, who give promise of becoming accomplished teachers, preachers, and workers, should be kept longer at school, or set apart wholly for study."[36] But even boys who cannot be reckoned among the brightest scholars should not be excluded from receiving a higher education, for he says: "But also the boys that are less promising should learn to understand, read, and write Latin. For we need not only learned doctors and masters in the Scriptures, but also ordinary pastors, who may teach the Gospel and the Catechism to the young and ignorant, baptize, administer the Lord's Supper, etc. If they are not capable of contending with heretics, it does not matter. For in a good building, we need both large and small timber; and in like manner we must have sextons and others to aid the minister and further the Word of God."[37] In order that adequate provisions may be made for such a general and spe-

---
36) Painter, op. cit., p. 200.
37) Ibid., p. 235.

cialized education, he urges the establishment of the best possible schools in every city, the establishment and maintenance of a sufficient number of universities, with faculties in theology, law, medicine, science and arts, and the use of the cloistral foundations and endowments or the granting of special stipends to help promising young men who have no other means of support to carry them through school.

THE SCHOOL CURRICULA.—Luther has in a general way indicated in a number of his writings what in his opinion should enter into the curricula of the various grades of schools. "As for myself," he says, "if I had children[38] and were able, I would have them learn not only the languages and history, but also singing, instrumental music, and the whole course of mathematics. For what is all this but mere child's play, in which the Greeks in former ages trained their children, and by this means became wonderfully skilled people, capable for every undertaking. How I regret that I did not read more poetry and history, and that no one taught me these branches."[39] Under languages he included German, Latin, Greek, and Hebrew, but he would not have the children burdened with the learning of too many languages at the same time; hence it is provided in the school plan for Saxony, prepared by Melanchthon but approved by Luther, that Latin shall be first taught. To the subjects already mentioned, he would add logic, rhetoric, and dialectics, natural science, and gymnastics. He would not have natural science studied according to the books of Aristotle, however, but by observing nature herself, in fact, he would do away with all of Aristotle's books, excepting his works on logic, rhetoric, and poetry, for in all the others he teaches what is contrary to the

---
38) Luther was not yet married.
39) Painter, op. cit., p. 198.

teachings of the Word of God, and Luther deplores that the philosophy of Aristotle had so long held sway in the Church and the school.[40] Concerning the importance of two of the new elements he adds to the school curricula, music and gymnastics, he says: "Music is a semi-disciplinarian and school-master; it makes men more gentle and tender-hearted, more modest and discreet."[41] "Music is a delightful, noble gift of God, and closely related to theology. I would not give up what little skill I possess in music even for something great. The young are to be continually exercised in this art; It makes good and skilful people of them."[42] "It was well considered and arranged by the ancients that people should practice gymnastics, in order that they might not fall into revelling, unchastity, gluttony, intemperance, and gaming. Therefore these two exercises and pastimes please me best, namely, music and gymnastics, of which the first drives away all care and melancholy from the heart, and the latter produces elasticity of the body and preserves the health."[43] But the two most important subjects in which the children are to be instructed are the Scriptures and the Catechism. They are to give foundation and tone to the whole educative scheme. "Above all in both higher and lower schools the chief and most common lesson should be the Scriptures, and for the young boys, the Gospel; and would to God that each town had also a girls' school, in which girls might be taught the Gospel for an hour daily, either in German or Latin."[44] And yet the Saxony school plan calls for specific instruction in the Scriptures and the Catechism only once a week, either on Wednes-

---
40) *Werke*, Erlangen ed., vol. XXI, pp. 344-6.
41) Painter, op. cit., p. 165.
42) Ibid., *Werke*, Er. ed., vol. LXII, pp. 308-9.
43) Painter, p. 166.
44) Painter, op. cit., pp. 138-9; *Werke*, Erlangen ed., vol. XXI, p. 349.

days or Saturdays.[45] In commenting on this fact, Karl Weber observes that it must be borne in mind that the plan calls for one hour's instruction each day in singing, which means instruction in singing spiritual or religious songs, and that the children were also frequently required to attend a brief daily service in the churches, both of which should be considered as part of the religious instruction provided for the children.[46] It is interesting to note in this connection, that an effort is made to maintain somewhat af a balanced proportion between the religious and purely secular instruction, for it is specifically stated, that "some teach the children absolutely nothing from the Scriptures, while others teach absolutely nothing but the Scriptures, neither of which is to be suffered." [47]

The Saxony School Plan prepared by Melanchthon in 1528, which was in part revised by Luther, who also wrote an introduction for it, was by Luther published in revised form and with a new introduction in 1538. It is an interesting document in the history of education, because it gives a fairly complete plan of instruction for a common public school, and a plan according to which a number of such schools were established. It divides the school into three departments or classes and prescribes the curriculum and the methods of procedure for each department. The first department includes those children who are just beginners and are learning to read; the second department, those who have learned to read, and are now ready for "grammatica," and the third group, the more advanced students, who are to be drilled in Latin grammar, speaking, and writing, and taught such other subjects as may be suitable. The teacher is

---

45) *Werke*, Erlangen ed., vol. XXXIII, p. 68.
46) *Melanchthons ev. Kirchen- u. Schulordnung*, p. 152, note 39.
47) Ibid., p. 110; *Werke*, Ibid., p. 68.

admonished to insist on the students speaking nothing but Latin, and he must himself as much as possible speak only the Latin language, in order that the pupils may acquire facility in speaking that language. Among the subjects studied in the first two departments are included *Aesop's Fables*.[48]

Luther was quite modern in his insistence on making the education practical and relating it to actual life. He anticipates the objections which some people would be ready to raise against his plan of general education, by putting into the objector's mouth the question: "Who can do without his children and bring them up in this manner to be young gentlemen?" To this question Luther replies: "It is not my idea that we should establish schools as they have been heretofore, where a boy has studied Donatus and Alexander twenty or thirty years, and yet has learned nothing. The world has changed, and things go differently. My idea is that boys should spend an hour or two a day in school, and the rest of the time work at home, learn some trade and do whatever is desired, so that study and work may go on together, while the children are young and can attend to both.—In like manner, a girl has time to go to school an hour a day, and yet attend to her work at home."[49] The principle here laid down was very slowly applied, and it is really only in our day that it has been given a fair chance to prove its value, but it nevertheless shows the broadness of vision and practical bent of Luther at a time when there was so much educational waste and pedantry and so little had as yet been done to relate education to practical, everyday life.

PUBLIC LIBRARIES.—Luther realized that if his plan

---
48) *Werke*, Ibid., pp. 64-70; Weber, op. cit., pp. 1-38; 106-112; 149-154. As noted on pages 209 and 288 Melanchthon's School Plan was undoubtedly prepared on the basis of Luther's School Plan of 1524.
49) Painter, op. cit., pp. 199-200.

of a general public educational system was to succeed, it would be necessary to establish public libraries. Therefore he also makes a strong appeal for the establishment of public libraries in connection with his appeal to the Councilmen in behalf of Christian schools. To him good schools and good libraries go together. "Finally," he says, "this must be taken into consideration by all who earnestly desire to see such schools established and the languages preserved in the German states: that no cost nor pain should be spared to produce good libraries in suitable buildings, especially in the large cities, which are able to afford it. For if the knowledge of the Gospel and of every kind of learning is to be preserved, it must be embodied in books, as the prophets and the apostles did, as I have already shown. This should be done, not only that our spiritual and civil leaders may have something to read and study, but also that good books may not be lost, and that arts and the languages may be preserved, with which God has graciously favored us."[50] He gives directions as to how the books for these libraries are to be selected and what fields of knowledge they are to cover, and in these he again shows both broadness of vision and keenness of insight. "But my advice is," he goes on to say, "not to collect all sorts of books indiscriminately, thinking only of getting a vast number together. I would have discrimination used.—In the first place, a library should contain the Holy Scriptures in Latin, Greek, Hebrew, German, and other languages. Then the best and most ancient commentators in Greek, Hebrew, and Latin. Secondly, such books as are useful in acquiring the languages, as poets and orators, without considering whether they are heathen or Christian, Greek or Latin. For it is from such works that grammar must be

---
50) Ibid., p. 203.

learned. Thirdly, books treating of all the arts and sciences. Lastly, books on jurisprudence and medicine, though here discrimination is necessary. A prominent place should be given to chronicles and histories, in whatever language they may be obtained; for they are wonderfully useful in understanding and regulating the course of the world, and in disclosing the marvelous works of God." [51]

TEACHERS AND TEACHING.—Luther regarded the teaching profession very highly and considered it of vital importance. "An industrious, pious school-master or teacher, who faithfully trains and educates boys, can never be sufficiently recompensed, and no money will pay him, even as the heathen Aristotle says. Yet this calling is shamefully despised amoung us, as if it were nothing—and at the same time we pretend to be Christians! If I had to give up preaching and my other duties, there is no office I would rather have than that of school teacher. For I know that next to the ministry it is the most useful, greatest, and best; and I am not sure which of the two is to be preferred. For it is hard to make old dogs docile and old rogues pious, yet that is what the ministry works at, in great part, in vain; but young trees, though some may break in the process, are more easily bent and trained. Therefore, let it be considered one of the highest virtues on earth faithfully to train the children of others, which duty but few parents attend to themselves." [52] For this position young men, and women, too, should be carefully trained, so that they not only know the subjects they are to teach, but also have had experience in the world of affairs, and know how to deal with children. He also maintains that no one should be

---

51) Ibid., pp. 206-7.
52) Ibid., pp. 263-4.

ordained to the ministry who has not for some time served as a school teacher.

As has already been mentioned earlier in this volume, Luther was a keen observer of children and their habits, and he put the knowledge of child life thus gleaned into good use both in dealing with his own children and the children of others, as well as in instructing others how to deal with children, in the home and in the school. "Now, since the young must leap and jump, or have something to do, because they have a natural desire for it, which should not be restrained (for it is not well to check them in everything), why should we not provide them such schools, and lay before them such studies? By the gracious arrangement of God, children take delight in acquiring knowledge, whether language, mathematics, or history. And our schools are no longer a hell or purgatory, in which children are tortured over cases and tenses, and in which with much flogging, trembling, anguish, and wretchedness they learn nothing."[53] Activity and inquisitiveness being natural to the child, the teacher should capitalize these innate tendencies, but in such a way that the learning process is made pleasant to the child and no undue pressure is brought to bear upon it in order to make it study, for "what must be forced with rods and blows will have no good results."[54] The teacher must come down to the level of the child, play with it and prattle with it, for "if we are to teach children, we must become children."[55] Lessons should not only be drawn from books, but also direct from nature. "We are at the dawn of a new era," he declares, "for we are beginning to recover the knowledge of the external world that we lost through

---
53) Ibid., p. 198.
54) Ibid., p. 155.
55) Ibid., p. 155; Richard and Painter, *Christian Worship*, pp. 186-88.

the fall of Adam. We now observe creatures properly, and not as formerly under the Papacy. Erasmus is indifferent, and does not care to know how fruit is developed from the germ. But by the grace of God we already recognize in the most delicate flower the wonders of divine goodness and omnipotence. We see in His creatures the power of His Word. He commanded, and the thing stood fast. See that force display itself in the stone of a peach. It is very hard, and the germ it encloses is very tender; but when the moment has come, the stone must open to let out the young plant that God calls into life. Erasmus passes by all that, takes no account of it, and looks upon external objects as cows look upon a new gate."[56] He emphasized the necessity of concreteness in teaching, and made liberal use of pictures, stories, and examples. His *Small Catechism* appeared with twenty wood cuts in its first edition of 1529, the number was increased to twenty-three in the edition of 1531, and later to twenty-four. His examples and stories were drawn from daily life, folk-lore, and especially from history. "The celebrated Roman Varro affirms that the best way to teach," says he, "is to unite examples with words. This results in a clearer apprehension of what is taught, and secures also better retention; otherwise, when statements are heard without examples, no matter how good the doctrine may be, the heart is not so deeply moved, and the subject is not so clearly understood nor so firmly retained."[57] He knew the value of the story both to interest the child and to teach a lesson, and recommended *Aesop's Fables*, some of which he himself translated and published.

In the introduction to his *Small Catechism* he gives definite instructions as to the method of teaching to

---
56) Ibid., p. 163.
57) Ibid., p. 155.

be employed. "In the first place, let the preacher take the utmost care to avoid changes or variations in the text and wording of the Ten Commandments, the Lord's Prayer, the Creed, the Sacraments, etc.—For young and inexperienced people cannot be successfully instructed unless we adhere to the same text or the same forms of expression. They easily become confused when the teacher at one time employs a certain form of words and expressions, and at another time, apparently with a view to make improvements, adopts a different form. The result of such a course will be that all the time and labor which we have expended will be lost.—In the second place, when those whom you are instructing have become familiar with the words of the text, it is time to teach them to understand the meaning of those words, so that they may become acquainted with the object and purport of the lesson.—In the third place, when you have reached the end of the *Short Catechism*, begin anew with the *Large Catechism*, and by means of it furnish the people with fuller and more comprehensive explanations. Explain here at large every Commandment, every Petition, and, indeed, every part, showing the duties which they severally impose, and both the advantages which follow the performance of those duties, and also the dangers and losses which result from a neglect of them." [58] In judging these teaching rules or principles, it must be borne in mind that it was not Luther's idea that the Catechism should be placed in the hands of the child as a text-book; he intended it as a guide or manual for the pastor, teacher, or parent, who was to teach the child orally its contents, first leading the child to commit a certain part to memory and then leading it to understand what it had already learned by heart. Hence the em-

---

58) *Book of Concord*, pp. 360-361.

phasis laid upon definiteness and fixedness of the forms of expression to be used and the simplicity of the language to be employed. It is the principle of repetition and drill which here comes into play. The explanation that followed would be either in the form of a simple, familiar conversational talk or in the form of questions and answers, with a number of illustrations drawn from history or life freely used. The manner of conducting the explanatory part of the teaching process, Luther well illustrates in his *Deutsche Messe* by giving several sample questions and answers. Personally, he supplemented these with his informal *Catechismussprüche*, short and pointed statements of truth learned or the conclusion drawn, clearly and definitely put.[59] He appears himself to have been a master in the use of both the informal, familiar lecture form of instruction and the use of the Socratic method of questioning. It should also be noted that in the directions as quoted above, he points out that teaching should be progressive, proceeding from the simple to the more difficult and complex.

Luther encouraged self-activity on the part of the pupils by means of play, discussions, debates, and even dramatics. Disputations or debates he would have weekly, because they not only test the resourcefulness of the pupil and give practice both in public appearance and public speech, but also lead him to carry on a research into the subject to be debated with greater interest and diligence. Luther, however, wanted the work in debating to be more for the purpose of searching after truth and stimulating the student in this search than a mere seeking after honor.[60] We have here stressed some of the essential principles on which the supposedly modern project method of teaching

---
59) *Werke*, Erlangen ed., vol. LVIII, pp. 251-258.
60) *Tischreden, Werke*, op. cit., vol. LXII, pp. 304-5.

rests. Strange as it may seem, Luther also advocated dramatics as a method of teaching and learning.[61] Whether he would approve of the modern Biblical and religious dramatics advocated by present-day educators is questionable, but at any rate he had no objection to the staging of the dramas of secular literature. Dr. Johann Collarius came to him once and asked his advice on this matter. There was a school teacher in Schlesien who had arranged to play one of the comedies of Terence, and many of the people had objected, contending that it was wrong for a Christian to carry out a play written by a heathen poet. Luther answered that the pupils should be permitted to carry out such plays, since in the first place it gave them an excellent practice in speaking the Latin language, and in the second place, because of the valuable instruction that the people in general might receive from seeing such a play, which would portray manners, customs, ideals, and conduct of people in the various stations of life. To him dramatics portrayed life as pictures and living examples, and hence he found no good reason to object to them.

This brief survey of the pedagogical principles of Luther indicates at least in a fair degree the breadth of vision, keenness of insight, and whole-hearted devotion which characterized this man and tended to make him the power that he was in advancing the cause of a broad, general Christian education and establish it on such foundations that it would endure and continue to unfold and develop under the influence of deepening insight, increasing knowledge, and ripening experience of the generations of educators that were to follow him.

---

61) Ibid., pp. 336-37.

CHAPTER XII

LUTHER'S CONTRIBUTIONS TO CHRISTIAN WORSHIP

In their stimulating and helpful little book, *Training the Devotional Life*, Weigle and Tweedy say: "Training in worship is an essential element in the religious education of our children. It is not enough that they be taught about God and about the issues of life, nor even that they be trained in Christian ways of living. They must be brought into the presence of God, they must learn to know Him for themselves. They must be helped to seek Him and to find Him and to experience the joy of His love and grace." [1]

There has been a growing recognition of these truths stated in this quotation during the past decade among pastors and religious educators. Worship in home and school, its nature, means, methods, and purpose, as well as the training in worship, has recently received an unusual degree of attention in religious periodical literature, and a veritable library of books on the subject has recently appeared fresh from the press, both in this country and abroad. And yet these truths are not new, though given a new emphasis in many quarters in our day. They were known and practiced in Old Testament times, they are stressed throughout the entire New Testament. Jesus both taught them and exemplified them in His life. The early Church knew them and observed them, both in the individual and the congregational life. Worship

---
1) p. 5.

has always been the deepest and fullest expression of the spiritual life and the source of its nurture, inspiration, beauty, and power. But with the development of ecclesiasticism and ceremonialism came also externalism and formalism in worship. The rise of sacerdotalism changed the essential nature of worship, from being a sense of personal fellowship with God, dependence upon Him, satisfying one's spiritual needs, and yielding one's self to God, to become a mere rite, a cultus-act, on the part of the worshipers as a sacred duty toward God, mediated through the Church and its priesthood, and meritorious in character. This was especially the case with the most highly developed form of ceremonialism in the Church, the Mass.

This unevangelical conception of worship manifested itself quite early in the Church in spite of the strenuous opposition by many of the leading churchmen of the day. Already Clement of Alexandria observes: "The disciples of Christ ought so to appear and so to shape their conduct in their daily living, as, for the sake of propriety, they strive to appear in the Church; they should really *be* and not merely *seem* to be such—so gentle, so devout, so amiable. But I know not how it is, that with the place, they change their appearance and their manners, just as it is said of the polypus, that it changes its color with the roots to which it clings. They lay aside the spiritual demeanor which they assumed in the Church as soon as they leave it, and put themselves on a level with the multitude with whom they mingle. They convict themselves of insincerity and show what was really the temper of their hearts, by laying off their assumed mask of decorum. They profess to honor the Word of God, but leave it behind them in the place where they heard it."[2] The Word of God became dethroned from its

---

2) Quoted by Richard and Painter, *Christian Worship*, p. 62.

important place in the public worship, and tradition and elaborate ritual took its place. The devotion and fidelity to the Church and its man-made ordinances were substituted for the personal relation, devotion, and fidelity to Christ and His Word. Saints and Saints' Days, rites, and ceremonials were multiplied, and the language of the Church was substituted for the vernacular, until the whole public worship had become one endless round of external and formal legalistic ordinances and observances. To observe these ordinances and practices was regarded as meritorious and counted towards salvation, while the failure to observe them necessitated the infliction of penalties on the part of the Church and led even to the forfeiture of salvation on the part of the individual. "Christ was practically forgotten or ignored. Salvation was linked to the supposed divinely appointed order of the Church. Worship was little else than the formal execution of that order. In all its parts it was essentially a doing and giving unto God for reconciliation. The Church, led by the Holy Ghost, it was said, had canonized the saints and had constituted the divine order of worship. It was necessary to salvation to believe what she taught, to do what her priests prescribed, to die under her benediction." [3]

It was such ideas and such practices of worship which Luther had to contend with throughout his reformatory work. He was thoroughly familiar with the theory and practice of worship, in the home and the school, in the convent, and the Church, and he had learned by painful experience how unscriptural, hollow, and unsatisfying such worship was. But he had also a keen appreciation of the many significant and abiding values, the forms of public worship possessed when properly purged, truly understood, and rightly

---

3) Ibid., p. 102.

used and cultivated. He also realized the psychological difficulties involved in drastic and radical reforms. Hence, he proceeded slowly and cautiously with his reforms of Christian worship. In his *Formula Missae* he says, regarding this matter: "Hitherto in my books and sermons to the people I have tried first to call away their hearts from impious opinions in regard to ceremonies, and thought that I was doing something Christian and advantageous by causing the destruction, without violence, of the abomination which Satan had set up in the holy place by the Man of Sin. Hence I attempted nothing by violence or by authority, nor did I exchange the old for the new, for I always hesitated and feared on account of persons weak in faith, from whom the old and familiar mode of worshiping God cannot suddenly be taken away in favor of a new and untried mode." [4]

LUTHER'S CONCEPTION OF WORSHIP.—To Luther worship was the natural outgrowth and constant expression of the personal religious life. It expresses itself in confession of faith, confession of sin, prayer, supplication, praise, thanksgiving, and offering or sacrifices on the part of the worshipers. In the public worship, God meets His people through His means of grace, and they come to Him with their joint confession, prayers, praises, thanksgiving, and sacrifices. The Word and the Sacraments have, therefore, the chief place in the divine worship. Through them God bestows His grace and spiritual blessings. The worshiper is instructed, edified, and inspired, experiences the divine fellowship, and gives expression to his needs, dependence, joy, and gratitude. The social element had a high place in Luther's conception of the public worship, and he stresses again and again the fact that fellowship with Christ also means fellow-

---
4) Ibid., p. 165.

ship of believers. He even asserts that to do good to one's fellow man and render him service is true worship. "How can God," he says, "place the service to be rendered to Himself nearer to you and make it easier for you than by counting your love to your neighbor and the good done to him as if rendered to Himself. That is a wonderful doctrine, that if you do good to your neighbor, that is an act of worship and done unto God Himself. . . . Know this, that to serve God is nothing else than to serve your neighbor with deeds of love, whether child, woman, servant, friend, or foe, without the least distinction, whoever needs your help in body and soul and where you are able to help physically and spiritually, that is worship and good works." [5]

Luther laid special emphasis on the pedagogical value of worship. Hence the stress he lays on preaching and catechisation in the church and the reading and meditation on the Word and the instruction of the children in the home. In his Order of Service he especially provides for the catechisation of the children as a part of the divine service. The whole worship was to be designed so as to train and nurture the Christian life. The missionary character of the worship he also emphasized. The worship was to be conducted in the language of the people in order that they might join in it and thoroughly appreciate it. Yet he advocated the use of more than one language whenever possible. He in no way desires to banish the Latin language from the church service. He says in his *German Mass*: "For it concerns me to do everything for the young, and if I were able, and the Greek and the Hebrew language were as familiar to us as the Latin, and had as much

---

5) Rietschel, *Lehrbuch der Liturgik*, vol. I, p. 33. See also Kretzmann, *Christian Art*, pp. 275-83.

fine music and hymnology as the Latin has, then should Mass be celebrated, sung, and read one Sunday after another in all four languages—German, Latin, Greek, and Hebrew. I do not at all agree with those who give themselves to only one language and despise all others. For I should like to bring up such youth and people as could be of service to Christ also in foreign lands and speak with the people so that it may not go with us as with the Waldenses in Bohemia, who have so confined their faith to their language that they cannot talk clearly and intelligently with anyone unless he learned their language beforehand. But not so did the Holy Ghost in the beginning. He did not wait until all the world came to Jerusalem and learned Hebrew, but gave all kinds of tongues to the preaching office so that the apostles could speak wherever they came. I prefer to follow this example; and it is also proper to exercise the young in many languages. Who knows how God may use them in the course of time?" [6]

FIXED ORDER OF SERVICE.—Luther believed in a fixed order of service, since he desired to secure the highest possible degree of objectivity and uniformity in the worship and to educate the people in general, but especially the young, in true Christian worship and pious devotional exercises. He stressed the pedagogical and missionary value of a fixed and regular order, holding that those who are already Christians need no such order, but that it is necessary for those who are not yet Christians in order that they may become so. Yet he does not want a fixed order of service to become an infringement of personal liberty or a burden to the conscience. Absolute uniformity is not essential. He desires, however, to guard against uncontrolled subjectivism, fads, and whims in the con-

---

6) Richard and Painter, *Christian Worship*, p. 187.

gregational worship of God. His views of the order of service are well and quite fully stated in his preface to the *Deutsche Messe* in the following words: "Before all things I kindly beseech, even for God's sake, all those who desire to see or follow this our order in divine service, that they, by no means, make a necessary law out of it, nor entangle or bind any one's conscience therewith; but that in accordance with Christian freedom they use their pleasure, how, where, and when, and how long the circumstances suit or demand it. For we also do not publish it with the intention to control any one therein, or to rule with laws, but because everywhere the German Mass and divine service are insisted upon, and great complaint and scandal exist concerning the manifold forms of the new Masses. Everyone makes his own, some with good intention, some also from forwardness, that they also may bring something new into vogue, and shine among others, and not be bad workmen. Thus it everywhere turns out with Christian liberty, that few use it otherwise than to their own pleasure or advantage, and not to the glory of God and the good of his neighbor.

"But although it rests upon every one's conscience how he uses such liberty (and no one is to hinder or forbid the same), yet it should be seen to, that his liberty is and shall be the servant of charity and one's neighbor. Wherever it, therefore, happens that men take offense or go astray because of such various usage, we are truly bound to restrict liberty, and as far as it is possible, to labor and to forbear, in order that people may be made better and not be offended in us. Since, therefore, there is nothing in this external service involving our conscience before God, and yet it may be made useful to our neighbor, we should in love, as Paul teaches, endeavor to be of one mind, and in the best way possible to be of like forms and ceremonies, just as all Christians have one Baptism, one Sacrament, and to no person is given of God a special one.

"Yet I will not ask those who already have their good order of service, or who through God's grace can make a better one, to let it go and yield to us. For it is not my intention that all Germany should accept precisely our Wittenberg order. It has indeed never been in the past that the endowed institutions, cloisters, and parishes were the same in all points; but it would be excellent if in every principality divine service were conducted in the same form, and the surrounding towns and villages directly shared with a city; whether those in other provinces also held the same, or added something special thereto, should be free and uncensured. For, in short, we institute such orders not for the sake of those who already are Christians. For they need none of these things, for which also one does not live; but they live for the sake of us, who are not Christians, that they may make us Christians, for these have their worship in spirit.

"But we must have such order of service for the sake of those who are yet to become Christians or to become stronger, just as a Christian does not need Baptism, the Word and sacraments as a Christian (for he already has all things), but as a sinner. But most of all it is done on account of the simple and the young, who are to be and must be exercised daily and educated in the Scripture and God's Word, that accustomed to Scripture they may become skilful, fluent and versed therein, in order to represent their faith, and in the course of time to instruct others and help to increase the Kingdom of Christ: for the sake of such must we read, sing, preach, write and poetize, and if it would be helpful and advantageous thereto,

I would let all the bells ring, and all the organs play, and everything sound that can sound."[7]

CHURCH BUILDINGS.—While Luther did not develop and lay down any new principles of church architecture, he clearly pointed out the essential elements that enter into the true worship of God as the preaching of the Word, the administration of the sacraments, hymn singing, prayer and offering, and thus directed the future trend in church building away from the idea of providing for the purely liturgical performance on the part of priests merely, which was chiefly to be seen by the congregation, to the preaching type of church buildings, the type which would best facilitate the preaching and the hearing of the Word of God. He also did away with the Catholic distinction between clergy and laity, and consequently obliterated the Catholic distinction between the choir section and the auditorium section of the church. The former was the place of the altar, the clergy, and the choir, and was regarded as more holy than the latter. There was in Luther's time no immediate need of any new church buildings, so the question of church architecture did not arise. The first church to be built in Germany after the beginning of the Reformation was the church or chapel of the Castle of Torgau, which Luther himself dedicated in 1544. It was unlike the churches of the time in not having a closed off choir or the altar placed to the west, but this difference was due rather to practical considerations than any new architectural principles.[8]

ART IN WORSHIP.—Luther was himself a great lover of art and believed in its use both in the church buildings and church worship. In this respect he dif-

---

7) Richard and Painter, *Christian Worship*, pp. 185-6.
8) Rietschel. *Lehrbuch der Liturgik*. vol. I, p. 109: Kretzmann, *Christian Art*, pp. 74-76.

fered materially from the Reformed leaders. "I am not of the opinion," he says, "that through the Gospel all art shall be struck to the ground and destroyed as certain super-spirituals pretend, but I will that all art, especially music, shall be used in the service of Him who has created and given it." [9] As to pictures he held that, since there are many word paintings given in Scripture of God, angels, man and beast, it is not wrong to have paintings on the walls to aid the memory and give clearer and better conceptions.[10] Luther's views on art in Christian worship have had a far reaching influence not only within the branch of the Church which bears his name but also within the various branches of the Reformed churches which were for a long time strongly opposed to the use of art in any form whatsoever in connection with the church and church worship.

SUNDAYS AND HOLIDAYS.—The legalistic and meritorious conception of Sundays and holidays current in his day, Luther rejected entirely, and he removed from the calendar a large number of saint and other festive days. No wonder a recent Catholic writer regards the havoc Luther wrought in the calendar of saints' days with such concern.[11] Already in 1520 Luther in his *Sermon on Good Works* expresses the wish that all holidays but Sunday might be done away with in the interest of thrift, morality, and godliness. In his letter to the German nobles of the same year he expresses similar sentiments. He retained Sunday and the chief festivals of the Church Year as Christmas, Easter, Pentecost, the Day of the Circumcision of Jesus (New Year), Epiphany, and Ascension. He also favored the retention of such festivals as the Annun-

---

9) Rietschel, *Lehrbuch der Liturgik*, vol. I, p. 69.
10) Ibid., vol. I, pp. 69-70; Zöckler, *Handbuck d. th. Wissenschaft*, vol. IV, p. 410.
11) See p. 277.

ciation, the Purification of Mary, the days of John the Baptist and the apostles, and Saint Michael's Day. But on all these days God alone should be praised and glorified for the benefits He bestowed upon His people through these servants.[12]

His views on Sunday and its observance are clearly set forth in his explanation of the Third Commandment (Fourth, Reformed) in his *Large Catechism*. "The word Sabbath (Feiertag) is derived from the Hebrew word which properly signifies to rest (feiren), i. e., to abstain from labor. Hence we are accustomed to say, in German, Feier-abend machen, i. e., to cease working, or give a holy evening (sanctify the Sabbath). Now, in the Old Testament, God separated the Seventh Day, and appointed it for rest, and commanded that it should be regarded holy above all others. According to this external observance, this commandment was given to the Jews alone, that they should abstain from toilsome work, and rest, so that both man and beast might recuperate, and might not be debilitated by unremitting labor. Although they afterwards interpreted this too strictly, and grossly abused it, so that they traduced and could not endure in Christ those works which they themselves were accustomed to do thereon, as we read in the Gospel; just as though the commandment were fulfilled in this, viz., that no external (manual) work whatever be performed, which was not the meaning, but, as we shall hear, that they sanctify the Sabbath or Day of Rest.

"This commandment, therefore, according to its gross sense, does not pertain to us Christians; for it is altogether an external matter, like the other ordinances of the Old Testament, which were bound to

---

12) Rietschel, *Lehrbuch der Liturgik*, vol. I, pp. 205-6; Kretzmann, *Christian Art*, pp. 369-78.

particular customs, persons, times, and places, and all of which have now been made free through Christ.

"But to derive hence Christian instruction for the simple as to what, in this commandment, God requires, let it be observed that we keep the festal days, not for the sake of intelligent and learned Christians (for they have no need of this observance) but first of all for bodily causes and necessities, which nature teaches and requires; and for the common people, man-servants and maid-servants, who are occupied the whole week with their work and trade, that for a day they may forbear, in order to rest and be refreshed.

"Secondly, and most especially, that on such day of rest (since otherwise it cannot be accomplished) time and opportunity be taken to attend divine service, so that we meet to hear and treat of God's Word, and afterward to praise God in singing and prayer.

"But this, I say, is not so limited to any time, as with the Jews, that it must be just on this or that day; for in itself no one day is better than another, and this should indeed occur daily; but since the mass of people cannot give such attendance, there must be at least one day in the week set apart. But since from of old Sunday (the Lord's Day) has been appointed for this purpose, we also should continue the same, that everything be done in harmonious order, and no one, by unnecessary innovation, create disorder.

"Therefore the simple meaning of the commandment is this, viz., since holidays are observed, such observance be devoted to hearing God's Word, so that the special employment of this day be the ministry of the Word for the young and the mass of poor people; yet that the observance of rest be not so strictly interpreted as to forbid any other incidental and necessary work." [13]

---

13) *Book of Concord*, p. 401-2.

FAMILY WORSHIP.—Luther himself set his followers a splendid example of family worship. Morning and evening he conducted devotions at the table, using especially the *Psalter* and the *Small Catechism* as devotional books.[14] His children were taught to say their table prayers and often received religious instruction from him at the table.[15] On Sundays, especially when he was ill and could not go to church himself, he gathered his family and other members of his household about him for singing, prayer, and a brief exposition of some Scripture passage. Thus arose the collection of sermonettes known as his *Hauspostille*, published in 1542.[16] Both this collection of sermons and Luther's *Kirchenpostille* have been used very extensively in family worship and are still in use in many quarters.

Even before he established his home, Luther sought to promote both individual and family devotional life. His *Betbüchlein*, prayer book, appeared as early as 1522. In the preface to this devotional book he complains of the spirit and content of the current prayer books, of which he mentions two by name, and offers his own as a substitute and help to the cultivation of the devotional life on the purely evangelical basis. This prayer book contains brief explanations of the Ten Commandments, the Creed, and the Lord's Prayer, prayers for various occasions, a number of psalms translated into German, a few meditations, and the story of Christ's Passion.[17] In 1535 he prepared a brief devotional guide for his friend Peter, a barber.[18] In a number of his sermons and Scripture expositions he stresses the importance of family prayer, the Chris-

---
14) Mathesius, *Historien*, p. 210.
15) Ibid., p. 230.
16) Ibid., p. 210. See chapter X, p. 195.
17) *Werke*, Weimar ed., vol. X. 2, p. 375 seq.
18) *Werke*, St. Louis ed., vol. X, p. 1394 seq.

tian father and mother being a priest and priestess. By his hymns as well as by his devotional books, Luther made contributions to the daily devotions before the family altar of inestimable value.

LITURGICAL WRITINGS.—The liturgical writings of Luther are numerous and important. Only the more significant of these can be mentioned here. We shall first notice his three orders of divine service.

1. *Concerning the Arrangement of Divine Service in the Congregation.* This order of service was prepared at the request of the congregation of Leisnig in the spring of 1523. It was perhaps the first attempt to introduce a German order of service. Whether it was prepared before or after Carlstadt had introduced German services on week-days at the castle church of Wittenberg, March 23, 1523, or not, is a mooted question.[19] In the introduction Luther mentions three serious abuses which had crept into the church service, namely, the setting aside of the Word of God, the introduction of fables and lies to take its place, and the making of the divine service a meritorious work. These abuses, he contends, must be removed. God's Word must be given its proper place; fables and lies and the doctrine of works must be banished, and the principles of worship, according to Psalm 102:21-22, and I Cor. 14:31, must be observed, for "where God's Word is not preached, it is better neither to sing, read, nor assemble."[20] The order of service provided is very simple, and is intended primarily for week-day services, early in the morning and in the evening. It provides for hymn singing, the reading of lessons from the Old Testament in the morning, and from the New Testament in the evening, a half-hour exposition of the lesson read, and prayer. While it may not be pos-

---
19) *Werke*, Weimar ed., vol. XII, pp. 31-32.
20) Ibid., p. 35.

CHRISTIAN WORSHIP

sible for the whole congregation to be present at these daily services, he urges that the ministry, teachers, and pupils at least be present. The Sacraments may also be administered during these services if so desired. On Sunday the service should be fuller, removing legends and other objectionable features and retaining in the main the hymns and responses. The congregation is given free hands in determining how much or how little of the former order is to be used. The principal thing, however, is to give the preaching of the Word the most prominent place.[21]

2. The Latin Order of Worship (*Formula Missae et Communionis*). This order of service was prepared especially at the urgent request of Luther's intimate friend, Nicolaus Hausmann, pastor at Zwickau. A copy was sent to Hausmann under date of December 4, 1523. In the letter which accompanied it Luther says: "I am sending you the *Formula Missae* which I have been able to get up. It is a short but easy book."[22] This order of service was composed in the Latin and followed the traditional Catholic order, the objectional features being removed and the preaching of the Word given its proper place. At the request of Hausmann, a German translation was later provided, not by Luther himself, but under his direction and approval, by Paul Speratus, and published at Wittenberg. Another German translation appeared about the same time at Nuremberg. The translator of the Nuremberg edition is unknown, but generally supposed to have been Osiander. The first edition of the translation by Speratus contained a hymn by Agricola, and subsequent editions contained hymns both by Luther and Agricola.

---
21) Ibid., pp. 35-37; Richard and Painter, *Christian Worship*, pp. 159-163.
22) Smith and Jacobs, *Luther's Correspondence*, vol. II, p. 210.

3. The German order of Service (*Deutsche Messe*). German orders of service had already been introduced at various places[23] before Luther composed his *Deutsche Messe*, so his was not the first such order provided. Luther was pressed, however, on every hand, both by the clergy and the civil authorities, to prepare a German order of service which might be generally accepted and thus bring about some degree of uniformity in the church services throughout Lutheran Germany. His friend Hausmann, at whose urgent request the *Formula Missae* was composed, was just as insistent that Luther prepare a German order and take steps to bring about uniformity. Luther was busy with other very pressing matters and also felt that he was not equal to the task, as such an order had to be provided with the necessary music for the chants and also with proper hymns. In a letter to Hausmann under date of November 17, 1524, he says concerning this matter: "I hope for a German mass, but can scarcely promise it, for I am unequal to the task, which calls for music as well as the spirit. Meanwhile I grant any one permission to use his own judgment until Christ shall give us something else. I do not think it well to hold a council of our party for the purpose of establishing unity in ceremonies. It would set a bad example, however zealous and well-meant the effort were, as all the councils of the Church, from the very beginning prove. Even the Apostolic

---

[23] Carlstadt introduced the German language into the services at Wittenberg as early as 1521. Wolfgang Wissenberg of Basel and Johann Schwebel of Pforzheim introduced German services into their churches in 1522, but nothing is known as to the form and content of these services. Kaspar Kantz of Nördlingen prepared a German service the same year. It was published in revised form two years later. In 1523 Thomas Münzer prepared a German service for the church at Alstedt. The following year German services were introduced in Wertheim, Wendelstein, Reutlingen, Sonnewalde, Reval, Altenburg, Leisnig, Hirschburg, Weimar, Schweinitz, Strassburg, Nuremberg, and Königsberg, and during the year 1525 in Erfurt and other places. See *Werke*, Weimar ed., vol. XIX, pp. 43-52; Rietschel, *Lehrbuch der Liturgik*, vol. I, pp. 402-409.

CHRISTIAN WORSHIP

Council dealt more with works and traditions than with faith, but in later councils there was no discussion of faith, but always of opinions and questions, so that the very word 'council' is to me almost as suspicious and distasteful as the word 'free will.' If one church does not wish to imitate another in these external things, why should it be compelled to do so by decrees of councils which are soon converted into laws and snares for souls? Let one church, therefore, imitate another of its own accord, or else let it be allowed to use its own customs; only let the unity of Spirit be preserved in faith and Word, however great the diversity and variety in the flesh and in the elements of the world." [24]

About a year later he replies to another urgent request from Hausmann for a German order of service in the following words: "Keep on with what you are doing and put up with what you can, my dear Nicholas. I am altogether taken up with my reply to Erasmus. I know that the parishes must be reformed and uniform ceremonies introduced. I am now wrestling with the problem and shall ask the aid of the elector." [25] Not very long after this letter was written, the first draft of the *Deutsche Messe* was sent to Elector Frederick the Wise, who, at Luther's request, sent him his court musicians, Konrad Ruppf and Johann Walther, to assist him with the musical part of the service. On Sunday, October 29, 1525, the first step to introduce the new German order of service at Wittenberg was taken. At the conclusion of his sermon on that day Luther laid the matter before the whole congregation. The following Christmas Day it was used in full and finally accepted. Hausmann had also expected to introduce the service on Christmas

---
24) Smith, op. cit., p. 259.
25) Ibid., pp. 337-38.

Day in his own church, but the printing of the service was delayed, so that the first copies did not come off the press until the first week of January, 1526. So great was the demand for this order of service that no less than three editions and at least seven reprints were published during the year 1526. Separate reprints were also made of three parts of the service, the one dealing with how to lead the children to God's Word and worship, another on the brief exposition of the Lord's Prayer, and the third an abridgment prepared especially for the laity of the order of service proper. In the Erfurt Hymnal of 1527 and the Zwichau Hymnal of the following year this brief order of service was printed.

The *Deutsche Messe*, like the *Formula Missae*, follows the traditional order in the main throughout. The German service is, however, a more free rendering and more thoroughly evangelical. The German language is employed throughout. It was not always carried out in the actual worship in the German language in full, not even in the city of Wittenberg. Music was provided for the hymns to be sung as well as for the chanting of the collects, the Epistle, and Gospel lessons. This order has become the basis of all later Lutheran orders of service.[26]

MINOR LITURGICAL WRITINGS.—Besides the three principal liturgical works described above, Luther also wrote some minor ones of considerable importance.

1. The Latin and German Litany. Luther worked over the Latin Litany of the Catholic Church, purging it from some of its objectionable features. This was published as *Latina Litania Correcta*. From this cor-

---

26) *Werke*, Weimar ed., vol. XIX, pp. 43-133; Rietschel, *Lehrbuch der Liturgik*, vol. I, pp. 409-412; Richard and Painter, *Christian Worship*, pp. 184-202.

rected or revised Latin Litany, he prepared a German translation. Both were published in 1529, but no copies of the original edition is extant so far as known. The exact date of publication is not known, but this work was ready and in use at Wittenberg as early as February 13, 1529. The Litany was provided with music throughout, and in addition was supplied with five versicles and three prayers in the German version and five versicles and five prayers in the Latin. It was early printed in the *Small Catechism*, the hymn books, church ordinances, Luther's Prayer Book, and the Marriage Service, so that it was given considerable publicity.[27]

2. Baptismal Service (*Taufbüchlein*). This was a form provided to be used in administering the Sacrament of Baptism. It followed almost immediately upon the publication of the first order of service noted above, being published in 1523. A new and thoroughly revised edition was published in 1526. The first edition was essentially a free translation of the Catholic baptismal ritual then in use, some parts, as the *Ave Maria*, being omitted. It followed the form generally used at Wittenberg at the time. The revised form of 1526 is considerably briefer than the original. It contains the exorcism, but some of the symbolic actions contained in the original form are omitted. The appendix to the version of 1523, in which Luther gives some reasons for the translation of the baptismal formula into German and some general admonitions regarding Baptism, appears somewhat reconstructed as an introduction in the version of 1526.[28] A very brief baptismal formula, differing from the two already mentioned, is also attributed to Luther by some, but

---

27) *Werke*, Weimar ed., vol. XXX. 3, pp. 1-42.
28) Ibid., vol. XII, pp. 38-48; vol. XIX, pp. 531-54.

it is rejected by the best of Luther scholars as not being genuine.[29]

3. Marriage Service (*Traubüchlein*). When this service was composed is not definitely known. It was in all probability published separately in 1529. In the same year it appears as an appendix to the *Small Catechism*. It consists of a brief introduction on the nature of marriage, the Christian's entrance into it, and gives reasons for composing this form. The service itself is very simple, only one question being addressed to each of the parties. Will you have N. N. to be your wedded husband (or wife)? Then follow in succession the exchange of rings, the declaration by the pastor, that the parties are husband and wife, Scripture reading, admonition, and prayer. It has become the pattern of all subsequent forms of the marriage service used in the Lutheran Church.[30]

LUTHER'S PRINCIPLES OF WORSHIP.—Briefly stated, we may summarize Luther's principles of worship as set forth in his liturgical writings as follows:

1. Christian worship is not a legal institution imposed upon man by God, by his relation to which man may either merit or forfeit salvation, but it is an intercommunion and fellowship between God and His people.

2. In the Christian worship God meets His people, the congregation, with His divine grace and power through the means of grace, the Word and sacraments, for their instruction and edification, and the people meet Him with their supplications, praise, thanksgiving, adoration, and offerings.

3. The chief objective elements of worship are the reading and preaching of the Word and the administration of the Sacraments.

---

29) Ibid., vol. VI, pp. 49-52.
30) Ibid., vol. XXX, 3, pp. 43-80.

4. The chief subjective elements of worship are the personal faith, devotion, and self-surrender on the part of the members of the congregation expressed in terms of prayer, praise, thanksgiving, and offerings.

5. The worship is pedagogical, instructing, correcting, and edifying the believers, young and old, and it is missionary, proclaiming God's truths and exemplifying them in the faith and devotion of the believers as a testimony and invitation to the unbelievers.

6. Fixed forms and stated times of worship are necessary not because of any merit attached to them, but because they promote good order and decency in the worship of God and instruct the young and ignorant.

7. Orders of service, clerical vestments, and church ordinances are to be regarded as adiafora and must not be insisted on, so as to burden the conscience, yet chaos and unbridled subjectivism must be guarded against.

8. Orders of divine worship must provide for the fullest possible participation of the congregation as a whole, especially through the congregational singing and responses.

9. Public worship must be so arranged and carried out that the instruction and edification of the children and young people are not neglected.

10. Art, especially music, should be given a large place in the Christian worship.

11. Private and family devotions are necessary to the cultivation and sustentation of the Christian life and the Christian nurture of children.

12. The outcomes of worship are increasing knowledge of spiritual things, deeper and firmer convictions, spiritual edification, and pious and dutiful living.

INFLUENCE OF THESE PRINCIPLES.—Even a casual examination of works on liturgics and Christian worship, Reformed as well as Lutheran, and the common practices within the various branches of the Protestant Church, will reveal the fact that Luther's principles of Christian worship have had a far-reaching and beneficent influence on Christian worship generally. Even the Catholic Church has benefitted by them, especially in regard to preaching. While the relative importance of the sermon and the liturgy remains essentially the same, the liturgy still being of the greater importance, yet the amount and quality of preaching and even the general tenor of the whole worship have been considerably affected. Dargan very truly says: "Neither the Catholic Church as a whole nor its preaching in particular was the same after the Reformation as before it, not what they would have been without that great movement."[31] It is, of course, true that a number of these principles were also held by many of Luther's contemporaries, both Lutheran and Reformed, but none of them succeeded as well as Luther to hold to the essentials and strike a happy balance between two opposite extremes, a fanatical subjectivism on the one hand and an equally fanatical superspiritualism on the other, the former emphasizing feeling, spirit, and freedom, thus undervaluing both Word and Sacraments, the latter placing a one-sided emphasis upon the Word and its preaching as the only legitimate part of divine service, rejecting liturgy, art, and historic continuity in form, time, and place. It is interesting to note how these extremes have tended toward modification in the direction of Luther's position, except in the case of the high church party in the Church of England, which has tended more and more toward Roman Catholic ritualism.

---

31) *History of Preaching*, vol. I, p. 525.

CHRISTIAN WORSHIP

While many leaders in the Lutheran Church have not always been true to Luther's great principles of Christian worship, but have tended either in the direction of ritualism and formalism or toward a disregard for ritual altogether, many Reformed leaders have been tending away from both extreme spiritualism and extreme liturgical bareness toward embracing more and more the principles of worship enunciated by Luther. The following words of two distinguished Methodist theologians express essential agreement with Luther's principles of worship: "The essential elements of Protestant worship are the sermon, which is based upon the Word of God, the united prayer, and singing of the congregation, and the benediction, which concludes the service. The highest point of Protestant worship is attained in the periodical celebration of the Lord's Supper, whose leading characteristic is that of a feast. The distribution of the various liturgical observances, the relation they are to sustain toward each other, and the more or less festal character they are to bear will be determined by the ecclesiastical year, the periodically recurring festal season which it includes, and the wisdom and care of the pastor, all forms of art which have no immediate relation to the living Word are referred to the background at this point and are designated at most to promote an auxiliary object, not directly aiming at an increase of devotion." [32]

One of the significant trends of the present time, when ultra-liberalism in theology is sweeping over the country, robbing the pulpit of its vital message and substituting stones for bread in the form of an abstracted religion of humanitarianism, destructive criticism, sowing seeds of doubt and skepticism, modern

---

32) Crooks and Hurst, *Theological Encyclopedia and Methodology*, p. 506.

Pelagianism, and the doctrine of salvation by character, greater and greater efforts are being put forth to embellish churches and forms of worship, placing special emphasis upon music and art in worship and the introduction of clerical and choral vestments. With the vaning of the pulpit and its Gospel message, there comes into play a new emphasis upon ritualism, with a strong esthetic and emotional appeal. Omitting, as this tendency does, the essential objective elements in Christian worship, and catering primarily to the esthetic and emotional in man, it will of necessity ultimately develop into a mere esthetic and emotional cult and numerous varieties of religious subjectivism.

HYMN SINGING AND WORSHIP.—"Be filled with the Spirit," says Paul, "speaking one to another in psalms and hymns and spiritual songs, singing and making melody with your heart to the Lord." [33] Singing has always been an indispensable part of Christian worship, the public worship in particular. As a result the rich treasury of Hebrew psalms and the hymns and chants of the Church have arisen. As Sachsse observes, the religious feeling has always found expression in song, and song has again ever been a powerful means for kindling similar religious emotions in others. In a rich heritage of psalms and hymns, believers have always found expression for their varied religious emotions and experiences, and through their hymn singing they have wielded a potent, wholesome, and significant educational, evangelizing, and edifying influence. "Christian hymns," says Sachsse, "form a constituent part of Christian instruction, both because they are capable of kindling and enlivening the religious emotions and because an appreciation of the hymns enables the pupils to enter into the very spirit

33) *Eph.* 5:19.

of the public worship. It is a well known fact that many evangelical Christians derive their spiritual edification in their homes mostly from the hymn book, and that they in times of spiritual crises find in them their chief consolation. It would, therefore, be a serious lack in the Christian instruction if the church hymns were to be neglected." [34]

LUTHER'S HYMNS.—As a true educator, Luther recognized the educational and devotional value of Christian hymns and their significance in the public worship. He therefore very early in his work of reformation set himself the task to provide suitable hymns in the vernacular for both home and church, set to such melodies as the people cherished and were able to sing. It is generally conceded that his activity as a hymn writer began in 1523. He may have made some attempts before this time, but there seems to be no hymns of earlier date among those attributed to him. His deep concern about providing appropriate hymns for the people is clearly indicated in his letter to Spalatin under date of January 14, 1524, in which he says: "There is a plan afoot to follow the example of the prophets and the fathers of the early Church and compose for the common people German psalms, that is spiritual songs, so that the Word of God may remain among the people in the form of song also. We are seeking everywhere for poets, and since you are gifted with such knowledge of the German language and command so elegant a style, cultivated by much use, I beg that you will work with us in this matter and try to translate some one of the psalms into a hymn, like the sample of my own which you have here. But I wish that you would leave out all new words and words that are only used at court. In order to be understood by the people, only the

---
34) *Die Lehre von der kirchlichen Erziehung*, p. 366.

simplest and commonest words should be sung, but they should also be pure and apt and should give a clear sense, as near as possible to that of the Psalter. The translation, therefore, must be free, keeping the sense, but letting the words go and rendering them by other appropriate words. I lack the gift to do what I wish to see done, and so I shall try you and see if you are a Heman or an Asaph or a Jeduthun. I would make the same request of Johann von Dolzig, whose German is also rich and elegant, but only in case you both have leisure, which I suspect is not the case just now."[35]

Neither Spalatin nor Dolzig complied with Luther's request, but he secured some assistance from others. At the time when Luther wrote this letter he had undoubtedly already published at least four of his hymns in the so-called *Achtliederbuch* (Book of Eight Hymns), the first evangelical hymnbook to be published. This collection was published by a Nuremberg printer and contained, besides four hymns by Luther, three by Paul Speratus and one by an anonymous writer.[36] These hymns were, no doubt, composed in 1523 and printed separately for use in the church at Wittenberg.

The event which appears to have caused Luther to discover his poetic abilities was the martyrdom of two young Augustinians at Brussels, July 1, 1523, the first Lutheran victims of the Dominican inquisition. These men were burned to death at the stake, courageously reciting the Apostles' Creed and singing the ancient doxology of the Church, "Te Deum Laudamus" (Thee God We Praise, Thy Name We Bless). The news of the martyrdom of these two young men, Heinrich Voes and Johannes Esch, spread like wild-fire

---
35) *Luther's Correspondence*, vol. II, pp. 211-12.
36) *Werke*, Weimar ed., vol. XXXV, pp. 1, 14, 97.

by letter and pamphlet. Luther was quite familiar with the persecutions of his followers in Holland and had already written them several letters of encouragement. When news of the burning at the stake of these two Augustinian followers reached him, he was touched to the quick and wrote the Christians in Holland a very comforting and encouraging letter.[37] About the same time as he wrote this letter, he also wrote a poem about the martyrdom of his followers, "Ein neues Lied wir heben an," which, like the letter mentioned, is full of praise and joy because of the victorious faith of the two martyrs. From now on Luther manifests a remarkable poetic productivity, in spite of his many cares and labors, revealing another aspect of his many-sided genius. In addition to the hymns already mentioned, there appeared in print no less than nineteen during the year 1524. Eighteen hymns, including the martyr hymn and the four in the Book of Eight Hymns, appeared in a hymnbook called the *Erfurt Enchiridion*, and the Wittenberg hymnbook of Johann Walther contained six more.

It is not definitely known how many hymns Luther composed, some hymns attributed to him not being regarded as genuine. In a hymnbook published in 1545, Luther himself disclaims authorship of a hymn ascribed to him.[38] There are thirty-six or thirty-seven hymns which are generally regarded as being Luther's. Besides these, he composed a number of German and Latin rimes and poems.

LUTHER'S BEST KNOWN HYMN. — Luther's best

---

37) See Smith and Jacobs, *Luther's Correspondence*, vol. II, p. 194.
38) The Erlangen edition of Luther's works, vol. LVI, credits him with thirty-nine hymns, and the Weimar edition, vol. XXXV, with only thirty-six. Julian, in his *Dictionary of Hymnology*, p. 414, ascribes thirty-seven hymns to Luther, while the collection of *Hymns of Luther* by Bacon & Allen contains only thirty-six. This is also the number of hymns credited to Luther by the Lutheran hymnologist, Prof. John Dahle, in his recent work, *A Library of Christian Hymns*, vol. I, pp. 68-82, and by Lambert, *Luther's Hymns*.

known hymn is "Ein feste Burg ist unser Gott" (A Mighty Fortress is Our God), the Battlehymn of the Reformation. Just when this hymn was written is still a mooted question. It has been assigned dates varying from 1521 to 1529, as it first appeared in Klug's Hymnal on the latter date. It is most likely that it was written shortly after the Diet of Spires in 1529, at which further unjust and oppressive strictures on religious liberty and freedom of conscience were enacted. It is based on Psalm 46, whose spirit and sentiments it reflects. This "Marseillaise of the Reformation" has become the most popular and most widely disseminated Christian hymn. It appears in every church hymnal of any consequence, except, of course, Catholic hymnals. It has been translated into no less than 167 languages and dialects. "Only two other hymns have passed the hundred mark in the number of their translations, namely, Toplady's 'Rock of Ages,' with 128 versions, and Martin Rinkert's, 'Now Thank We all Our God,' with 104 versions." [39] The first translation into the English language was made by Miles Coverdale in 1539, "Our God is a Defense and Toure." Since then over seventy translations into English have been made. The following reproductions of the first two lines give some idea of the variations in the English translations of the hymn:

> *God is our refuge in distress,*
> *Our strong defence and armor.*
>
> *A fortress firm is God our Lord,*
> *A sure defence and weapon.*
>
> *A mountain fastness is our God,*
> *On which our souls are planted.*
>
> *A safe stronghold our God is still,*

---

[39] Carl Doving, *Lutheran World Almanac for 1928*, p. 88. Rev. Carl Doving of Chicago has for years carried on researches in hym-

*A tower of safety is our God,
His sword and shield defend us.
A fortress firm and steadfast rock*

The stirring music which is inseparable from this hymn, no matter into what language it has been translated, is Luther's own composition.

THE PURPOSE AND CHARACTER OF LUTHER'S HYMNS.—The hymns of Luther were primarily composed to enrich the German public worship, instruct, edify, inspire, and give expression to the new-found faith and consequent joy and praise of the believer. He states his purposes quite fully in his introduction to the Hymnal of Johann Walther, published in 1525, where he says: "These songs have been set in four parts for no other reason than because I wished to provide our young people (who both will and ought to be instructed in music and other sciences) with something whereby they might rid themselves of amorous and carnal songs, and in their stead learn something wholesome, and so apply themselves to what is good with pleasure as becometh the young. Besides this, I am not of the opinion that all sciences should be beaten down and made to cease by the Gospel, as some fanatics pretend; but I would fain see all the arts, and music in particular, used in the service of Him who hath given and created them. Therefore, I entreat every pious Christian to give favorable reception to these hymns, and to help forward my under-

nology. He has especially been interested in the history and translation of this hymn and has succeeded in assembling a unique and extensive collection of its translations. In *Teologisk Tidsskrift*, April, 1924, pages 216-17, he lists 140 translations, in the *Lutheran Church Herald*, October 27, 1925, 168, and in the *Lutheran World Almanac*, just quoted, 107. For the further history of this hymn, see *Werke*, Weimar ed., vol. XXXV, pp. 185-229; Dahle, *A Library of Christian Hymns*, vol. II, pp. 421-31; Lambert, *Luther's Hymns*, pp. 40-50. Pick, *Luther as a Hymnist*, contains sixteen versions of the English translation of this master piece.

taking, as God has given him more or less ability. The world is, alas, not so mindful and diligent to train and to teach our poor youth, but we ought to be forward in promoting the same." [40]

Luther's hymns are quite varied both in their origin and their contents. Some of them are original, others are based upon German or Latin originals, being either mere adaptations or more or less free translations. Many are based upon the Psalms or various Scripture texts, and a few on parts of the Catechism. Even in his hymn writing, Luther did not forget the children, several of them being especially written for the little folks. A writer in a recent number of the *International Journal of Religious Education* mentions Luther as having written one of the four best hymns for children, the well known *Cradle Hymn*.[41] All his hymns breathe forth his deep religious convictions, spiritual insight, strong faith and childlike reliance upon and trust in God. They are simple in language and thoroughly evangelical in tone, and were either adapted to popular melodies or set to suitable music written by himself or his musical assistants. They exerted a powerful influence over the people of that day and had no small part in furthering the cause of the Reformation. The abiding value of a large number of them is attested by the fact that they are still extensively sung in the various parts of the Lutheran Church, and quite a few of them are still found in Reformed hymnals.

THE POEM ON FRAU MUSICA.—This poetic exaltation of music Luther wrote as an introduction to the prize poem of his friend and musical co-laborer, Johann Walther, in 1538. Walther's poem was in praise of his own art, music. In Klug's Hymnal of 1543 it

---

40) Bacon & Allen, *Hymns of Luther*, p. 21; Lambert, *Luther's Hymns*, p. 13.
41) Helen L. Fisher, December number, 1926, p. 25.

appeared as the concluding number in the collection of hymns. The translation given below is by Catherine Winkworth and is taken from Bacon and Allen's *Hymns of Luther*. For the German text, see *Werke*, Weimar ed., vol. XXXV, pp. 483-484, or Crusius, *D. M. Luther's geistliche Lieder*, p. 25.

> *Of all the joys that are on earth*
> *Is none more dear nor higher worth,*
> *Than what in my sweet songs is found*
> *And instruments of various sound.*
>
> *Where friends and comrades sing in tune,*
> *All evil passions vanish soon;*
> *Hate, anger, envy, cannot stay,*
> *All gloom and heartache melt away;*
> *The lust of wealth, the cares that cling,*
> *Are all forgotten while we sing.*
>
> *Freely we take our joy herein,*
> *For this sweet pleasure is no sin,*
> *But pleases God far more, we know,*
> *Than any joys the world can show;*
> *The devil's work it doth impede,*
> *And hinders many a deadly deed.*
>
> *So fared it with King Saul of old;*
> *When David struck his harp of gold,*
> *So sweet and clear its tones rang out,*
> *Saul's murderous thoughts were put to rout.*
> *The heart grows still when I am heard,*
> *And opens to God's Truth and Word;*
> *So are we by Elisha taught,*
> *Who on the harp the Spirit sought.*
>
> *The best thing of the year is mine,*
> *When all the little birds combine*

*To sing until the earth and air
Are filled with sweet sounds everywhere;
And most the tender nightingale
Makes joyful every wood and dale,
Singing her love-song o'er and o'er,
For which we thank her evermore.*

*But yet more thanks are due from us
To the dear Lord who made her thus,
A singer apt to touch the heart,
Mistress of all my dearest art;
To God she sings by night and day,
Unwearied, praising Him alway;
Him I, too, laud in every song,
To whom all thanks and praise belong.*

CHAPTER XIII

EVALUATION OF THE MAN AND HIS WORK

No man was ever more cruelly hated and viciously maligned than was Luther, nor was ever a man more truly loved and sincerely appreciated. There is no historic character, save one, the Lowly Nazarene, whose life and work have been so closely scrutinized, so thoroughly weighed in the balances, and so variously estimated as the life and work of Luther. His enemies have ever sought to discredit him and minimize the character, extent, and value of his manifold and far-reaching services to mankind, and the wholesome, ennobling, liberalizing, reinvigorating intellectual and religious influences that have radiated from him, while friends, admirers, and adherents have vied with one another in paying tributes to his character, achievements, and services. As the various Luther anniversaries have come and gone, the number and volume of Luther encomiums have swelled by leaps and bounds. No Luther anniversary was so productive of such general and uniformly laudatory tributes to the life and work of Martin Luther as the Quadricentennial of his birth in 1883, nor was there ever given such incentive and impetus to fresh, intensive and searching re-investigation of Luther as a man and as a reformer as this anniversary supplied, resulting in thoroughgoing, comprehensive, and critical Luther researches, the production of Luther biographies and monographs, Catholic as well as Protestant, and, best of all, the beginning of the publication of the scholarly and critical collection of Luther's works, entitled *Luthers sämmtliche Werke, kritische Ausgabe*, published at Weimar, and hence generally known as the "Weimar Edition of Luther's Works."[1] This work has not yet been completed, though fifty-three volumes of general works, and, in addition, five on the translation of the Bible, and six on the *Table Talks*, have so far been published.

SOME GENERAL ESTIMATES OF LUTHER'S LIFE AND WORK.—"Luther," says the great German thinker and educator, Johann G. Herder, "was a patriotic, great man. As teacher of the German nation, as co-reformer, indeed of the whole of enlightened Europe, he has long been recognized; even people who do not accept his articles of religion, enjoy the fruits of his reformation. He, like Hercules, grappled with the spiritual despotism which annuls or undermines all free, healthy thinking, and restored to whole peoples the use of reason, and this, indeed, in the most difficult of all things, in spiritual. The might of his language and the upright spirit united itself with sciences, which burst into new life from him and with him, allied itself with the labors of the best men in all departments, who thought, in part, it may be, very differently from him; and so arose for the first time a popular literary public in Germany and the neighboring countries. Now those read who had otherwise never read, while those learned to read who were otherwise unable to read. Schools and academies were founded, German religious songs were sung, and sermons preached in the German language."[2]

Professor Egbert C. Smyth, of Andover Theological

[1] See M. Reu, *Thirty-five Years of Luther Research*, and Preserved Smith, *Recent Progress in the Study of Luther*, Am. Jour. Theol., vol. XIII, pp. 259-69.
[2] Quoted by Croll,*Tributes to Luther*, p. 30.

Seminary, writes: "A man so great and mighty deserves something very different from blind admiration. He had great faults. He cannot be regarded as a perfect exponent of the Reformation which he introduced. It is more important carefully to study the man and his work than to eulogize him. Yet we believe that the deeper the insight gained into his character, the more justly his actions are weighed, the more perfectly his nature is understood, the grander will he seem. There was more of humanity in him than in any other man of his time. Therefore he had more power than any other. Melanchthon was a better scholar, Zwingli a calmer and more sagacious reasoner, Calvin had a more systematic and organizing mind, Charles the Fifth is more renowned for his knowledge of men, especially their weaknesses; but no one ranks with Luther in his understanding of human nature, its needs and capacities, its ruin and its glory. No one touched men at so many points, helped them so much, entered so profoundly into the deepest secrets of their hearts, opened to them such sources of strength." [3]

Writes J. W. Hott, editor of the *Religious Telescope*, official organ of the Church of United Brethren, "To Luther the Christian world owes more than to any man who lived since the days of the Apostle Paul. He belongs to all churches, and the fruit of his toil to the ages. He is the father of Protestantism, the Nestor of free thought, and the uplifted hand which holds an open Bible before the gaze of the world." [4]

The great English historian, James A. Froude, speaking of Luther's mind says: "Luther's mind was literally worldwide: his eyes were forever observant of what was round him. At a time when science was scarcely out of its shell, Luther had observed nature

---

3) Article in *Christian Union*, Nov. 8, 1883, Croll, op. cit., p. 84.
4) Croll, op. cit., p. 163.

with the liveliest curiosity. He had anticipated by mere genius the generative functions of flowers. Human nature he had studied like a dramatist. His memory was a museum of historical information, of anecdotes of great men, of old German literature and song and proverb. Scarce a subject could be spoken of on which he had not thought, and on which he had not something remarkable to say." [5]

In a memorial address on Luther delivered in one of the churches of Hartford, the well-known New England writer, Chas. Dudley Warner, said: "The city of Hartford, the State of Connecticut, the United States, Great Britain and its world-encircling colonies, Holland and its dependencies, the German empire, are to-day what they are largely because of the life of Martin Luther. 'Had there been no Luther,' says Mr. Froude, 'the English, American, and German peoples would be thinking differently, would be acting differently, would be altogether different men and women from what they are this moment.' This city of Hartford, supposing it in existence without the Reformation, would have been a different place from what it is—different in its social, literary, religious, and civil economy. There is not a person in this audience who is what he would have been but for the influence of Luther. We may say this at any time of all preceding influences, of all great writers and actors in the world—they change human life after them; but no man, I think, has affected it so largely since the fall of the Roman Empire as Luther. There would probably have been a Reformation, though not at the time it did occur, without him; but it would have been different in character. Without him at that time it would probably have resulted in a compromise, and a compromise which years would have shown surrendered

---
5) *On Luther's Mind*, Croll, pp. 112-13.

that which we now regard as vital in the Reformation. It needed exactly such a fighter as Luther to win the battle in the great movement of the sixteenth century, and such a conservative as Luther to keep the movement within bounds." [6]

The foremost American Luther scholar and writer on Luther's life and work, though himself not a Lutheran, is unquestionably Dr. Preserved Smith. In a brief article on Luther in the *Outlook*, he gives the following estimate of the man and his work: Luther "needs not that we praise him. The work that he accomplished stands secure without that. The need is ours to understand him; to fathom as far as we are able, the personality that led and dominated his time as scarcely any other man has ever done. For if we judge historically by the results accomplished rather than by our own pert standards of what is 'modern', we must all admit that the Saxon reformer was one of the greatest of the sons of men. In all that momentous age of transition his brain was the most active, his heart the most passionately earnest, his will the most indomitable." [7]

To the above quoted estimates of Luther and his work, estimates with the exception of the one by Herder, given by scholars and writers outside the Lutheran Church, and such citations could be multiplied almost without number, it is but fitting that the estimate of at least one American Lutheran divine should be added, and we shall permit the late Dr. J. B. Remensnyder, a man well and favorably known both within and outside the Lutheran Church, to give this testimony. Says he: "Luther's fame, unlike that of other personalities, grows brighter with the lapse of years. The more he is studied and the keener the searchlight

---
6) Croll, op. cit., pp. 217-18.
7) Volume CXVII, p. 385.

is cast upon him the nobler he appears. More biographies have appeared of him in the last decade than in any other like preceding period, and he is more largely quoted to-day, and his influence is more deeply felt on current religious thought than ever. The personality of Luther appears to be the most unique, myriad-featured and powerful in history. He is not alone the author of a new era in the history of religion, but from him dates a new epoch in the progress of civilization.—Luther was a spiritual hero. He wielded no sword but the weapon of truth. He bore no scepter but the authority of the Word of God. He had for his only ideal, religion: his only aim, the good of men and the everlasting welfare of the soul. And because he was thus a warrior, a prince, and a hero of the realm of spirit, his fame is set upon a hill that cannot be hid, and his light shines like a mighty sea-mark into the far abyss of time." [8]

When we turn to Roman Catholic scholars and writers for an evaluation of Luther and his work, we find very little but unconcealed hatred of the monk who dared to defy the authority and attack the doctrines and practices of the "Holy Church," the most abusive vituperation, the most vicious assaults on the man's character and motives, the most remarkable distortion of history both before and after what is disdainfully referred to as the "so-called Reformation," and the most studious and ingenious attempts to defend the Church and belittle the achievements of Luther. Even Grisar, who aims to treat Luther and his work in a fair and objective manner, according to his own declaration, leaves no stone unturned to defame his character and belittle his work. The one outstanding Catholic scholar and writer who seems to have succeeded

---

8) *What the World Owes Luther*, pp. 03-4.

better than any one within the Catholic Church to give
a fair and somewhat appreciative portrayal of Luther
and a reasonably just estimate of his work is the historian Johann Döllinger, even long before he himself
was forced to separate from the same Church which
excommunicated Luther.[9] He speaks of the "Augustinian monk of Wittenberg" as the "mightiest man of
the people, the most popular character which Germany ever possessed."[10] "Germany is the birthplace
of the Reformation; in the spirit of a German man,
the greatest German of his age, the Protestant doctrine arose. In the presence of the superiority and
creative energy of this genius, the rising and enterprising part of the nation bowed down, in meek reverence and full confidence. Recognizing in him, this
union between force and guiding spirit, they acknowledged him as their master; they lived his thoughts;
and for them he was the hero in whom the nation itself was embodied, with all its peculiar traits. They
gazed upon him with admiration; they surrendered
themselves to his control; because they saw that it
was nothing but their own most profound experience
which was expressed in his writings, more clearly, more
eloquently, more powerfully than they could ever have
expressed it themselves. Accordingly, for Germany the
name of Luther is not simply the name of a distinguished man; it is the living germ of a period in the
national life, it is the center of a new circle of ideas,
the most direct and apt expression of the religious and
moral views that controlled the attention of the Ger-

---

9) Luther. *Eine Skizze; Kirche und Kirchen, Papstthum und Kirchenstaat.* Döllinger was among those Catholic scholars who objected most strenuously to the doctrine of papal infallibility at the Vatican Council and later withdrew from the Roman Church and organized the Old Catholic Church, whose very evangelical confession he was largely instrumental in drawing up. See Schaff, *Creeds of Christendom*, vol. II. pp. 545-51.
10) *Papstthum und Kirchenstaat*, p. 10.

man spirit, from the mighty influence of which even they who opposed them could not entirely escape."[11]

What a glaring contrast to Döllinger's graphic portrayal of the mighty and transforming influence wielded by Martin Luther, whom he recognizes as the greatest genius of his age, is the following recent pronouncement on Luther by a Catholic scholar: "Throughout the whole period of this activity (he refers to the Luther researches clustering about the 400 anniversary of Luther's birth), the Luther of fiction has been *relegated to the realm* of the unhistorical. Scholars can no longer satisfy themselves with the general platitude that the greatest achievement of the race to which he belonged and the most important event in history is the Protestant Rebellion (!) of the sixteenth century. We can no longer hold in the face of what modern scholarship has brought to light since 1883 that Luther's rebellion (!) was essentially the beginning of a new religious movement. The Protestant Rebellion (!) marked no new stage in human progress; it did not close the eyes of a dying medieval Church; it marked no new dawn of the modern era. Protestant scholars of repute no longer hold out to their disciples the old misconceptions that the Rebellion (!) in Germany secured greater purity and spirituality in religion. It did not contribute, as has been told so often, to the elevation of the laity and the advancement of woman. It did not fashion a separation of secular from ecclesiastical power. It gave no extraordinary impulse to literature or to science. It did not establish liberty of conscience. In a word, it had nothing in its principles or methods, which was to ennoble our modern civilization."[12] The same view of Lu-

---
11) *Papstthum und Kirchenstaat*, pp. 386-7. The translation, except the first sentence, which is the author's own, is the one given in Croll, *Tributes to Luther*, p. 56.
12) Peter Guilday, Ph. D., Catholic University of America, Washington, D. C., in his introduction to O'Hare's book, *The Facts About Luther*. The exclamation marks (!) are ours.

ther and his accomplishments is presented by another writer in the *Catholic World*, in which article he labors to prove that all was well with the Church at Luther's time and that the Church was fully *capable of having brought* about any necessary reformations within itself without Luther and his heretical innovations. He also claims that according to the verdict of history Luther accomplished nothing of real value.[13] To the Catholic mind, Luther is nothing but the lowest and meanest mischief-maker, the arch-heretic. "One of the most serious, if not absolutely the most serious, effect of Luther's movement and the so-called Reformation on the social life of Europe," says another Catholic writer, " was the obliteration from the calendar of the Saints' days." Of these, he says, there were at the time between thirty and forty, and on these the people were compelled to attend mass, and therefore had to abstain from all sorts of servile labor. One wonders if the man intends to be taken seriously or whether he is indulging in some dry humor![14] More serious are the accusations which appeared in the Catholic press of this country on the 400th anniversary of the beginning of the Reformation, when the World War was at its height, Luther being chiefly held responsible for having made this horrible war possible. Says the *Sacred Heart Review* of Boston: "The student of history with his knowledge of the Christian world before and after the so-called Reformation, can confirm this claim that the world in its present crisis is but Luther's world developed along lines suggested by Luther's principles."[15] Thus the great Heresiarch accomplished nothing at all worthy of mention, or whatever he did accomplish was only

---

13) Millar, *Justification of Luther by History Alone*, Catholic World, vol. CIV, pp. 768-80.
14) J. J. Walsh, M. D., Ph. D., *Luther and Social Service*, ibid., pp. 781-90.
15) Quoted by *Literary Digest*, Oct. 27, 1917, p. 29.

harmful and destructive of all that was best in social, cultural, and religious institutions according to the general Catholic interpretation of his life and work.[16]

ESTIMATES OF LUTHER AS AN EDUCATOR. It matters not what phase of Luther's life or work is studied, if one searches the works of both Catholic and Protestant writers, one is always struck by the fact that, with a few notable exceptions, Catholic writers invariably rate Luther and his work very low, while Protestant writers, though fully aware of his faults and short-comings, nevertheless rate him high as a man of deep spirituality, high ideals and noble aspirations, remarkable moral courage, powerful mind, matchless capacity for work in spite of his often delicate physical condition, and as a man of unselfish and persistent devotion to a great cause. They also, almost without exception, regardless of personal creed or church affiliation, place a very high estimate upon his work both as a religious reformer and as an educator. This same sharp distinction between Catholic and Protestant writers will also appear in the following evaluations of Luther's educational theories and achievements.

1. CATHOLIC ESTIMATES. Denifle in his three-volume arraignment of Luther pays no attention to his educational work. Not so Janssen. He devotes considerable space in his large *History of the German People* to show that as a result of Luther's work the schools declined, and deals at length with a comparison of Catholic schools both before and after the Reformation with the schools fostered by Luther and his reformation, showing the merits of the former and the faults of the latter, making it appear that Luther's educational influence was of a negative and harmful

---

[16] For refutation of Catholic charges against Luther and critical examination of Catholic interpretation of his accomplishments, see Boehmer, *Luther in the Light of Recent Research;* Kaverau, *Luther in katolischer Beleuchtung*, and Wilh. Walther, *Luther im neuesten römischen Gericht*, Heft. 1-4.

character rather than of a beneficial one.[17] Grisar pursues the same line of argument, although he treats Luther more fairly on many points than does Janssen. Luther's appeal for better schools, according to Grisar, "were not dictated so much by a love for humanistic studies as such or by the wish to further the interests of learning in Germany, as by the desire to fill the secular government berths with able 'Christian' men and above all to provide preachers and pastors for the work Luther had commenced and for the struggle against Popery. Melanchthon's attitude to the schools was more broad-minded. To some extent his efforts supplied what was wanting in Luther. His object was the education of the people, whereas in Luther's eyes the importance of the schools chiefly lay in their being 'seminaria ecclesiarum,' as he once calls them. With him their aim was too much the mere promoting of his specific theological interests, to the 'preservation of the Church.'"[18] Speaking of Luther's letters, he says: "They do not make of Luther 'the father of national schools,' as he has been erroneously termed, because what he was after was not the real education of the masses, but rather something different; still less do the booklets, with their every page reeking with the Word of God which he preached, make him the father of the modern undenominational schools."[19] As to the success of Luther's efforts to reform the old schools and establish new ones, he remarks: "On the whole his hopes were disappointed. The famous saying of Erasmus, 'Wherever Lutheranism prevails, there we see the

---

17) In vol. III, Janssen tries to show moral and educational decline due to Luther; in vol. XIII, he deals with schools and universities, and in vol. XIV, he compares Catholic and Protestant philosophy, naturally to the discomfiture of the latter.
18) *Luther*, vol. VI, pp. 9-10.
19) Ibid., p. 14.
NOTE.—The words quoted from Erasmus occur in a letter written by him to Pirkheimer from Basel in 1528, "Ubicumque regnat Lutheranismus, ubi litterarum est interitus," stronger even than the translation.

downfall of learning,' remained largely true throughout the 16th century, in spite of Luther's efforts."[20]

NON-LUTHERAN ESTIMATES. The non-Lutheran writers on the history of education and educational reformers have often excelled Lutheran writers in their eulogies on Luther and his work. As in everything else so also as an educator, Luther belongs to the world, for his services in this respect were world-wide, and this fact has been recognized by educational writers perhaps even more than by writers on religion and theology. Only a few representative writers are cited.

Professor Foster Watson of the University College of Wales says: "Luther touches on many points of educational theory and practice. All his education is subordinated to his religious motif, yet it includes the greatest questions, religious teaching, family, education, the vernacular. As the translator of the Scriptures into German, the author of the German Catechism, the writer of German hymns, and in pursuance of these aims, the teacher and trainer of his own children, Luther stands out as the Prophet of German popular education and the inspirer of princes and magistrates in the erection of popular schools. His sympathetic attraction to teaching is shown by his words: 'Let no man think himself so intelligent that he can despise children's play. When Christ wished to teach men, He had to become man. If we are to train children, then we must become children with them.'"[21]

The distinguished French pedagog, Gabriel Compayre, writes: "The German reformer Luther is, of all his co-religionists, the one who has served the cause of elementary instruction with the most ardor. He not only addressed a pressing appeal to the ruling classes in behalf of founding schools for the people, but, by

20) Ibid., p. 36.
21) Article on Luther in Monroe's *Cyclopedia of Education*.

his influence, methods of instruction were improved, and the educational spirit was renewed in accordance with the principles of Protestantism. . . . A remarkable fact about Luther is, that as a preacher of instruction, he does not speak merely from the religious point of view. . . . At the same time that he extends the program of studies, Luther introduces a new spirit into methods. He wishes more liberty and more joy in the school. . . . No one has more extolled the office of teacher." Referring to quotations from Luther which he has cited, he concludes: "These quotations will suffice to make appreciated the large and liberal spirit of Luther, and the range of his thought as an educator."[22]

Says Dr. F. P. Graves: "The purpose of education Luther everywhere holds to involve the promotion of the State's welfare quite as much as that of the Church. The schools were to make good citizens as well as religious men." (Compare Grisar's statements, pp. 176-7). "The most important innovation of Luther, however, was his desire to introduce schools in which the common people could be fitted for their occupations in life. He also wished to correlate the school more closely with the home. . . . The methods that Luther proposed were a decided advance upon those of the narrower humanism. They were to be less mechanical and memoriter, and appeal more to interest and rationality. He would utilize the natural activity of the children and not attempt to repress them, and would make use of concrete examples, wherever possible. . . . The organization, content, and method advocated by Luther in his Letter, Sermon, and other writings, were worked out in actual institutions by his friends and associates, especially Melanchthon."[23]

Dr. Paul Monroe is very cautious in his presentation of Luther's educational contribution, perhaps being

---
22) *The History of Pedagogy*, pp. 114-120.
23) *A History of Education* (Middle Ages), pp. 179-189.

largely influenced by Janssen, whom he cites as one of his authorities. Nevertheless, he credits him with having introduced music and gymnastics into the schools and placed a new emphasis upon the teaching of history and science. He also credits him with bringing education within the reach of all, rich and poor, and making provision for the education of girls as well as boys. "Thus," he concludes, "Luther contributed materially to the formulation of a new and broader conception of education and gave powerful impetus to practical changes already initiated."[24]

ESTIMATES OF LUTHERAN WRITERS. From Lutheran sources as from non-Lutheran sources volumes of estimates of Luther's contributions to education might be culled, but we shall limit ourselves to three, representing as many countries—Scandinavia, Germany, and America.

"By his German Bible and his Catechism Luther laid the foundation of the Protestant common school, and with his conception of spiritual liberty he combined his conception of the significance of the home, the mother-tongue, and reality, the object with the word, yea, he even had an appreciation for history, athletics, music, and song. The school also no longer remained an ecclesiastical affair, but became a matter of state concern."[25]

"Luther stands forth not only as a pedagogical writer, but through the entire work of his life and the power of his personality he takes first rank among pedagogs. He presented with eloquent words the aim and necessity of education in home, school, and church, and made earnest appeals for the improvement of the schools and in behalf of school attendance, the study of languages and the sciences, urged the better

---
24) Monroe. *History of Education*, p. 414.
25) Article "Pedagogik" in Salomonsens *Konversationsleksikon*. Translated by the author from the Danish.

training of teachers, established new schools, counselled and guided the visitation of schools, wrote text books for religious instruction, introduced better methods, and not only did he bring up his own children faithfully and successfully, but also by his many other activities in association with Melanchthon he trained excellent teachers, enthused pastors and teachers for the school work, and set in motion in behalf of the schools a thousand forces, ushering in a springtide rich in promises."[26]

Concluding his presentation of Luther and his contributions to education, Dr. Painter says: "Looking back over the ground traversed, we realize that the great Reformer accomplished scarcely less for education than for religion. Through his influence, which was fundamental, wide-reaching, and beneficent, there began for the one as for the other a new era of advancement. Let us note a few particulars:

"1. In his writings, as in the principles of Protestantism, he laid the foundation of an educational system, which begins with the popular school and ends with the university.

"2. He set up as the noble ideal of education a Christian man, fitted through instruction and discipline to discharge the duties of every relation of life.

"3. He exhibited the necessity of schools both for the Church and the State, and emphasized the dignity and worth of the teacher's vocation.

"4. With resistless energy he impressed upon parents, ministers, and civil officers their obligation to educate the young.

"5. He brought about a reorganization of schools, introducing graded instruction, an improved course of study, and rational methods.

"6. In his appreciation of nature and child life, he laid the foundation for educational science.

---
26) Schumann, *Luthers pädagogishe Schriften*, p. 101.

"7. He made great improvements in method; he sought to adapt instruction to the capacity of children, to make learning pleasant, to awaken the mind through skillful questioning, to study things as well as words, and to temper discipline with love.

"8. With a wise understanding of the relation of virtue and intelligence to the general good, he advocated compulsory education on the part of the State.

"In view of these facts, Luther deserves henceforth to be recognized as the greatest, not only of religious, but of educational reformers."[27]

---

27) *Luther on Education*, pp. 167-8. See also his work, *A History of Education*, pp. 140-147.

CHAPTER XIV

THE VERDICT OF HISTORY

The widely differing estimates given the character of Luther and the value of his work by Catholic and Protestant writers in the preceding chapter naturally compel the inquiring and reflecting reader to raise the question, What is the verdict of history respecting this man and his work? It goes without saying that personal bias or prejudice on the part of a writer will color to a greater or lesser extent his interpretation of historical data and the conclusions he draws from them, even though he may aim at the most objective, discriminating, and impartial presentation. The principle that the historian as the scientist should be objective and impartial in both presenting and interpreting his data is a splendid one in the abstract. But it is more easily stated than observed. Hence it is not strange that such widely divergent views as we have noticed may arise from the consideration of the same historical phenomena. And yet there is such a thing as a concensus of historical judgment which may serve as a guide and corrective for individual and subjective historical judgments. According to this consensus of historical judgment, a judgment from which only Roman Catholic writers in the main dissent, the life and work of Martin Luther did mark the beginning of a new era in the world's history. His place in history as a religious, social, and political reformer has been definitely established, and even the most searching and scholarly assaults by his enemies during the past four centuries have failed to dislodge him. Secular history, as well as ecclesiastical, ascribes to him a unique position of power and influence in both ecclesiastical and secular affairs. The high general estimates given of Luther and his work in the foregoing chapter are well supported by ascertained historical facts and the concensus of historical judgment and require no further argument and elucidation in this volume.

The place of Luther in the history of education is, however, a different matter and demands further consideration. He is commonly regarded both by scholars and the generally enlightened public only as a religious reformer, whose religious reforms merely indirectly affected thought and action in other fields of human enterprise and endeavor, among them education. This is, however, but a one-sided conception of this many-sided man. His great religious contributions are thus made to eclipse or overshadow more or less completely his other contributions to human progress and well-being. While the best writers on the history of education are constrained to devote some space to Luther and his contribution to education, they regard it more incidental to his work as a religious reformer than a direct contribution to educational theory and practice because of any special interest in education as such on his part. He is generally presented as though he were completely out-ranked as an educator by his contemporaries, such as Melanchthon and Sturm, to say nothing about the educational reformers of the seventeenth, eighteenth, and nineteenth centuries. It is a significant fact that the most widely known Teachers' College in the United States, that of Columbia University, whose latest building is inscribed to the memory of outstanding modern educators, omits the name of Luther entirely, beginning its inscriptions with the names of Melanchthon and Sturm. The place of Luther in the history of education is, therefore, still an open question.

While it has been indicated by some of the authorities quoted above and specifically stated by Painter, Schmidt, and Raumer, it has not yet attained to general recognition and acceptance.

We surveyed the educational movements and influences at work during the centuries immediately preceding the Reformation and noted the general status of education at the time when Luther enters the historic arena.[1] We have also considered in somewhat detail Luther's pedagogical writings and the principles he enunciated. It remains to inquire to what extent, if any, Luther was influenced by the educational theories of earlier and contemporary educators, whether he actually established any schools and otherwise directly promoted education, and what roots his educational ideas actually took. In so doing, it will be necessary to note the social, political, and religious forces with which he had to contend and which tended to negative his educational plans and efforts and neutralize his educational influences.

To what extent Luther was influenced by the earlier educators is difficult to say. Tracing influences is a subtle and delicate task. That he was aware of the educational efforts of others is plainly evident from what he said and wrote. Having attended a school of the Nüll Brethren, another name for the Brethren of the Common Life, as he himself tells us, he was, of course, familiar with the educational views and work of this order.[2] His great contemporary, Erasmus, he knew very well and corresponded with him for a time. He also read his works and therefore knew of the educational ideas of Erasmus. That he was acquainted with the educational leaders of the Italian Renaissance, such as Petrarch, Boccaccio, da Feltre, and da Verona, and the advanced educational ideas of the latter two,

---
1) See chapter I.
2) De Wette, *Briefe*, vol. I, p. 390.

is doubtful, except as these were slightly reflected in the writings of the Dutch Humanists, especially Erasmus. The educational ideas of Luther, however, stand out by themselves in many particulars, such as originality, freshness, boldness, practicability, and comprehensiveness, whatever debt he may owe to past and contemporary educators.

In spite of his multitudinous tasks and exacting labors and responsibilities as the active leader of the Reformation, Luther was actively engaged in the promotion of schools throughout Germany. The work of actually establishing schools he left mainly to his faithful and able associates, Melanchthon, Bugenhagen, and Brenz. While Melanchthon is generally credited with being the father of the German gymnasia or secondary schools, there is every reason to believe that Luther was the originator and the most powerful supporter of the movement for the establishment even of secondary schools. As early as 1524, as we have already mentioned, he sent a school plan to Spalatin to be presented to Elector Frederick the Wise, whose chaplain Spalatin was.[3] This school plan seems to have been lost. Four years later the school plan of Melanchthon appeared with an introduction by Luther. In 1538 Luther reissued this plan in a revised form under his own name. Of the actual establishment of schools he writes to Spalatin under date of April 16, 1525. "I am just now setting out with Philip and Master Agricola for Eisleben, whither we have been summoned by Count Albert to establish a Christian school, since you are so luke-warm and neglect our own. I am beginning to hope and to make some efforts that Philip may begin a similar school at Nuremberg. The Magdeburgers have called Casper Creutziger, the Dantzigers Master

---

3) De Wette, *Briefe*, vol. II, p. 554; Raumer, *Geschichte der Pädagogik*, vol. I, p. 185.

Arnold."[4] In his letter to Elector Johann of Saxony, dated November 22, 1526, he urges him to establish public schools either supported by the towns or villages themselves or by the proceeds of the monastic properties.[5] The Margrave of Brandenburg he urges to establish one or two universities in his domain and outlines plans for faculty and courses of study. He also urges upon him the importance of establishing good primary schools in all towns and villages.[6] His two great educational appeals have already been noticed.[7]

Luther was thus actively engaged in promoting the cause of education primary, secondary, and university throughout Germany.

Owing to the dissolution of the old cathedral and conventual schools, where the Lutheran Reformation took hold; the transition from church control to state control; the wide-spread notion that the removal of the authority and power of the Catholic Church would result in the uncertainty and instability of the various ecclesiastical offices, for the filling of which education had been principally maintained; the unwillingness of the people generally to assume the financial obligations involved in the establishment of public tax supported education; and the religious and political unrest and controversy, Luther's educational progress could not be realized as rapidly nor as fully as it otherwise would have been. That it did succeed, however, in spite of severe handicaps and great opposition is evidenced by the establishment of a large number of schools, primary and secondary, and at least one university, the University of Marburg, during Luther's lifetime. Other Lutheran universities were established later in Germany and other Lutheran countries. The University of Jena

---
4) Smith, *Luther's Correspondence*, vol. II, p. 305.
5) Ibid., pp. 383-4. See p. 197.
6) Ibid., pp. 486-8. See p. 196.
7) See chapter VIII.

was established in 1548 and 1557, Altdorf in 1575, and Helmstadt in 1576.

In addition to establishing schools and promoting the general cause of a broad Christian education, Luther and Melanchthon had a large share in the training of teachers for the new schools, at the University of Wittenberg, whose student body numbered as high as 2,000 students annually. Teachers were even provided for royal households outside of Germany. In a letter dated April 18, 1539, Luther writes to Gustavus I, king of Sweden, replying to his request for a tutor for his son. A young man by the name of Norman was sent to be the prince's instructor, accompanied by another young man by the name of Michael Agricola.[8]

Luther set a good example for others by sending his own children to the public schools. In August, 1542, he sent his son Hans, then sixteen years of age, to Torgau to attend the public school at that place. Writing to the school master at Torgau, Marcus Crödel, he says: "I send you my son Hans, as we arranged, my dear Marcus, so that he may be instructed in grammar and music along with the other boys, and at the same time I hope you will attend to his manners and morals. I am committing a great trust to you in the Lord. I shall never grudge the outlay, and you will report his progress and let me know what should be done with him. I send Florian, one of his schoolmates, with him, for it is important that boys should have others to vie with. But you must be more strict with the latter, and if you can, board him with a burgher; if not, send him back. God bless your efforts. If they succeed, then I shall, if spared, send the other two boys; for in the future we shall not easily find such unwearied instructors, especially in the languages, and such strict disciplinarians as you. Therefore, one must seize the op-

---

8) Currie, *The Letters of Martin Luther*, p. 369.

portunity, for time flies, and competent teachers disappear even more quickly. For more advanced studies they would be better here. Farewell in the Lord, and say to Hans Walter that I pray for his welfare, and commit my little son to his care in music. I can train theologians, but wish my children to have grammar and music."[9]

Johann Sturm of Strassburg is assigned a very prominent place in the history of education as an educator and a founder of a model secondary school at Strassburg, being not infrequently rated higher than either Luther or Melanchthon. There can be no question of Sturm's great abilities and success as a teacher and promoter of secondary education. It should be observed, however, that he had been influenced to a very large extent by the educational ideas of Luther and Melanchthon, and that he built upon the foundation already laid at Strassburg by Jacob Sturm, at whose instigation he was induced to come to Strassburg and begin his educational career there. The high school at Strassburg was founded in 1534 by Jacob Sturm and reorganized by Johann Sturm, upon his arrival in 1538. Strassburg was an important city and became early subject to Lutheran influence. Kurtz says of this city: "One of the first cities which opened its gates freely to the Gospel was Strassburg. Nowhere were Luther's writings more zealously read, discussed, printed, and translated than in that city."[10] Luther was in constant communication with Reformation leaders there both Lutheran and Reformed. He was well acquainted both with Jacob and Johann Sturm. The former took part in the Marburg Colloquy in 1529, and Luther sends warm greetings to the latter and Calvin in a letter written to Bucer in 1539.[11] That Sturm was

9) Currie, *The Letters of Martin Luther*, p. 415.
10) *Church History*, vol. II, p. 250.
11) Currie, *The Letters of Martin Luther*, p. 368.

to some extent dependent upon Melanchthon and therefore on Luther for his educational ideas is admitted by Dr. Ficker, who says of him: "Dependent on Melanchthon, he followed the principle of training in rhetoric and eloquence based upon Humanism and evangelical piety for the offices of the Reformation movement and the State."[12] Luther and Melanchthon began the establishment of schools in 1525. The school plan of Melanchthon was published in 1528, while Johann Sturm did not begin his school work at Strassburg until 1538. There is thus ample room for influence being exerted upon Sturm and his educational program both on the part of Luther and Melanchthon. A comparison of the plans of Luther and Melanchthon on the one hand and Sturm's on the other will also reveal considerable likeness with respect to scope, subject-matter, and aims, though Sturm's plan is more detailed.

Luther's educational influence could be traced still further, but this will suffice for our present purpose. Luther could work with men and he could work through men. With his gifted and devoted associate Melanchthon as his chief educational counsellor and co-worker at his side and the faithful support and assistance of Bugenhagen in North Germany and Brenz in South Germany, as leaders in the organization of the Church and school, he laid the educational foundations in Germany on solid ground, deep and secure, and built a broad and comprehensive school program. Rightly may Schmidt say of him: "Luther himself was one of the greatest educators and school masters."[13] And again: "Luther himself stood at the head of the workers in the field of education, because he called attention to a large number of grave abuses in the schools, brought new life to teachers and young people through the school visitation which he directed and commended,

---
12) Schaff-Herzog *Encyclopedia*, vol. II, p. 121.
13) *Geschichte der Pädagogik*, vol. III, p. 46.

urged a thorough language study as the basis of learning and culture, and, as the source of pure religious conceptions, wrote new books for religious instruction, proposed suitable methods of teaching the various branches of knowledge, and because, in association with Melanchthon, he trained a large number of excellent teachers for higher and lower schools and enjoined upon rulers and governments to provide for schools and the education of the young."[14]

Having thus, on the strength of the evidences, cumulatively presented in the foregoing pages, determined Luther's place in the history of education, it is fitting that we conclude our study of Luther as an educator by briefly summarizing his distinct and specific contributions to educational theory and praxis in the following points:

1. No educator before his day devoted so much time and attention to education in all its phases and wrote and spoke so extensively on educational matters as did Luther, and few, if any, have since excelled him as a writer and speaker in behalf of popular and universal Christian education, broad and comprehensive, yet balanced and practical. His strong pleas for popular Christian education in sermons and tracts are models of incisiveness, directness, and comprehensiveness, great in their convincing power and moving in their appeal. His great translation of the Bible into the language of the people became a tremendous educational influence. In his two Catechisms he has given to posterity manuals in religious education of permanent value, and through them he has contributed both directly and indirectly to the production of the great historic manuals of religious instruction written after his day, the *Heidelberg Catechism*, the two *Westminster Catechisms*, and even indirectly the *Catechismus Romanus*, to say

---

14) Ibid., p. 21.

nothing of the many text books on his own *Small Catechism*.

2. He pointed out with clearness and vigor the fundamental importance of Christian education to both Church and State, showing that education is not only necessary for the spiritual welfare of man, but also for his temporal, social welfare, and the proper character and permanence of all legitimate and beneficent social, political, and cultural institutions.

3. He conceived of education as affecting the whole life of man, and therefore regarded religious and secular education simply as integral parts of a complete and well-rounded Christian education. Furthermore, to him the work of the Church and the work of the school were inseparable. He was a firm believer in the idea that the educational method was the normal method of building and extending the Kingdom of God, and this idea he persistently and consistently pressed home. "For him," says Martig, "Church and school were inseparable; for according to his conviction the people could appropriate the true Christian religion only by means of a Christian education and through good schools."[15]

4. He gave a new meaning to the offices of parent, teacher, and pastor, drawn both from Scripture and human experience, and emphasized the great duties and vast opportunities of parents, teachers, and pastors in child training and home and nation building. As teacher, pastor, and parent he exemplified in his own life the ideals for which he stood, laying a concrete foundation, not only for the Protestant Manse and its far-reaching influence for good, but also for Christian family-life in general, and setting an exalted example for all parents, teachers, and pastors to take their God-given calling seriously, have definite aims, and

---

15) *Geschichte der Erziehung.* p. 31.

diligently utilize the means at their disposal for the successful attainment of these aims.

5. He made the provision for a broad and universal Christian education one of the prime functions of the State and lifted education as a whole out of the narrowness of ecclesiasticism both as to scope and content. It is therefore correct historically to say, in a relative sense at least, that Luther was the founder of the public common school system, and the originator of the system of compulsory education. While the Volksschule of his own country and the common schools of this country are the outgrowth of these principles so clearly enunciated by Luther, they are not such common schools as he would have established. As Professor Good well says: "Although he speaks of public schools, he did not mean to imply secularization of schools. To him secular schools would have been an abomination. He did not realize that in pleading for state support he was invoking state control; that those who provide for the maintenance of any work eventually come to determine the methods and objects of that work."[16]

6. He capitalized the best elements in Humanistic education, set them free from the tendency toward a narrow Latinolatry, the extreme of which was "Ciceronianism," and the further tendency to create merely an intellectual aristocracy, and related them to the life of the people in general, utilizing them in the interest of the education of the masses.

7. He was a man of the people and plead the people's cause in the matter of education as in religious and political causes. Therefore he stood for universal education, the education of all boys and girls, generally, in the home and in the elementary schools, and special training for men and women capable of be-

---

[16] Harry G. Good, *Position of Luther upon Education, School and Society*, vol. VI, p. 517.

coming efficient teachers, and promising boys for the various types of professional service in Church and State. "A worthy family life was, according to Luther, both an end of education and a means thereto. Education was to be in the family and for the family. The German people have greatly profited by this high value placed upon the family life by their first modern leader. That education was for girls as well as for boys was in itself a remarkable advance. In a word, education was to be universal."[17]

Frederick Andres, in a brief poem inscribed to Martin Luther as the "Father of Primary Education," says beautifully and with a touch of philosophy:

*Deep down beneath the surface of the earth
The miner finds a hard and lifeless mass;
Ignite it, and what wonders come to pass!
Lo, light and heat and power are given birth!
Deep down below the men and things of worth
A miner's son beheld a helpless class,
Inert and hopeless as are clods of earth.
"Set fire to these," he cried, and showed the ways
That schools could make the dormant force to blaze,
Producing light and heat and power. His aim
Is ours, though centuries have passed, the same;
His method ours, to kindle lifeless coals;
His motive ours, the love for human souls.*[18]

8. He stood for a practical education, an education which would fit for the everyday duties and experiences of life. Therefore he would combine schooling in religion and the languages, arts, and sciences with manual training at home. He thus pointed the way to manual training in connection with religious and intellectual education.

---
17) Ibid., p. 514.
18) *Education*, vol. XXVII, p. 549.

9. Luther observed child life and understood child nature, capacities, and modes of expression better than any one before him had done, and thus paved the way for child study and the due consideration of the child both in curriculum making and methods of teaching. "One of the most striking traits of Luther's character was his sympathy with childhood," says Professor Geo. L. Prentiss of Union Theological Seminary.[19]

10. His understanding of child nature and development naturally led him to hold forth as well as to practise improved methods of teaching. He wanted to substitute observation of nature for Aristotle's treatise on nature in nature study, and the teaching of language by living speech instead of merely by the letter of grammar. "Every one learns German and other languages more from speaking at home, at market, in church, than from books," says he. "Printed words are dead; spoken words are living. On the printed page they are not as forcible as when uttered by the soul of man. Tell me, Where has there even been a language that one could learn to speak from grammar alone?"[20] "Luther urged that children be given an opportunity for play and that studies should both interest the student and inform him about the world in which he lives."[21]

11. He provided for the improvement of existing schools and the establishment of new schools of all grades, and was instrumental, largely through the aid of Melanchthon, Agricola, and others, in the founding of a number of public schools which became models for similar schools.

12. He was the first exponent for the establishment of public libraries for every city and town for the free use of both scholars and the public generally, and he

---
19) *Luther with the Children, Symposiac on Luther*, 1883, pp. 31-36.
20) Painter, *Luther on Education*, p. 158.
21) Harry G. Good, *Position of Luther upon Education*, School and Society, vol. VI, p. 516.

gave a powerful impetus to the creation of free public libraries as adjuncts to free public schools.

13. Luther assigned to the Bible a prominent place in the education of the child. It was to be the primary source of all religious and moral instruction. But the schools he sought to establish were by no means merely Bible schools, but schools with a broad, comprehensive program. Says Professor Good: "While Luther emphasized religious instruction, his suggestions for a curriculum show that he desired no narrow ecclesiastical course of study, no mere reading, writing, and Bible school."[22]

14. He awarded song and music a large place in the education of the child, both at home and in school, as well as in church, and provided the people with suitable songs and appropriate music. "The leader of the Reformation," says Dr. Philip Schaff, "was also the first evangelical hymnist. To Luther belongs the extraordinary merit of having given to the German people in their own tongue the Bible, the Catechism, and the hymn book, so that God might speak directly to them in His Word, and that they might directly answer Him in their songs. He was also a musician and composed tunes to his best hymns. Some of them are immortal, most of all that triumphal war-cry of the Reformation which has so often been reproduced in other languages, and which resounds with mighty effects on great occasions: 'Ein' feste Burg ist unser Gott.' "[23]

The author's colleague, Professor John Dahle, an authority on hymnology, has this to say about Luther on the point under consideration: "Luther loved the Church and the language of his fathers. He loved the hymns and the music of the Church and often expressed his esteem and even admiration for the great poets and musicians of the Church. He loved the hymns of

---
22) Harry G. Good, *School and Society*, op. cit., p. 516.
23) Julian, *Dictionary of Hymnology*, p. 414.

the ancient Church and praised especially the use of the Latin language for its fine tone and musical cadence, and expressed the wish that the youth of his time might be trained in the language of the ancient Church. For this purpose he retained many of the four-part choir songs with Latin texts. He did not consider himself proficient enough to render these glorious hymns into his mother tongue, still less did he feel that he could create anything new to take their place."[24]

15. Luther, therefore, stands forth as the greatest educator of his age and in the very front rank of the world's greatest educators, whose educational theories have become the valued heritage of successive generations of educational leaders in Church and State and whose influence on educational thought and practice is still very marked throughout the entire field of educational endeavor, especially in that branch of the Christian Church which bears his name.

> *Lord, keep us steadfast in Thy Word;*
> *Curb those who fain by craft or sword*
> *Would wrest the Kingdom from Thy Son,*
> *And set at naught all He hath done.*
>
> *Lord Jesus Christ, Thy power make known,*
> *For Thou art Lord of lords alone;*
> *Defend Thy Christendom, that we*
> *May evermore sing praise to Thee.*
>
> *O Comforter, of priceless worth,*
> *Send peace and unity on earth,*
> *Support us in our final strife,*
> *And lead us out of death to life.*
> —MARTIN LUTHER, 1541.

---

[24] *Library of Christian Hymns,* vol. I, p. 73.

BIBLIOGRAPHY

I. LUTHER'S WORKS

Luthers sämtliche Werke, kritische Ausgabe, 60 volumes published to date, Weimar, 1883-
Dr. M. Luthers sämtliche Werke, 67 vols., Erlangen, 1826-1886.
Luthers sämtliche Werke, herausgegeben von J. G. Walch, 24 vols., Halle, 1740-1753. New and revised edition by Concordia Publishing House, St. Louis, Mo., 30 vols., 1880-
Small Catechism, trans. into Delaware Indian language by Johan Campanius, Swedish Lutheran pastor in Delaware, 1642-48. *Lutherii Katechismus öfversat på American-Virginske Språket*, Stockholm, 1696, with map of Nova Svecia, bearing the following legend: "Anno 1654 och 1655 är denna Nova Svecia Carta med dess Riviers och lands situation och beskaffenhet aftagen och till Carts förd af P. Lindström." This is an original copy of Campanius' translation of Luther's *Small Catechism* into the Delaware language made in 1648 and published in Stockholm in 1696. Copy in Library of Yale University, where it was carefully examined by the author. Another copy is listed at the City Library of New York.
Small Catechism, Quadri-centennial Jubilee Edition, trans. into English by an Inter-synodical Committee, Provisional edition, Columbus, Ohio, 1927.

BIBLIOGRAPHY

Currie, Margaret A., *The Letters of Martin Luther*, London, 1908.
DeWette, W. M. L., *Luthers Briefe*, 5 vols., Berlin, 1825-28; 6th volume by DeWette-Seidemann, Berlin, 1856.
Enders, E. L., and Kaverau, G., *Dr. Martin Luthers Briefwechsel*, 18 vols., Frankfurt, 1884-1923.
Hazlitt, William, *The Table Talk of Martin Luther*, with life of Luther by Alexander Chalmers, London, 1857.
Lenker, J. N., *Luther's Works in English*, selections from sermons, exegetical, and catechetical works, 13 vols., Minneapolis, 1903.
Smith, Preserved, *Luther's Correspondence and Other Contemporary Letters*, vol. I, letters from 1507 to 1521, Philadelphia, 1913; do. jointly with Jacobs, C. M., vol. II, letters from 1521 to 1530, Philadelphia, 1918. Vol. III in press.
Smith, Preserved, and Gallinger, Herbert Percival, *Conversations with Luther* (extracts from his *Table Talks*), Boston, New York, and Chicago, 1911.

II. BIOGRAPHIES OF LUTHER

Audin, J. M. V., *History of the Life, Writings, and Doctrines of Martin Luther*, translated from the French, Philadelphia, 1841 (Catholic).
Bayne, Peter, *Martin Luther, His Life and Work*, 2 vols., London and New York, 1887.
Berger, Arnold C., *Martin Luther in kulturgeschichtlicher Darstellung*, 2 vols., Berlin, 1895.
Bower, Alexander, *The Life of Martin Luther*, London, 1813.
Bunsen, Chevalier, *Life of Martin Luther with an Estimate of Luther's Character and Genius* by Thomas Carlyle, New York and Cambridge, 1870.
Denifle, Heinrich, *Luther und Luthertum in der ersten*

Entwickelung, 3 vols., Mainz, 1904-9. Volumes II and III completed by A. M. Weiss (Catholic).
Dose, Joh., *Der Held von Wittenberg und Worms*, Düsseldorf, 1906.
Döllinger, J. J. I., *Luther, Eine Skizze*, Freiburg, 1890, first published in 1851 (Catholic).
Freytag, Gustav, *Doktor Luther, eine Schilderung*, 3rd ed., Leipsic, 1884; Eng. trans. by G. C. L. Riesner, Philadelphia, 1916.
Froude, James Anthony, *Luther, a Short Biography*, New York, 1884.
Graebner, H. L., *Dr. Martin Luther*, Milwaukee, 1895.
Grisar, Hartmann, *Martin Luther*, German edition, 3 vols., Freiburg, 1911-12; English translation by E. M. Lamond, 6 vols., London, 1913-17 (Catholic).
Holl, Karl, *Luther*, 3rd ed., *Gesammelte Aufsätze zur Kirchengeschichte*, Tübingen, 1923.
Jacobs, Henry E., *Martin Luther*, New York and London, 1898.
Keil, Friedrich S., *D. Martin Luthers merkwürdige Lebens-Umstände*, Leipsic, 1764.
Keslerum, Andreum, *Lutherthumb*, Coburg, 1630.
Keyser, Friederich, *Reformations-Almanach für Luthers Verehrer auf das evangelische Jubeljahr 1817*, Erfurt, 1817.
Kolde, Theodor, *Martin Luther*, 2 vols., Gotha, 1884-1893.
Köstlin, Julius, *Life of Luther*, translated from the German, New York, 1883; do., *Luther, sein Leben und seine Schriften*, 2 vols., Elberfeld, 1883. Recent edition by G. Kaverau.
Lindsay, Thomas M., *Luther and the German Reformation*, New York, 1900.
Listov, A., *Martin Luthers Levnet*, Copenhagen, 1864.
Lorenz, Ottomar, *Luther-fest Almanach*, Erfurt, 1883.
McGiffert, Arthur Cushman, *Martin Luther, the Man and His Work*, New York, 1911.

BIBLIOGRAPHY

Mathesius, Johann, *Historien von des Ehrwirdigen inn Gott seligen theuren Manns Gottes, D. Martin Luthers Anfang, Lere, Leben, Standhafft, u. s. w.*, Nuremberg, 1576. Reprint by Concordia Publishing House, St. Louis, Mo., 1883.

Michelet, Jules, *The Life of Luther*, translated from the French by William Hazlitt with notes and additions, especially from Audin, 2nd ed., London, 1862 (Catholic).

Nuber, Georg, *Lutherus Redivivus, Das ist: Die Ganze Historia von dem auszerwehlten u. s. w., D. Martino Luthero*, Stuttgart, 1658.

O'Hare, Patrick F., *The Facts About Luther*, New York and Cincinnati, 1916 (Catholic).

Plitt-Petersen, *D. Martin Luthers Leben und Wirken*, Leipsic, 1883.

Rein, Vilhelm, *Das Leben D. Martin Luthers*, Leipsic, 1883.

Smith, Preserved, *The Life and Letters of Martin Luther*, Boston and New York, 1911.

Steinhaeuser, A. T. W., Editor, *Leaders of the Lutheran Reformation*, Philadelphia, 1907.

Ukert, G. H. A., *Dr. Martin Luthers Leben*, Gotha, 1817.

Weiser, R., *Luther by a Lutheran*, Baltimore, 1848.

III. MISCELLANEOUS WORKS ON LUTHER AND EDUCATIONAL HISTORY

Achelis, E. Chr., *Lehrbuch der praktischen Theologie*, 3 vols., Vol. II. on Catechetics, Leipsic, 1911.

Adams, George Burton, *Civilization During the Middle Ages*, New York, 1901.

Bacon and Allen, *The Hymns of Martin Luther*, New York, 1883.

Bang, A. Chr., *Dokumenter og Studier vedrørende den*

lutherske Katekismus' Historie i Norden, 2 vols., Christiania, 1893-99.

Bang, A. Chr., *Den norske Kirkes Historie*, Christiania and Copenhagen, 1912.

Barnard, Henry, *German Teachers and Educators*, Hartford, 1878.

Bauslin, David H., *The Lutheran Movement of the Sixteenth Century*, Philadelphia, 1919.

Boehmer, Heinrich, *Luther in the Light of Recent Research*, New York, 1916.

Cave, Alfred, *Introduction to Theology and its Literature*, 2nd ed., Edinburgh, 1896.

Cohrs, Ferdinand, *Die evangelischen Katekismusversuche vor Luthers Enchiridion*, 5 vols., Berlin, 1900-07.

Compayre, Gabriel, *History of Pedagogy*, translated from the French by W. H. Payne, Boston, 1892.

Creighton, M., *History of the Papacy During the Period of Reformation*, 5 vols., London, 1887-94.

Croll, P. C., *Tributes to the Memory of Martin Luther*, Philadelphia, 1884.

Crooks, G. R., and Hurst, J. F., *Theological Encyclopedia and Methodology*, New York, 1891.

Crucius, D. M., *Luthers Geistliche Lieder*, Magdeburg, 1846.

Cubberly, E. P., *The History of Education*, Boston, 1920.

Cubberly, E. P., *Readings in the History of Education*, Boston, 1920.

Dahle, John, *Library of Christian Hymns*, 3 vols., Minneapolis, 1924-28.

Dargan, E. C., *A History of Preaching*, 2 vols., New York, 1906-11.

Dau, W. H. T., *Luther Examined and Re-examined*, St. Louis, 1917.

D'Aubigne, J. H. Merle, *History of the Reformation of the Sixteenth Century*, Milwaukee, Wis., 1901.

BIBLIOGRAPHY

Davidson, Thomas, *A History of Education*, New York, 1900.
Draper, John W., *History of the Intellectual Development of Europe*, 2 vols., New York, 1876.
Döllinger, J. J. I., *Kirche und Kirchen, Papstthum und Kirchen-Staat*, München, 1861.
Farrar, F. W., *History of Interpretation*, New York, 1889.
Fisher, George Park, *History of the Christian Church*, New York, 1900.
Fisher, George Park, *The Reformation*, 1906; Revised ed., 1926.
Gerberding, G. H., *The Lutheran Catechist*, Philadelphia, 1910.
Gerberding, G. H., *The Lutheran Pastor*, Philadelphia, 1903.
Graul, Karl, *Distinctive Doctrines*, from 12th German ed. by D. M. Martens, 1897.
Graves, Frank P., *A History of Education During the Middle Ages*, New York, 1910.
Guericke, H. E. F., *Allgmeine Christliche Symbolik*, Leipsic, 1861.
Günther, M., *Populäre Symbolik*, St. Louis, 1872; New ed., 1912.
Hallam, Henry, *History of Europe During the Middle Ages*, 3 vols., The Colonial Press, New York, 1899.
Hallam, Henry, *View of the State of Europe During the Middle Ages*, Harper, New York, 1893.
Hardeland, A., *Luthers Katechismusgedanken in ihrer Entwickelung bis zum Jahre 1529*, Gütersloh, 1913.
Hartshorn, Hugh, *Worship in the Sunday School*, New York.
Haskins, C. H., *The Renaissance of the Twelfth Century*, Cambridge, 1927.
Haskins, C. H., *The Rise of Universities*, New York, 1923.
Hofmann, Rudolf, *Symbolik*, Berlin, 1857.

Horn, E. T., *Outlines of Liturgics*, Philadelphia, 1890.
Hönecke, Adolf, *Dogmatik*, 5 vols., Milwaukee, 1909-1917.
Jacobs, Henry E., *The Book of Concord, Historical edition*, 2 vols., Philadelphia, 1882; do., *Popular edition*, texts only, Philadelphia, 1912.
Jacobs, Henry E., *The Lutheran Movement in England*, Philadelphia, 1916. First edition in 1890.
Jacobs, Henry E., *A Summary of the Christian Faith*, Philadelphia, 1907.
Janssen, Johannes, *History of the German People at the Close of the Middle Ages*, 14 vols., London, 1896-1909. Translated from the original German edition of 1888-94 (Catholic).
Kaverau, Gustav, *Luther in katolischer Beleuchtung, Glossen zur H. Grisars Luther*, Leipsic, 1911.
Kemp, E. L., *History of Education*, Philadelphia, 1912.
Ker, John, *Lectures on the History of Preaching*, New York, 1889.
Kessel, Robert, *Der kleine Katechismus Dr. Martin Luthers als Glaubens-und Lebensbuch für Schulpraxis anschaulich-geschichtlich erklärt und gewürdigt*, Leipsic, 1919.
Klotsche, E. H., *An Outline of the History of Doctrines*, Burlington, Iowa, 1927.
Knoke, K., *Grundriss der Pädagogik*, Berlin, 1902.
Krauth, Chas. Porterfield, *The Conservative Reformation and its Theology*, Philadelphia, revised ed., 1913.
Kretzmann, P. E., *A Brief History of Education*, St. Louis, no date, about 1925.
Kretzmann, P. E., *Christian Art in the Place and in the Form of Lutheran Worship*, St. Louis, 1921.
Köstlin, Julius, *The Theology of Luther*, 2 vols., Philadelphia, 1897.
Kurtz, Johann Heinrich, *Church History*, 3 vols.,

translated from the German by John Macpherson, New York, 1888.
Lambert, J. F., *Luther's Hymns*, Philadelphia, 1917.
Laurie, S. S., *The Rise and Early Constitution of the Universities*, New York and London, 1912.
Leitzmann, Albert, *Martin Luthers Geistliche Lieder*, Bonn, 1907.
Lindbergh, C. E., Christian Dogmatics, Rock Island, Ill., 1922.
Lindemann, J. C. W., *Dr. Martin Luther als Erzieher der Jugend*, St. Louis, 1881.
Lindsay, Thos. M., *A History of the Reformation*, 2 vols., New York, 1906. New edition, 1916.
Luthardt, C. E., *Compendium der Dogmatik*, Leipsic, 1882.
Lökensgaard, Knute, *Kateketik*, Minneapolis, 1913.
Lökensgaard, Knute, *Outlines of the Catechism*, Canton, S. D., 1923.
Madsen, P., *Den kristelige Troslaere*, Copenhagen, 1912-13.
Martig, Emanuel, *Geschichte der Erziehung in ihren Grundzügen*, Bern, 1901.
McCormick, P. J., *History of Education*, Washington, 1915 (Catholic).
Mertz, Georg Karl, *Das Schulwesen der deutschen Reformation im 16 Jahrhundert*, Heidelberg, 1902.
Monroe, Paul, *A Text-Book in the History of Education*, New York, 1906.
Monroe, Paul, *Thomas Platter and the Educational Renaissance of the Sixteenth Century*, New York, 1904.
Munro, D. C., and Sellery, G. C., *Medieval Civilization*, New York, 1910.
Neve, J. L., *Introduction to Lutheran Symbolics*, Columbus, Ohio, 1917; new edition, *Introduction to Symbolical Books of the Lutheran Church*, 1927.
Norlie, O. M., and Kiefer, G. L., *Lutheran World Al-*

manac and Encyclopedia, New York, 1921, 1922, 1924-26, 1926-28.

Norton, A. O., *Readings in History of Education, Medieval Universities*, Cambridge, 1909.

Otto, Rudolf, *The Idea of the Holy (Das Heilige)*, Oxford, 1926.

Painter, F. V. N., *A History of Education*, New York, 1900.

Painter, F. V. N., *Luther on Education*, Philadelphia, 1889.

Pattison, T. H., *The History of Christian Preaching*, Philadelphia, 1903.

Paulsen, Friedrich, *German Education, Past and Present*, translated by T. Lorenz, New York, 1908.

Pfleiderer, Otto, *The Development of Christianity*, translated by Daniel A. Huebsch, New York, 1910.

Pick, Bernhard, *Luther as a Hymnist*, Philadelphia, 1875.

Pieper, F., *Christliche Dogmatik*, 3 vols., St. Louis, 1917-1920.

Ranke, Leopold, *History of the Reformation in Germany*, 1845.

Rashdall, Hastings, *The Universities of Europe in the Middle Ages*, Oxford, 1895.

Raumer, Karl von, *Geschichte der Pädagogik*, 4 vols., Gütersloh, 1890.

Reisner, Edward H., *Historical Foundation of Modern Education*, New York, 1927.

Remensnyder, Junius B., *What the World Owes Luther*, New York, 1917.

Reu, M., *Thirty-five Years of Luther Research*, Chicago, 1917.

Reu, M., *Catechetics*, Chicago, 1918.

Reu, M., *Quellen zur Geschichte des kirchlichen Unterrichts im evangelischen Deutschland zwischen 1530 und 1600*, 7 vols., Gütersloh, 1904-20.

Reu, M., *Homiletics*, Chicago, 1922.

Richard, J. W., and Painter, F. V. N., *Christian Worship, its Principles and Forms*, Philadelphia, 1892. Contains Luther's *Deutsche Messe* in English translation.
Richard, J. W., *The Confessional History of the Lutheran Church*, Philadelphia, 1909.
Rietschel, G., *Lehrbuch der Liturgik*, 2 vols., Berlin, 1909.
Roalkvam, Halvard, *Kateketik*, Minneapolis, 1898.
Sachsse, E., *Die Lehre von der kirchlichen Erziehung*, Berlin, 1897.
Schaff, Philip, *Creeds of Christendom*, 3 vols., New York, 1877.
Schaff, Philip, *History of the Christian Church*, 7 vols., New York, 1882-1910.
Schaff, Philip, *Theological Propedeutic*, New York, 1909.
Scharling, E. H., *Evangelisk Luthersk Dogmatik*, Copenhagen, 1913.
Schiller, Johann, *Dr. M. Luther über christliche Kinderzucht*, Frankfurt and Erlangen, 1854.
Schmauck, T. E., Bentze, C. T., and Kolde, T., *The Confessional Principle and the Confessions of the Ev. Luth. Church*, Philadelphia, 1911.
Schmid, Heinrich, *Doctrinal Theology of the Ev. Lutheran Church*, 2nd Eng. ed. from 6th Germ. ed. by C. A. Hays and H. E. Jacobs, Philadelphia, 1889.
Schmidt, Hermann, *Handbuch der Symbolik*, Berlin, 1895.
Schmidt, Karl, *Geschichte der Pädagogik*, 4 vols., Göthen, 1883.
Schumann, J. C. C., *Dr. Martin Luthers pädagogische Schriften*, Wien, 1884.
Sclater, J. R. P., *The Public Worship of God*, New York, 1927.
Seeley, Levy, *History of Education*, 3rd ed., New York, 1914.

Severinsen, P., and Vognsböl, N. *Martin Luthers Liv og Hovedvärker*, 5 vols., Copenhagen, 1910-14.
Sinding, E., *Luther som Opdrager*, Christiania, 1904.
Slattery, C. L., *Problems of Faith and Worship*, New York, 1926.
Smith, Preserved, *Luther's Table Talk*, New York, 1907.
Stevenson, George M., *The Conservative Character of Martin Luther*, Philadelphia, 1921.
Symposiac on Martin Luther by the Professors of Union Theological Seminary, New York, 1883.
Tanner, Jacob, *Ten Lessons in the Catechism*, Minneapolis, 1927.
Van Oosterzee, J. J., *Praktisk Theologie*, trans. from the Dutch, Copenhagen, 1881.
Wackernagel, Philipp, *Luthers Geistliche Lieder*, Stuttgart, 1848.
Wagner, E., *Luther als Pädagog*, Langensalza, 1892.
Walther, Wilh., *Lehrbuch der Symbolik*, Leipsic, 1924.
Waring, Luther Hess, *The Political Theories of Martin Luther*, New York and London, 1910.
Weber, Karl, M. Phil., *Melanchthons evangelische Kirchen- und Schulordnung vom Jahre* 1528, Schlüchtern, in Kurhessen, 1844.
Weidner, F. W., *Christology*, Chicago, 1913.
Weidner, F. W., *The Doctrine of Man*, Chicago, 1912.
Weidner, F. W., *Theological Encyclopedia*, 3 vols., Chicago, 1910.
Weigle, L. A., and Tweedy, H. H., *Training the Devotional Life*, Boston, 1919.
Williams, S. G., *The History of Medieval Education*, Syracuse, 1903.
Woodward, W. H., *Vittorino da Feltre and Other Humanist Educators*, Cambridge, 1921.
Woodward, W. H., *Education During the Renaissance*, Cambridge, 1906.

Zöckler, Otto, *Handbuch der theologischen Wissenschaften*, 5 vols., Nördlingen, 1889-1890.

IV. ENCYCLOPEDIAS

Catholic Encyclopedia, 16 vols. and Supplement, New York, 1907-1914.
Cyclopedia of Education, edited by Paul Monroe, 5 vols., New York, 1911-13.
Encyclopedia of Education, edited by Foster Watson, 4 vols., London and New York, 1921-22.
Realencyklopädie für protestantische Theologie und Kirche, 24 vols., Leipsic, 1896-1913.
Schaff-Herzog, *The New Encyclopedia of Religious Knowledge*, 12 vols., New York and London, 1908-12.
Salomonsens Konversationsleksikon, 19 vols., Copenhagen, 1893-1911.

V. PERIODICAL LITERATURE

Andres, F., *Martin Luther*, poem, *Education*, vol. XXVII, p. 549.
Doving, Carl, *Ein' Feste Burg*, *Teologisk Tidsskrift*, April, 1924, pp. 216-17.
Elert, Doctor, *Luther og vor Tid*, *Skandinaven*, Dec. 3, 1926.
Fiedler, George, *Luther's Views and Influence on Schools and Education*, *Modern Quarterly of Language and Literature*, vol. I., pp. 211-16.
F. B., *Der Religionsunterricht in der modernen Pädagogik*, *Lehre und Wehre*, vol. XLV., pp. 193-218.
Good, H. G., *Position of Luther upon Education*, *School and Society*, vol. VI., pp. 511-18.
Harvey, Andrew Edward, *Luther in the Estimate of Modern Historians*, *Am. Jour. of Theol.*, vol. XXII., pp. 321-48.

Kiefer, G. L., *Luther Bibliographies*, Teologisk Tidsskrift, vol. X., pp. 506-8.
Körner, Emil, *Luther und die Schrift*, Kirchliche Zeitschrift, vol. L., pp. 509-80.
Luther Anniversary, editorial in Nation, vol. CV., pp. 503-4.
Luther for To-Day, Literary Digest, vol. LV., pp. 28-29.
Millar, M. I. X., *Justification of Luther by History Alone*, Catholic World, vol. CIV, pp. 768-80.
Pury, R. B., *Luther's Influence on Education*, Education, vol. XXXVII, pp. 30-35.
Reu, M., *A New Translation of Luther's Small Catechism*, Kirchliche Zeitschrift, vol. L., pp. 626-689.
Reu, M., *Der Siegeszug von Luthers Katekismus durch Europa*, Kirchliche Zeitschrift, November and December, 1927.
Smith, Preserved, *English Opinion of Luther*, Harvard Theol. Review, vol. X, p. 129 seq.
Smith, Preserved, *Luther, 1517-1917*, Outlook, vol. CXVII, pp. 335-6.
Smith, Preserved, *Recent Progress in the Study of Luther*, Am. Journ. of Theol., vol. XIII, pp. 259-69.
Smith, Preserved, *A Decade of Luther Study*, Harvard Theol. Review, vol. XIV, pp. 107-35.
Walsh, J. J., *Luther and Social Service*, Catholic World, vol. CIV, pp. 781-790.

# INDEX OF SUBJECTS

Absolution, Luther's doctrine of, 127
Address to nobility, Luther's, 152, 221
Appeals, three stirring, 152

Baptism, Luther's doctrine of, 124
Babylonian Captivity of the Church, 210
Bible, discovery of by Luther, 48, 49, 71
Bible, Luther's translation of, 131
Bible, German translations before Luther's, 132
Bible translations and Catholic Church, 133
Bible translations, revision of, 143
Bible translation, faithfulness of, 144
Bible translation, influence on German language, 146
Bible translation, adverse criticism of, 147
Bible, use of in schools, 48, 49
Bible, Luther's views of, 107
Bora, Catharina von, 95
Brethren of the Common Life, see Hieronymians
Buildings, church, 245

Catechisms, Luther's, 172
Catechisms before Luther, 173
Catechisms, sources of Luther's, 174
Catechisms, preparation and publication of, 175, 176
Catechism, Large, 109, 110, 126, 127, 239, 247
Catechism, Small, 109, 176, 233, 234, 249
  contents of, 176
  form of, 176
  purpose and value of, 177
  subject-matter, arrangement of, 180

  pedagogical value of, 182
  translation of, 185
  first book translated into Indian language, 187
Catechism, Heidelberg, 183, 184
Catechism, Westminster, 183
Catholic views of Luther's marriage, 91
Charlemagne, reformation by, 26, 27, 42
Chivalry, 28
Christ, Luther's doctrine of, 111
Christian life, Luther's doctrine of, 121
Christian education, importance of, 211
Christian education, aim of, 212
Church, Luther's doctrine of, 127
Cotta, Ursula, 63
Crusades, the, 27
Curricula, school, 226

Education, general and specialized, 225
Erfurt, city of, 66
  University of, 31, 49, 66, 67, 68
  student life at, 69
  studies and degrees at, 70
Estimates of Luther's life and work, Protestant, 270
  Catholic, 274
  of Luther as an educator, 278
  Catholic, 278
  Reformed, 280
  Lutheran, 282
Exegetical works, Luther's, 189

Fables, Aesop's, Luther's translation of, 204, 229, 233
Faith, Luther's doctrine of, 118
Formula of Concord, 117
Formula missae, 240, 251

God, Luther's doctrine of, 109

Hieronymians, the, 35, 52, 61, 287
Holidays, 246
Holy Ghost, Luther's doctrine of, 115
Holy orders, Luther's doctrine of, 122
Home training, character of, 215
Hymnal, Walther's, 265
Hymnal, Klug's, 266
Hymns, Luther's, 261
Hymn, Luther's best known, 263

Introductions to books by Luther, 205

Justification, Luther's doctrine of, 118

Last things, Luther's doctrine of, 128
Letter to councilmen, Luther's, 155, 211, 221, 230
Letters, Luther's, 196
Letter on Bible translation, 149, 150, 209, 210
Liberty of a Christian man, the, 210
Lord's Supper, Luther's doctrine of, 126
Litany, 254
Luther, Martin, birth, 54
  parentage, 55
  name, 55
  home training, 57
  at Mansfeld, 59
  at Magdeburg, 61
  at Eisenach, 62
  at Erfurt, 66, 80
  a Bachelor of Philosophy, 72
  a Master of Philosophy, 72
  studies law, 72
  enters cloister, 73
  as a monk, 74
  becomes a priest, 75
  journey to Rome, 76
  at Wittenberg, 78, 80
  becomes a Baccalaureus Biblicus, 80
  returns to Erfurt, 80
  lectures on Lombard, 81
  back at Wittenberg, 82
  a Doctor of Theology, 82
  lectures on the Bible, 83
  success as a teacher, 84
  marriage, 86, 87, 90, 92
  children, 97
  letter to son, 99
  at the table, 102
  home scenes, 102
  closing days, 103
  death, 104
  as a theologian, 105
  teachings concerning the Bible, 107
  doctrine of God, 109
  doctrine of the person and work of Christ, 111
  doctrine of the Holy Ghost, 115
  doctrine of the Trinity, 115
  doctrine of man, 116
  doctrine of original sin, 117
  doctrine of faith and justification, 118
  doctrine of Christian life, 121
  doctrine of Holy orders, 122
  doctrine of means of grace, 123
  doctrine of sacraments, 124
  doctrine of Baptism, 124
  doctrine of the Lord's Supper, 126
  doctrine of confession and absolution, 127
  doctrine of the church, 127
  doctrine of the state, 128
  doctrine of the last things, 128
  private confession, 122, 129
  pedagogical works, 131
  Bible, translation of, 131
  and earlier Bible translations, 138
  faithfulness of Bible translation, 144
  address to nobility, 152
  letter to councilmen, 155
  sermon on sending children to school, 164
  catechisms, 172

INDEX OF SUBJECTS

idea of catechetical instruction, 178
exegetical works, 189
sermons, 192
postils, 195
letters, 196
table talks, 200
translation of Aesop's Fables, 204
introductions to books, 205
prayer book, 208
baptismal book, 208, 255
German order of service, 208
wedding book, 208
visitation instruction, 209
letter on Bible translation, 149, 150, 209, 210
liberty of a Christian man, 210
Babylonian captivity of the Church, 210
pedagogical principles, 211
an observer of children, 99, 232
contributions to Christian worship, 237
conception of Christian worship, 240
principles of worship, 256
hymns, 261
best known hymn, 263
place in history of education, 286, 299
what he accomplished for education, 288-299

Man, Luther's doctrine of, 116
Means of grace, Luther's doctrine of, 123
Messe, deutsche, 179, 208, 235, 252
Middle Ages, schools in, 21, 22, 23, 24, 25, 43
social classes of, 25, 44
teachers in, 45
methods of instruction in, 45, 46, 50
education in, 51
Moors, the, 31
Music, value of, 227
Music, Luther's poem on, 266

New Testament, translation of, 140
Null Brethren, see Hieronymians.

Old Testament, translation of, 141
Orders, religious, 29
Order of service, fixed, 242
Order of divine worship, Luther's, 250
Original sin, Luther's doctrine of, 117

Paper, invention of, 39
Parents, duty of, 213
Pastors, duty of, 219
Postils, Luther's, 195, 249
Prayer Book, Luther's, 208, 249
Principles of worship, influence of Luther's, 258
Printing, invention of, 39
Protestant views of Luther's marriage, 93

Renaissance, the, 33

Sacraments, Luther's doctrine of, 124
Saxony school plan, the, 209, 227, 228, 288, 292
Scholasticism, 28
Schools, elementary, 41
cathedral, 45
conventual, 45
Sermon on sending children to school, Luther's, 164, 211
Sermons, Luther's, 192
Sermon on good works, Luther's, 246
Service, baptismal, 255
Service, marriage, 256
Significance, the, of Luther's marriage, 92
Smalcald articles, the, 120
State, Luther's doctrine of, 128
State, duty of, 220
Sundays, 246

Table Talks, Luther's, 200

Teachers and teaching, 231
Trinity, Luther's doctrine of, 115

Universities, rise of, 30
  faculties of, 47
  curricula of, 47
University of Erfurt, 31, 49, 66, 67, 68
University of Wittenberg, 78, 79

Visitation instructions, Luther's, 209

Wedding book, Luther's, 208, 256
Wittenberg, city of, 78
Wittenberg, University of, 78, 79
Worship, Christian, 237
  Luther's conception of, 240
  art in, 245
  family, 249
  principles of, 256
  and hymn singing, 260
Writings, Luther's liturgical, 250
Writings, Luther's pedagogical, 131

INDEX OF NAMES

Achelis, E. Chr., 181
Adams, George B., 40
Agricola, Rudolph, 34, 38, 174, 297
Albrecht, O., 164
Amsdorf, Nicholaus, 79, 159
Andres, Frederick, 296
Aquinas, Thos., 29, 48
Audin, J. M., 144
Averroes, 32

Boccaccio, 33, 287
Bacon, Roger, 48
Bauslin, David H., 94
Bora, Catharina, 95, 96, 104
Brenz, Johann, 174, 288
Bugenhagen, Johann, 89, 143, 174

Calvin, John, 192, 271
Campanius, John, 187
Carlstadt, Andreas, 79, 156
Charlemagne, 26, 27, 42
Collarius, Johann, 236
Collet, John, 33
Compayre, Gabriel, 23, 27, 280
Cotta, Ursula, 63
Cranach, Lucas, 56, 89
Cubberly, E. P., 43, 50
Cuyler, Theo. L., 94

Dahle, John, 298
Dargan, E. C., 193, 258
Dau, W. H. T., 135
Denifle, H., 91, 278
Dietrich, Veit, 195
Döllinger, Johann, 275

Elector, Friedrich of Saxony, 159, 199
Elector Johann of Saxony, 197, 199, 221, 289
Emser, Jerome, 150, 159, 209
Erasmus, Disiderius, 34, 38, 39, 190, 279, 287

Farrar, F. W., 190, 191
Frederick the Wise, 79, 253, 288
Froude, James A., 271

Galeatius Capella, 207
Gerberding, G. H., 178, 181
Graves, F. P., 38, 281
Grisar, Hartmann, 81, 82, 83, 145, 146, 147, 148, 149, 184, 274, 279
Groote, Geert, 35
Grocyn, Wm., 33
Guarino da Verona, 35, 287

Haskins, C. H., 46
Hausmann, Nicholas, 251, 252, 253
Herder, J. G., 270
Hess, Eobanus, 69, 157, 198
Hott, J. W., 271
Hummelberg, Michael, 156

Janssen, Johannes, 21, 22, 24, 48, 91, 278

Kemp, E. L., 24
Kempis, Thos. 37
Ker, John, 192, 193
Klotsche, E. H., 111
Köstlin, Julius, 57, 59, 107, 112, 120, 129
Kurtz, J. H., 121

Lang, Johann, 69, 139, 140
Laurie, S. S., 30
Linacre, Thos., 33
Link, Wenzel, 142, 209
Lombard, Peter, 48
Luder, Peder, 34
Luther, Hans, 54, 64, 75
Luther, Jakob, 103
Luther, Margaretha, 54
Luther, Martin, see subject index

Mackintosh, H. R., 112
Martig, Emanuel, 86
Mathesius, Johann, 61, 72, 84, 85, 142, 182, 194, 195, 200, 201
McCormick, P. J., 21, 24
McGiffert, Arthur C., 182

Melanchthon, Philip, 34, 90, 103, 141, 142, 153, 165, 174, 204, 226, 228, 271, 279, 286, 288, 293, 297
Menius, Justus, 165, 207
Michelet, Jules, 91
Monroe, Paul, 20, 22, 281

Nestle, Eberhard, 138
Norton, A. O., 51

O'Hare, P. F., 91, 132, 133, 150

Painter, F. V. N., 24, 44, 283
Paulsen, Friedrich, 22
Petrarch, 33, 287
Platter, Thos., 45
Prentiss, Geo. L., 297

Radewin, Florentius, 35
Rashdall, Hastings, 49, 51
Raumer, Karl, 24
Remensnyder, J. B., 94, 273
Reu, M., 181
Reuchlin, Johann, 34, 38, 39
Rörer, Georg, 143, 195

Sachsse, E., 260
Schaeffer, C. F., 186
Schaff, Philip, 93, 182, 298
Schmidt, Karl, 24, 45, 171
Schumann, J. C. C., 202

Smith, Preserved, 81, 83, 202, 203, 273
Smyth, Egbert C., 270
Spalatin, Georg, 56, 68, 69, 88, 97, 140, 142, 152, 199, 209, 261, 288
Spengler, Lazarus, 167
Speratus, Paul, 251, 262
Staupitz, Johann, 74, 76, 78, 79, 80, 82
Sturm, Jakob, 291
Sturm, Johann, 286, 291, 292

Tanner, Jacob, 173
Trebonius, Johann, 64, 65
Trutvetter, Jodocus, 68

Usingen, Bartholomew, 68

Vergerio, Pier, 35
Vittorino da Feltre, 35, 287

Walther, Johann, 205, 253, 265
Warner, Charles Dudley, 272
Watson, Foster, 280
Weber, Karl, 228
Weigle, A. L., 237
Wentz, A. R., 172
Wessel, Johann, 34, 38, 39

Zütphen, Gerhard, 37
Zwingli, H., 111, 126, 191